Costs L
Report

2010 Part 3

Note on Citation

Costs Law Reports should be cited as Costs LR,
e.g. *1-800 Flowers Inc* v *Phonenames Limited* [2001] 2 Costs LR 286.

Note that cases and paragraphs are also numbered to allow for easier online referencing. (Where possible, paragraph numbering from original transcripts will be maintained.) Using this method, paragraph one of the *1-800 Flowers Inc* v *Phonenames Limited* judgment would be cited as: *1-800 Flowers Inc* v *Phonenames Limited* [2001] Costs LR Case 21 at [1].

Also, where neutral citation numbers are given, the original transcript numbering has always been maintained, allowing the neutral citation method to be used. Using this method, paragraph two of *1-800 Flowers Inc* v *Phonenames Limited* would be cited as: *1-800 Flowers Inc* v *Phonenames Limited* [2001] EWCA Civ 721 at [2].

Costs Law Reports

2010 Part 3

Peter Rogers
LL B
Deputy Costs Judge of the Senior Courts Costs Office

Michael Bacon
MA (Cantab), FALCD, MAE, QDR

Text © Michael Bacon and Peter Rogers 2010
Typography © Class Legal 2010

COPYRIGHT

All rights reserved. No part of this publication may be reproduced in any material form (including photocopying or storing it in any medium by electronic means and whether or not transiently or incidentally to some other use of this publication) without the written permission of the copyright holder except in accordance with the provisions of the Copyright, Designs and Patents Act 1988 or under the terms of a licence issued by the Copyright Licensing Agency www.cla.co.uk. Applications for the copyright owner's written permission to reproduce any part of this publication should be addressed to the publisher.

ASSERTION OF MORAL RIGHTS

The author/editor asserts his/her right as set out in ss 77 and 78 of the Copyright Designs and Patents Act 1988 to be identified as the author/editor of this work wherever it is published commercially and whenever any adaptation of this work is published or produced including any sound recordings or films made of or based upon this work.

DISCLAIMER

The information presented in this work is accurate and current to the best of the author's/editor's knowledge. The author/editor and publisher, however, make no guarantee as to, and assume no responsibility for, the correctness or sufficiency of such information or recommendation.

Class Legal
Owl House, Carr Farm, Cadney, BRIGG,
Lincolnshire, DN20 9HP, UK
Tel: 01652 652222 Fax: 01652 651050
DX 24360 Brigg
Email: Info@ClassLegal.com
Website: www.ClassLegal.com

Class Legal is an imprint of Class Publishing Ltd, a company registered in England No. 2993127. VAT No: GB 503 5208 87

Registered Office: 7 Melrose Terrace, London W6 7RL, UK

PRINTING HISTORY

First published 2010

ISBN 978 185959296 0 ISSN 1366-8617

A CIP Catalogue for this book is available from the British Library

Typeset by: Stephen Theaker

Printed and bound by: Good News Digital Books

Contents

Table of Cases — *vii*

Case 25
Barr and Others v Biffa Waste Services Ltd
 and Another (Westmill Landfill Group Litigation) — 291

Case 26
Barr and Others v Biffa Waste Services Ltd
 (No. 2) (Westmill Landfill Group Litigation) — 317

Case 27
Shah v Ul-Haq and Others — 336

Case 28
Widlake v BAA Ltd — 353

Case 29
MasterCigars Direct Ltd v Withers LLP — 374

Case 30
Sulaman v Axa Insurance plc and Another — 391

Case 31
Pankhurst v White and Another — 402

Case 32
Richard Buxton (Solicitors) v Mills-Owens
 and The Law Society — 421

Case 33
HR Trustees Ltd v German and Another
 (In the Matter of the IMG Pension Plan) — 443

Case 34
R v Splain — 465

Case 35
R v Jones   469

Case 36
R v O'Cuneff   476

Index of Reported Cases (1910–2010)

Index

Table of Cases

Agapitos v Agnew [2002] EWCA Civ 247,
 [2003] QB 556 349
Aiden Shipping Co Ltd v Interbulk Ltd
 [1986] AC 969 ....446, 454
Alsop Wilkinson v Neary
 [1995] 1 All ER 431 ....450–451, 458, 461
Arrow Nominees v Blackledge
 [2001] BCLC 167 ....339, 345,
 ....345–348, 351
Atos Consulting Ltd v Avis plc
 [2007] EWHC 323 (TCC) 302
Axa General Insurance Ltd v Gottleib
 and Gottleib [2005] EWCA Civ 112....................................341, 349

Barnes v Time Talk UK Ltd [2003] EWCA Civ 402 367
Barr and Others v Biffa Waste Services Ltd
 and Another (Westmill Landfill Group
 Litigation) [2010] 3 Costs LR 291 291–316
Barr and Others v Biffa Waste Services Ltd
 (No. 2) (Westmill Landfill Group Litigation)
 [2010] 3 Costs LR 317 317–335
Beddoe, Re [1893] 1 Ch 547 ....448, 455, 456
Bekhor v Bilton [1991] QB 923 297
Biddencare 458
Blakes Estates Ltd v Government of Montserrat
 [2005] UKPC 46, [2006] 1 WLR 297 368
Bristol and West Building Society v Evans
 Bullock and Co, unreported, 5 February 1996 408
Buckton, Re [1907] 2 Ch 406 ....447, 450, 451,
 ....455, 456, 457,
 ....458, 459

Campbell v MGN Ltd (No. 2)
 [2006] 1 Costs LR 120; [2005] 1 WLR 3394............319, 320, 323

Capital Bank v Stickland [2004] EWCA Civ 1677 412
Chapman v Chapman [1954] AC 429 449
Chessels v British Telecommunications plc
 [2002] PLR 141 ....453–457, 458,
 ....459, 460, 461, 462
Churchill Car Insurance v Kelly
 [2006] EWHC 18 (QB)..343
Corby Group Litigation [2008] EWHC 619...................321, 323, 329
Cox v Bankside Members Agency,
 unreported, 29 November 1994, CA 297
Cresswell v Byron (1807) 33 ER 525 441

Earl of Radnor's Will Trusts, Re
 (1890) 45 ChD 423 ....451, 457
Expandable Ltd and Another v Rubin
 [2008] EWCA Civ 59 ....301, 302, 303,
 ....306, 309

Fitzpatrick v Tyco (No. 3)
 [2010] 2 Costs LR 115; [2009] EWHC 274 (TCC) 333

Garbutt v Edwards [2006] 1 Costs LR 143,
 [2006] 1 WLR 2907 387
Geberan Trading Co Ltd v Skjevesland
 [2002] EWCA Civ 1567, [2003] 1 WLR 912 434
Ghalib and Ghaffur v Hadfield,
 Preston County Court, 2004..339, 340
Grupo Torras 394, 395, 399

Hall and Others v Stone
 [2008] 3 Costs LR 450; [2007] EWCA Civ 1354 ......365–366, 369
Harcourt v FEF Griffin
 [2007] EWHC 1500 (QB) 297–298
Henry v British Broadcasting Corporation
 [2006] 3 Costs LR 412;
 [2005] EWHC 2503 (QB) 294, 295, 300,
 ....300–301, 303,
 ....304, 306, 307,
 ....308, 310, 311, 322

Table of Cases

Hobson v Ashdown Morton Slack Solicitors
and Others [2006] EWHC 1134 (QB) 299, 301, 304,
....305, 306, 308
HR Trustees Ltd v German and Another
(In the Matter of the IMG Pension Plan)
[2010] 3 Costs LR 443 443–464
Hunter and Others v Canary Wharf Ltd
[1997] 1 AC 655..324

Irwin v Liverpool City Council
[2005] 1 WLR 2557 388

Jackson v Ministry of Defence
[2006] EWCA Civ 46 ....364–365, 369
Jones v Associated Newspapers
[2007] EWCA 1489 (QB)...417

Khan, Shah and Mayat v Hussein,
Ashraf and the MIB, Huddersfield
County Court, May 2007 ....339, 340–341
King v The Daily Telegraph Group Ltd
(Practice Note) [2004] 3 Costs LR 449;
[2005] 1 WLR 2282 ....319, 320, 323,
....325, 331
Knight v Beyond Properties Pty Ltd
[2007] 1 Costs LR 5; [2007] 1 WLR 625 ....319, 322, 323, 332

Laws v National Grid plc [1998] 20 PBLR (1)..............445, 449–451,
....451–453, 457,
....458, 459, 461
Leigh v Michelin Tyre [2004] 1 Costs LR 148;
[2003] EWCA 1766 (Civ)..333, 381
Logicrose Ltd v Southend United
Football Club Ltd (1988) The Times, March 5 345
Lord Chancellor v Michael J Reed Ltd
[2010] 1 Costs LR 72 ....469, 473, 474
Lord Chancellor v Purnell
[2010] 1 Costs LR 81; [2009] EWHC 3158 (QB)....................480

Manifest Shipping Co Ltd v Ini-Polaris
Co Ltd (The Star Sea) [2001] UKHL 1 349

MasterCigars Direct Ltd v Withers LLP
[2008] 1 Costs LR 72 374–390
MasterCigars Direct Ltd v Withers LLP
[2009] 3 Costs LR 393 374–390
MasterCigars Direct Ltd v Withers LLP
[2010] 3 Costs LR 374 374–390
McDonald v Horn [1995] 1 All ER 961 .... 445–449, 450,
.... 451, 452, 454,
.... 455, 456, 458,
.... 459, 460, 461
McPhilemy v Times Newspapers
[2001] 2 Costs LR 295;
[2001] EWCA Civ 933 417
Molloy v Shell UK Ltd [2001] EWCA Civ 1271 .... 342–343, 358,
.... 359, 360, 361,
.... 362, 368, 369
Morgan v UPS [2009] 3 Costs LR 384;
[2008] EWCA Civ 1476 367

Painting v University of Oxford
[2005] 3 Costs LR 394;
[2005] EWCA Civ 161 .... 358, 359, 363–364,
.... 365–366, 369, 398
Pankhurst v White and Another
[2010] 3 Costs LR 402 402–420
Patel and Others v Ali 340
Peacock v MGN Ltd [2009] 4 Costs LR 584;
[2009] EWHC 769 (QB) 322–323, 332
Petrotrade v Texaco, unreported, 23 May 2000, CA 413, 417
Pitchmastic v Birse Construction,
unreported, 19 May 2000 .... 408–409, 410

R (Buglife – The Invertebrate Conservation
Trust) v Thurrock Thames Gateway
Development Corporation [2009] 1 Costs LR 80;
[2008] EWCA Civ 1209 314
R v B&Q plc [2005] EWCA Crim 2297 467
R v Jones [2010] 3 Costs LR 469 469–475
R v O'Cuneff [2010] 3 Costs LR 476 476–480

R v Splain [2010] 3 Costs LR 465 465–468
Reynolds v Stone Rowe Brewer
 [2008] 4 Costs LR 545;
 [2008] EWHC 497 (QB)...382, 388
Richard Buxton (Solicitors) v Mills-Owens
 and The Law Society [2010] 3 Costs LR 421
 (reversing [2008] 6 Costs LR 948) 421–442

Scammell v Dicker [2001] 1 WLR 631 409–410
Shah v Wassim Ul-Haq [2010] 3 Costs LR 336;
 [2009] EWCA Civ 542..336–352,
 ....361–363, 369
Smart v East Cheshire NHS Trust
 [2004] 1 Costs LR 124; [2003] 80 BMLR 175..........319, 322, 323
Stokes Pension Fund v Western Power
 Distribution [2005] 1 WLR 3595 ....404, 411–412
Straker v Tudor Rose
 [2008] 2 Costs LR 205; [2007] EWCA Civ 368 366–367,
 ....369, 370
Sulaman v Axa Insurance plc and Another
 [2010] 3 Costs LR 391 391–401

Underwood, Son, & Piper v Lewis
 [1894] 2 QB 306 ....436, 437, 441

Vansandau and Tindale v Browne
 (1832) 9 Bing 402...441

Wallersteiner v Moir (No. 2) [1975] QB 373................446, 448, 449,
 ....452, 458
West London Pipe Line Storage Ltd v
 Total UK Ltd and Others
 [2008] EWHC 1296 (Comm)............................298–299, 304,
 ....307, 310
Widlake v BAA Ltd [2010] 3 Costs LR 353;
 [2009] EWCA Civ 1256 ....353–373, 398, 399
Willis v Nicolson [2007] EWCA 199 (Civ) 320–321, 323, 333
Winterthur Swiss Insurance Co and Another v AG
 (Manchester) Ltd (In Liquidation) and Others
 [2006] EWHC 839 (Comm) 302, 308

Wong v Vizards [1997] 2 Costs LR 46;
[1997] 2 HLR 46 ....381, 382, 387, 388

Case 25
Barr and Others

v

Biffa Waste Services Ltd and Another (Westmill Landfill Group Litigation)

[2010] 3 Costs LR 291

Neutral Citation Number: [2009] EWHC 1033 (TCC)
High Court of Justice, Queen's Bench Division,
Technology and Construction Court
15 May 2009

Before:
Coulson J

_____ **Headnote** _____

The disclosability of a staged ATE policy of insurance where that policy is an integral element of Group Litigation and was mentioned in statements in support of an application for a Group Litigation Order was considered by the court, which had to deal with issues including relevance, privilege and the provisions of the Civil Procedure Rules.

_____

Judgment

1. The Application

1. COULSON J: On 3 March 2009, the claimants applied to Ramsey J for a Group Litigation Order ("GLO") in respect of their claims in nuisance and negligence against the defendant arising out of odour omissions from the defendant's site at Westmill, near Ware, in Hertfordshire. In the run-up to the hearing of that application, the

defendant made it clear that, whilst it did not necessarily object to the making of the GLO, it sought, as a condition of such an order, disclosure of the claimants' After The Event ("ATE") Insurance Policy.

2. At the hearing before Ramsey J on March 27, the claimants sought to defer consideration of the defendant's application for disclosure of the ATE Policy because the Insurers concerned, QBE Insurance Ltd, wanted to intervene and be heard on the issue. Accordingly, Ramsey J granted the GLO, and deferred the application in relation to the disclosure of the ATE Insurance until April 23. The GLO has now been approved by the President of the Queen's Bench Division. Schedule 2 of the GLO states that the claimants' liability to pay costs "shall be several and not joint". The GLO also includes a so-called mail shot letter, common in these cases, to be sent to other residents on the estate, which referred to the no win no fee agreement with the solicitors and the existence of the ATE Policy "to cover any potential cost liability".

3. At the hearing on April 23, the defendant renewed its application for disclosure of the ATE Policy. That application was resisted by the claimants and by the Intervening Insurers. The parties' respective submissions took the entirety of that day and I therefore reserved judgment. I am very grateful to all of the advocates for their considerable assistance in dealing with the interesting issues that arise from this application.

4. I set out briefly the background in **Section 2** below. At **Section 3** I set out what seem to me to be the relevant principles of law. At **Section 4**, I summarise the parties' submissions. Thereafter, at **Section 5** I consider the application pursuant to CPR 31 and at **Section 6**, the application under the court's general case management powers, particularly Parts 3 and 19 of the CPR. There is a short summary of my conclusions at **Section 7**.

2. The Factual Background

5. As noted above, these claims in private nuisance/negligence arise out of alleged odour omissions from the defendant's Westmill Landfill Site. There are around 140 claimant households in all, residents of a single housing estate on the other side of the A10 from the Westmill Site. The defendant is a well-known waste contractor.

6. During the course of his introductory remarks, Mr Croxford QC, on behalf of the defendant, made it clear that the defendant regarded

this as an important test case, and that there were a variety of factual and legal issues which would need to be resolved at the trial. He also indicated that, as the defendant saw it, there would be a need for expert evidence relating to (amongst other things) the historic land use in the area; the proper operation of a landfill site such as this; and, possibly, European law and policy relating to waste disposal and recycling. Mr Cooksley QC was doubtful as to whether expert evidence in all these fields would be either permissible or required.

7. It is not possible for me to say, at this early stage, what the scope of any expert or indeed factual evidence in this case is likely to be. On some issues, expert evidence may not be appropriate at all and, even if it was, a single joint expert might well be sufficient. However, I can certainly see that expert evidence on each side relating to the proper operation of this site will be of critical importance. Such evidence is likely to be extensive (and therefore relatively costly). Thus, whilst Mr Croxford's estimate of the costs of the litigation (at £2 million for each side) might be exaggerated, I am sure that the total costs will be well over £1 million. This is significant, because the parties are agreed that, but for the GLO, this action would probably not have been pursued at all. Even if sustained, each of the claimant's individual claims is likely to be worth only a few thousand pounds, whilst the costs to pursue each claim would have been so high that, without the GLO, it is most unlikely that any of them would have been pursued. I accept that the costs of any individual claim would have grossly outweighed the value of the claim itself.

8. On 9 July 2008, prior to the commencement of proceedings, the claimants' solicitors sent the defendant's solicitors a letter of claim, in accordance with the Pre-Action Protocol. At that time, the solicitors acted for 134 households and said that they were in the process of securing instructions from the remaining 98 households. As to funding, the solicitors said:

> "Please be advised that our clients have secured a policy of insurance in support of the Conditional Fee Agreement. The policy provides for a staged premium, the stages being pre-issue, post-issue and 60 days prior to trial. We will provide you with specific details as to the policy in due course as further notice of Funding Form N251 are served."

9. In a follow-up letter of 4 August 2008, the claimants' solicitors gave further information about the ATE Policy as follows:

"As you will be aware from previous correspondence we represent our clients under the terms of a conditional fee and agreement which provides for a success fee. Our clients now have the benefit of ATE policy with QBE Insurance (Europe) Ltd in support of the conditional fee agreement. The QBE policy provides for a staged premium policy. There are three stages. Premium (i) is payable if the claim is concluded before the issue of proceedings; premium (ii) is payable if the claim is concluded after the issue of proceedings but more than 60 days before the date listed for the commencement of the trial or the trial window; premium (iii) is payable if the claim is concluded 60 days or less before the beginning of the trial or the trial window as listed by the court or is heard at trial."

10. On 26 September 2008, the defendant's solicitor wrote, dealing with a variety of matters, and commented on the draft GLO that they had been sent. The letter concluded:

"Finally, we note that your clients now have the benefit of ATE Insurance. Our client is concerned about the claimants' ability to meet its costs should the claimants be unsuccessful at trial.

The decision of *Marion Henry* v *British Broadcasting Corporation* [2005] EWHC 2503 (QB) confirms that our client has a legitimate interest in knowing the extent of protection provided by the ATE policy and whether the ATE policy contains any exclusion clauses.

Accordingly, to allow our client to assess its potential financial exposure in this claim, please provide a copy of the ATE policy by return."

11. In their letter of 6 October 2008, the claimants' solicitors rejected this request. They maintained that they had provided the defendant's solicitors with Notice Funding Form N251, together with other details of the Policy, and that no further information was necessary. Importantly, in my judgment, they went on to say this:

"We can confirm that there are no exclusion clauses which are likely to render the policy invalid by reference to any anticipated defence to this claim.

Furthermore we confirm that the policy provides an adequate level of cover and that this will be continuously reviewed as the litigation advances and as the parties file the appropriate Estimate of Costs at the appropriate stages of the litigation."

The letter maintained that the decision in *Henry* was not authority for disclosure of the ATE policy and that in any event the judge's comments in that case were *obiter*, and the facts could be distinguished. The letter concluded that the claimants' solicitors did not believe that the defendant was "entitled to a copy of the policy at this stage".

12. Thereafter, the correspondence consisted of renewed requests by the defendant's solicitors for the document (see, for example, the letters from the defendant's solicitors of 9 October and 26 November 2008) and repeated rejections by the claimants' solicitors (see, for example, the letter of 28 October 2008). That explains why, when the claimants made their application for a GLO, the defendant responded immediately by saying that one of the conditions of such a GLO should be the disclosure of the ATE policy. The fact that the GLO in this case was made in advance of the determination of the disclosure issue was because of the need to accommodate the Intervening Insurers, and it seems to me that, in such circumstances, the existence of the GLO cannot now operate to the defendant's disadvantage in pursuing this application.

3. The Relevant Principles

3.1. The Provisions of the CPR Relating to Group Litigation and Funding Arrangements

13. The relevant provisions concerning the making of a GLO can be found at CPR 19.10 and onwards. Rule 19.13 deals expressly with case management and makes clear that CPR Part 3, which contains general provisions concerning the case management powers of the court, are applicable to Group Litigation. Of course, the court's case management powers under CPR Part 3 must be exercised in accordance with the overriding objective at CPR 1.1, to deal with cases "justly" and in ways which are proportionate (amongst other things) to the importance of the case and the financial position of each party. The court also has the power to order the disclosure and inspection of documents pursuant to CPR 31. Rule 31.14 deals expressly with documents "mentioned in", amongst other things, a witness statement. That is said to be relevant here because the ATE Policy has been mentioned in two witness statements relied on, for different purposes, by the claimants.

14. Many of the provisions of the CPR relevant to this application

can be found in Parts 43 and 44 which, although expressly concerned with costs, contain a number of provisions relating expressly to the effect of a GLO, including arrangements as to a possible Conditional Fee Agreement ("CFA"), percentage increases on basic fees to reflect success, and litigation (after the event or "ATE") insurance.

15. CPR 44.15 is entitled: "Providing information about funding arrangements". It provides:

> "(1) A party who seeks to recover an additional liability must provide information about the funding arrangement to the court and other parties as required by a rule, practice direction or court order."

An "additional liability" is defined at CPR 43.2(1)(o) as meaning:

> "the percentage increase, the insurance premium, or the additional amount in respect of provision made by a membership organisation, as the case may be."

16. The Practice Direction attached to Part 44 contains important guidance as to the provision of information as to funding arrangements. Section 19 contains the relevant paragraphs (44 PD.13). They are as follows:

> "19.1(1) A party who wishes to claim an additional liability in respect of a funding arrangement must give any other party information about that claim if he is to recover the additional liability. There is no requirement to specify the amount of additional liability separately nor to state how it is calculated until it falls to be assessed. That principle is reflected in rules 44.3A and 44.15, in the following paragraphs and in Sections 6, 13, 14 and 31 of this Practice Direction. ...
>
> 19.2(1) ...
>
> (a) A claimant who has entered into a funding arrangement before starting the proceedings to which it relates must provide information to the court by filing the notice [Form N251] when he issues the claim form.
>
> b) He must provide information to every other party by serving the notice. If he serves the claim form himself he must serve the notice with the claim form. If the court is to serve the claim form, the court will also serve the notice if the claimant provides it with sufficient copies for service. ...

19.4

(1) Unless the court otherwise orders, a party who is required to provide information about a funding arrangement must state whether he has
   – ... taken out an insurance policy to which s 29 of the Access to Justice Act 1999 applies ...

(2) Where the funding arrangement is a conditional fee agreement, the party must state the date of the agreement and identify the claim or claims to which it relates ...

(3) Where the funding arrangement is an insurance policy, the party must state the name and address of the insurer, the policy number and the date of the policy, and must identify the claims to which it relates...

19.5. Where the court makes a Group Litigation Order, the court may give directions as to the extent as to which individual parties should provide information in accordance with rule 44.15 (Part 19 deals with Group Litigation Orders)."

3.2. *The Traditional Approach to Disclosure of Liability Insurance Policies*

17. The terms of any liability insurance policy held by one party to litigation will often be of practical interest to the other parties. For example, a claimant may consider that a defendant is not worth pursuing in litigation unless he has cover, and so may request sight of any relevant insurance policy. However, the traditional approach has always been to treat such policies as a private matter between the insured and the insurer, with the result that such policies are not generally disclosable. That was the position in *Bekhor v Bilton* [1991] QB 923 and *Cox v Bankside Members Agency* (an unreported decision of the Court of Appeal dated 29 November 1994). This approach was confirmed by the Law Commission in their paper on Third Parties – Rights Against Insurers (Cm 5217 2001), when they stated that information about cover held by a solvent insured was not available to a claimant unless it was volunteered. It was accepted that the details of such insurance were private matters between an insurer and an insured, and that the mandatory production of such insurance policies might encourage speculative litigation.

18. More recently, in *Harcourt v FEF Griffin* [2007] EWHC 1500 (QB), Irwin J was dealing with a potentially large personal injury claim

where the insurance position (if any) of the first defendant, an unincorporated association, was of considerable significance. A Part 18 request was made designed to discover the extent of its insurance cover. Irwin J accepted that the nature and extent of the first defendant's insurance cover was not in itself a matter for dispute in the proceedings, but he adopted what he described as liberal interpretation to CPR Rule 18 and allowed the request. He said:

> "The purpose of the jurisdiction must be taken to be to ensure that the parties have all the information they need to deal efficiently and justly with the matters which are in dispute between them. Moreover, the wording need not be taken to imply that there must be a live disagreement about the relevant issue, since on very many occasions parties are properly required to furnish information pursuant to CPR Rule 18 precisely to discover that there is or there is not a live disagreement between the parties on a given point. The whole thrust of the new approach in civil litigation enshrined in the Civil Procedure Rules is to avoid waste of time and cost and to ensure swift and, as far as possible, proportionate and economical litigation. Therefore, I have no hesitation in finding that if there was no rule of law or significant rule of practice to the contrary, then the wording of CPR Rule 18 is broad enough to cover information of this kind."

19. Subsequently, in *West London Pipe Line Storage Ltd v Total UK Ltd and Others* [2008] EWHC 1296 (Comm), the first in a series of decisions by David Steel J in connection with the Buncefield disaster, the learned judge had to address a similar application, although it might be observed that, there, the application was patently more "tactical" than in *Harcourt*. He doubted whether *Harcourt* could have been correctly decided because, *inter alia*, a number of the relevant cases had not been cited to Irwin J. He set out the traditional position, which I have endeavoured to summarise at para 17 above, and went on:

> "30. It follows that there is in my judgment no jurisdiction to make the order sought. I reach this conclusion with some considerable hesitation – not least because it is contrary to the view of Irwin J in *Harcourt*. The trend is strongly towards an open approach to litigation. Albeit the potential for prejudice to the defendant and his insurers must be borne in mind, in the modern age of 'cards on the table' the question is readily

posed: why should not the one factor which may be key to the claimant's view of the merits of pursuing a claim, namely what is the limit of cover and will the costs eat it up anyway, be-known? By the same token, concerns as to the appropriate share of court resources to be allocated to a case ought to include allowance for the prospects of an effective recovery. But I am not persuaded that the provisions of CPR, however liberally interpreted, have led to a significant change in law and practice."

3.3. The Approach to ATE Insurance Policies

20. ATE Insurance is a relatively modern creation, and it therefore follows that there are far fewer decisions dealing with the proper approach to the disclosability (or otherwise) of such policies. However, leading counsel have identified two cases that touch on this issue, and whilst neither of them are directly applicable to the present facts, they are, in my judgment, of considerable assistance in identifying the proper approach to the disclosure of such policies. In particular, they illustrate that the existence of an ATE Policy is very often a critical element of the litigation itself because, as in the present case, without the existence of the ATE Policy, there could be no claim at all. They demonstrate that different considerations may therefore apply to the disclosure of the ATE Policy.

21. *Hobson* v *Ashdown Morton Slack Solicitors and Others* [2006] EWHC 1134 (QB) was a decision of Sir Michael Turner in which, in trenchant terms, he rejected the claimants' application for a GLO. He had numerous criticisms to make of the claimants' entire approach to the application in that case. Some, at least, of those criticisms related to the ATE Insurance.

22. Although the facts in *Hobson* are not entirely easy to follow, it appears that, on the first day of the hearing, the judge ordered the disclosure of the ATE Policy. It seems that, given the difficulties that the claimants faced, they did not object to the making of that order, which the judge clearly regarded as crucial to his deliberations. The Policy revealed that the sum insured was £1 million maximum in respect of adverse costs, and the insurance could become voidable after inception in certain specified circumstances. When the learned judge set out his reasons for refusing the GLO, one of them was "the lack of any certainty about the sufficiency of the ATE Insurance in terms of the amount of cover and its enforceability" (see para 71.7 of the

judgment). It does not appear that, in that case at least, there was ever any suggestion that the ATE Insurance Policy was not a relevant document which required to be disclosed for the court's consideration prior to the making of a GLO, or was in some way privileged.

23. The second authority on the point, *Henry*, was cited by the defendant's solicitors in their letter of 26 September 2008 (para 10 above). In that case, Gray J was dealing with an application for a cost-capping order, and Mr Croxford therefore properly accepted that Gray J's comments about the ATE Policy were strictly *obiter*. However, it appears that Gray J was in no doubt at all that the ATE Policy was disclosable.

24. The critical paragraphs of his judgment were as follows:

"23. Both the amount of cover and the existence of material exclusions in the policy are of obvious relevance to the opposite party, who must be in a position to make informed choices as to the conduct of the litigation. If the discrepancy between the amount of cover and the updated estimate of costs up to and including trial had been made known promptly to the BBC (as they could and should have been) the present application could have been mounted far sooner. It is said on behalf of the claimant that exclusions such as those contained in the Temple policy are commonplace in this field. If so, that is a further reason for candour on part of the insured's solicitors about the possible limits on the ability of the opposite party to recover under the policy. It is also said on behalf of the claimant that insurers such as Temple would be unlikely to seek to avoid liability by reference to the exclusion clauses summarised above. I see no reason why this or any defendant should proceed on any such assumption particularly in a high cost case.

24. As to the claim for privilege made in CR's letter of 14 July 2005, it was utterly misconceived. As the Litigation Department pointed out in its letter of 19 September 2005, the BBC must be entitled to see the provisions of the policy in order to assess its financial exposure in any action and to consider whether to apply for a costs capping order. The letter stressed the urgency of the request. Despite that and despite a reminder letter having been written to CR on September 23 it was not until after the BBC on October 4 issued an application seeking disclosure of the policy and a cost cap that CR finally disclosed the policy."

Both Mr Cooksley and Mr Cox accepted that, if I considered that the approach in *Hobson* and/or *Henry* was relevant to the present case, then they were bound to argue that the judges in both those cases were wrong to reach the conclusions that they did.

3.4. Documents Referred to in a Witness Statement

25. I have referred at para 13 above to the provisions of CPR 31.14, which provides that a document mentioned in a witness statement is disclosable. The principal exception to this would be if the document in question was in some way privileged (**Section 3.5** below).

26. The most recent consideration of CPR 31.14 can be found in *Expandable Ltd and Another* v *Rubin* [2008] EWCA Civ 59. In that case, the Court of Appeal said that the principal issue on an application such as this would be whether the document could be said to have been "mentioned" in the witness statement. Rix LJ said:

> "24. The second matter is that, subject to my first comment, the expression 'mentioned' is as general as could be. This is not to my mind intended to be a difficult test. The document in question does not have to be relied on, or referred to in any particular way or for any particular purpose, in order to be mentioned. Subject to Mr Lightman's second point, that the mention of a document within CPR 31.14 amounts to automatic and absolute waiver of privilege in it, which if correct would give to that rule a most important effect, I do not see why there should be need for a strict approach to a request for inspection of a specific document mentioned in one of the qualifying documents. The general ethos of the CPR is for a more cards on the table approach to litigation. If a party thinks it worthwhile to mention a document in its pleadings, witness statements or affidavits, I do not see why, subject to as I say to the question of privilege, the court should put difficulties in the way of inspection. I look upon the mention of a document in pleadings etc as a form of disclosure. The document in question has not been disclosed by list, or at any rate not yet, but it has been disclosed by mention in what, for the purposes of litigation, is another important and formal category of documents. If so, then the party deploying that document by its mention should in principle be prepared to be required to permit its inspection, and the other party should be entitled to its inspection. What in such circumstances is the virtue of coyness?"

26. For completeness, I should note that, on behalf of the claimants, Mr Cooksley also contended that, as a matter of principle, a document

referred to in a witness statement was not disclosable if it could be shown that it was not relevant. He cited no authority in support of that proposition (*Atos Consulting Ltd* v *Avis plc* [2007] EWHC 323 (TCC), the case he did rely on, was concerned with redactions generally, not allegedly irrelevant documents mentioned in pleadings or statements). On one view, by setting up a further "difficulty" in the way of the disclosure of "mentioned" documents, the claimants' reliance on relevance is contrary to the Court of Appeal's approach in *Expandable*. Moreover, in practice, it will always be rather difficult for a claimant to argue that a document which has been expressly referred to in support of an earlier application to the court is not, in fact, relevant at all. Be that as it may, for the purposes of this application, I am prepared to accept that, in theory, it may be possible to avoid disclosure of a mentioned document on the ground of relevance. I deal with the detailed submissions on relevance below.

3.5. Litigation Privilege

27. In *Winterthur Swiss Insurance Co and Another* v *AG (Manchester) Ltd (In Liquidation) and Others* [2006] EWHC 839 (Comm), Aikens J (as he then was) sets out a very helpful summary, at para 65 and following, of the definition of legal professional privilege. He identifies two sub-types, namely legal advice privilege and litigation privilege. It is the latter with which we are concerned with in this case. He defined it as follows:

> "68. The rationale for ... litigation privilege rests, in modern terms, on the principles of access to justice, the proper administration of justice, a fair trial and equality of arms. Those who engage in litigation or are contemplating doing so may well require professional legal advice to advance their case in litigation effectively. To obtain the legal advice and to pursue the adversarial litigation efficiently, the communications between a lawyer and his client and a lawyer and a third party and any communication brought into existence for the dominant purpose of being used in litigation must be kept confidential, without fear that what is said or written might be disclosed. Therefore those classes of communication are covered by 'litigation privilege'."

He went on at para 71 to identify what fell within the scope of litigation privilege. He said:

> "The privilege obviously covers legal advice given by a lawyer to his

client for the purposes of such existing or contemplated litigation. It also extends to communications between the lawyers and his client and the lawyer and third parties, provided that those communications are made for the sole or dominant purpose of obtaining legal advice or conducting that litigation. In deciding whether a communication is subject to 'litigation privilege', the court has to consider objectively the purpose of the person or authority that directed the creation of the communication."

28. Two of the decisions already identified above also deal with privilege. In *Expandable*, the Court of Appeal reasoned that the terms of CPR 31.14 did not automatically apply to documents which were privileged. More pertinently perhaps, in *Henry*, Gray J rejected in clear terms any suggestion that an ATE Policy was a privileged document (see the passage quoted in para 24 above).

4. An Outline of the Parties' Submissions

4.1. *The Defendant's Submissions*

29. Mr Croxford's submissions can be summarised as follows:

a) The defendant is concerned to protect itself, at the end of the trial, against a result whereby it wins the litigation, but then fails to recover its costs because the ATE Policy does not cover its costs or is limited in some way. There is no doubt that such a situation would lead to significant costs of enforcement against the claimants "severally", and may prove fruitless if the claimants are not worth pursuing.

b) The defendant is presently unable to make any assessment as to the realistic value of the claimants' cover. It therefore cannot know whether the policy provides proper cover for the defendant's costs if the defendant is successful. Likewise, it does not know if there are any exclusion clauses within the policy which may invalidate that policy altogether, or whether there are limits which might affect its coverage or value.

c) Whilst the defendant might wish to seek a costs-capping order, or to amend the standard provision within the GLO that costs be borne by the claimants severally, these are difficult applications to make in the absence of information about the ATE Policy.

d) The practical advantages to the defendant of seeing the Policy, so that it can work out what its potential exposure might be, are obvious, as per Gray J in *Henry*. On the other hand, there is no detriment to the claimants if the Policy is disclosed. The defendant points out that the claimants have not identified any prejudice to them should the Policy be disclosed. In addition, the defendant has made it plain that, if the claimants wish to do so, the amounts of the premiums can be redacted from the version of the ATE Policy that is disclosed, just in case it is said that the amount of the premiums themselves might indicate the nature of any advice given to the claimants as to the strength or value of their claims.

30. As a matter of law, the defendant puts its application for disclosure and inspection of the ATE Policy in two principal ways. First, it maintains that, since the policy has been mentioned in the witness statements of Ms Evans and Mr Stockdale, the claimants' solicitors, it is entitled to see the policy pursuant to CPR 31.14. The defendant rejects any suggestion that the policy is either a privileged document or is somehow irrelevant. Alternatively, the defendant seeks disclosure of the Policy pursuant to CPR 3, and/or CPR 18 and/or CPR 19, that is to say, by reference to the court's general case management powers. Unsurprisingly, in making this application, the defendant relies in particular on the decisions in *Hobson* and *Henry*.

4.2. *The Submissions of the Claimants and the Intervening Insurers*
31. The claimants and the Intervening Insurers did not identify any actual detriment if the ATE Policy was disclosed. But they maintained that, as a matter of principle, the policy was not disclosable. In answer to the application under CPR 31.14, the claimants submitted that, although the ATE Policy was mentioned in the witness statements, it was not relevant and/or it was covered by litigation privilege. Furthermore, in answer to the wider claim put by reference to the court's case management powers, both the claimants and the Intervening Insurers relied on the decision of David Steel J in *Total* (set out above), to argue that an insurance policy can never be a disclosable document, because it is a private matter between insured and insurer and irrelevant to the issues between the parties.

32. In the light of these submissions, I propose to deal first with the application under CPR 31.14 (**Section 5** below), before going on to consider the wider application pursuant to the court's general case management powers (**Section 6** below).

5. The Application Pursuant to CPR 31.14

5.1. The Mention of the ATE Policy

33. The claimants' application for a GLO was supported by a witness statement signed by Gwen Evans, the claimants' solicitor, dated 23 February 2009. At para 15 of that statement, Ms Evans said this:

> "My firm has the necessary resources to deal with this case and are experienced in handling environmental group actions involving allegations of private and public nuisance. We have entered into Conditional Fee Agreements (CFA) with the claimants in these proceedings and are also able to assist in relation to the funding of disbursements. The CFA is supported by a policy of insurance."

34. Following the application by the defendant for disclosure of the ATE Policy (because, amongst other reasons, it was expressly referred to in Ms Evans' statement) the claimants served a further statement from Neil Stockdale, the partner in charge of the case. His evidence is important. He said:

> "7. The ATE policy was referred to at para 15 of the witness statement of Gwen Evans dated 23 February 2009. However, it was not the intention of the claimants or Gwen Evans in making reference to the policy in the statement to waive privilege.
>
> 8. Gwen Evans has informed me, and I recall when discussing the preparation of the statement at the relevant time, that the reference to the policy was included to address comments made by Sir Michael Turner in *Hobson v AMS Solicitors* [2006] EWHC 1134.
>
> 9. The *Hobson* matter concerned an application for a Group Litigation Order where there was a lack of certainty about the extent of any After the Event Insurance Protection said to be awarded to the claimants. Sir Michael Turner was extremely critical of the litigation and dismissed the application for a Group Litigation Order.
>
> 10. In the circumstances given Sir Michael Turner's comments concerning ATE Insurance both Gwen Evans and I felt it appropriate that the claimants' application for a Group Litigation Order provide information relating to the way in which the claimants were funding their case."

35. It seems to me that the following must flow from this evidence.

First, the ATE Policy has plainly been mentioned in these witness statements, so that a claim for disclosure under CPR 31.14 has been properly triggered. Secondly, it seems to me clear beyond doubt that the policy was deliberately referred to in Ms Evans' statement, for a particular purpose. It was not merely mentioned in passing. It was deliberately deployed by the claimants in support of their application for the GLO.

36. It follows therefore, that unless I am persuaded that the ATE Policy is either irrelevant or is covered by litigation privilege, then I should order disclosure of the policy pursuant to CPR 31.14, and follow the approach outlined by the Court of Appeal in *Expandable*.

5.2. Relevance

37. There are, so it seems to me, three reasons why the ATE Policy is relevant. First, the fact of the policy was regarded as an important matter by the claimants' solicitors for the reasons explained by Mr Stockdale. They deliberately referred to the Policy in Ms Evans' statement. It is not suggested by Mr Stockdale that the Policy was irrelevant; on the contrary, he accepts that it was relevant to the application for a GLO. The claimants cannot now argue that the Policy is somehow irrelevant.

38. Secondly, it seems to me that the ATE Policy is obviously relevant to this Group Litigation. The parties are agreed that, if there was no GLO, this litigation would not be pursued, because the value of each individual claim is modest, whilst the costs (and therefore the costs risk) would be likely to be very significant. If there was no GLO, there would be no proceedings. And there would be no GLO without the existence of the ATE Policy: that is why it was referred to in Ms Evans' witness statement in the first place. It is therefore relevant to the very existence of this litigation.

39. Thirdly, it seems to me that the terms of the Policy are relevant to the issues before the court. In this regard, I respectfully agree with the approach of Sir Michael Turner in *Hobson*, as well as the approach of Gray J in *Henry*.

40. Furthermore, were there any remaining doubt about it, it seems to me that the claimants' solicitors have already accepted that the terms of the Policy are a relevant matter. I have referred at para 11 above to their own letter of 6 October 2008. That letter acknowledges that questions such as the existence of possible exclusion clauses and

the level of cover, *are* relevant. It is for that reason that the letter purported to summarise the contents of the Policy on both topics. It seems to me that, since the claimants' solicitors have acknowledged the relevance of the terms of the Policy, they cannot reasonably expect either the defendant or the court to accept their summary of the document, as opposed to the disclosure of the Policy itself. Again, this very point was made by Gray J in *Henry*: it is wrong in principle to make the defendant continue to incur costs merely on the assumption that the Hugh James letter is an accurate summary of the ATE Policy.

41. What would be the position if, contrary to Hugh James' advice, there was a relevant exclusion clause which meant that, at the end of this potentially expensive litigation, the policy was avoided and the defendant was unable to recover its costs without pursuing 140 different claimants? Would the defendant then have a claim in negligence against the claimants' solicitors because the letter of October 6 was misleading? It seems to me that this would be encouraging satellite litigation of the worst sort. Given the contents of the letter, I conclude that the ATE Policy, which is there summarised, should be provided to the defendant so that it can form its own view as to its limits and exclusion clauses.

42. This point can also be illustrated by reference to a dispute that arose during the hearing. Although the letter purported to confirm that the Policy provided an adequate level of cover, during his submissions Mr Cooksley said that the level of cover was irrelevant because it might be limited and might be altered. He also suggested that the sum insured was meaningless and might not be the whole amount. In reply on that point, Mr Croxford expressed the defendant's concern that the letter of 6 October 2008 (which of course said that the cover was adequate) might in fact be wrong or misleading, and he made the point that in those circumstances, the defendant was even more concerned to see the actual ATE Policy. In the light of this argument about the important issue of the possible level of the Policy limit/cover, it seemed to me that this submission was well-founded.

43. Finally, on the question of relevance, I should address the reliance by the claimants, and also by the Intervening Insurer, upon the decision in *Total* and the other cases referred to in **Section 3.1** above. It seems to me that there is a difference between liability insurance, which may well have been in place years before the events which gave rise to the subsequent litigation and have absolutely nothing to do with

those events, and ATE Insurance (particularly in the context of Group Litigation), the inception of which may be a critical factor in the existence of the proceedings themselves. In the former situation, it is easy to see why the courts have been reluctant to order the disclosure of a commercial transaction which was and remains an entirely private matter between the insured and the insurers, the inception of which had nothing whatsoever to do with the events which later formed the subject matter of the litigation. But, in my judgment, that approach is of no assistance in the consideration of an application for the disclosure of an ATE Insurance Policy which, depending on the facts, will have been taken out for the sole purpose of allowing a claimant to pursue litigation which would otherwise not be possible.

44. In circumstances such as these, where the GLO depends on the ATE Insurance Policy, and where, without such a Policy, there would be no proceedings at all, it does not seem to me that the traditional approach to liability insurance is of direct relevance. On the contrary, I consider that the correct approach to the disclosure of the ATE Insurance Policy is that set out in both *Hobson* and *Henry*.

45. For all these reasons, therefore, I conclude that the ATE Insurance Policy is a relevant document, which is why it was referred to in the witness statement of Ms Evans in the first place. Thus, unless it can be shown that the document is covered by privilege, it is disclosable pursuant to CPR 31.14.

5.3. Litigation Privilege

46. In my judgment, the ATE policy is not covered by litigation privilege. I note that, during the course of his able submissions, Mr Cooksley was unable to identify any case in which an ATE Policy has been found to be a privileged document. Although he relied on *Winterthur*, that was a case about documents created after the inception of the Policy, and whether they were privileged. It was not concerned with a claim for privilege in the Policy itself. On the contrary, as far as I am aware, the only authority in which this point has been considered is *Henry*. It is fair to say that Gray J was not overly troubled by the suggestion that the ATE Policy was privileged, rejecting the argument in a few crisp lines (see para 24 above). I respectfully agree with him.

47. The type of documents covered by litigation privilege are summarised in para 71 of the judgment of Aikens J in *Winterthur*

(para 27 above). In my judgment, the ATE Insurance policy in this case does not fit into any of these categories. It is not a document containing legal advice. It is not a communication between the claimants' solicitors and the claimants, or between the claimants' solicitors and third parties. It is simply not caught by this description.

48. The one potential exception to that is the information within the ATE Policy as to the amount of the premiums. It is rightly accepted by Mr Croxford that, as a matter of principle, privilege will extend to material which would allow the reader to work out what legal advice had been given. Here, the claimants have indicated that the amount of the premiums stated in the Policy could be said to reflect legal advice as to the claimants' prospects of success and, although I regard that as a little far-fetched on the facts, I can see circumstances in which that point might have at least some force. Accordingly, it seems to me that the amounts of the premiums should be redacted from the disclosed ATE Policy document.

49. Apart from the amounts of the premiums, the claimants and the Intervening Insurer were unable to identify any other parts of the Policy which would otherwise fall within the category of litigation privilege. For the reasons which I have set out above, I am in no doubt that the Policy itself is not so caught.

5.4. *Summary*

50. The ATE Insurance Policy was clearly mentioned in Mr Evans' first statement, which was made in support of an application for a GLO, and referred to again in Mr Stockdale's later statement. Following the approach of the Court of Appeal in *Expandable*, those "mentions" made the document disclosable pursuant to CPR 31.14 unless it could be shown that the document was privileged. This document was not privileged.

51. Although there is no authority for the proposition that CPR 31.14 does not apply if the document is irrelevant, I have assumed that there is such a principle for the purposes of this application. However, it is plain that on the facts the Policy was indeed relevant, and considered by the claimants' solicitors to be so.

52. Accordingly I consider that, pursuant to CPR 31.14, the Policy is a disclosable document and should be disclosed for inspection. In this way, the defendant will be able to form its own view of the terms of the Policy, and not be forced to rely on the claimants' solicitors'

summary. I do, however, order that the amounts of the premiums should be redacted from the version of the Policy that is disclosed.

53. In the light of this conclusion it is, strictly speaking, unnecessary for me to go on to consider the alternative basis for the application, pursuant to the court's general case management powers. The CPR 31.14 application is decisive in this case, which means, amongst other things, that Mr Cox's submissions – which were limited to the secondary case – were ultimately immaterial to the result. However, in the light of the detailed submissions that I have heard from all parties, and on the assumption that I am wrong to allow the application under CPR 31.14, I go on to deal with the application pursuant to the court's case management powers.

6. The Application Pursuant to the Court's Case Management Powers

6.1. *Disclosure of Insurance Policies*

54. For the reasons outlined in paras 43 and 44 above, I consider that different considerations apply to the disclosure of a pre-existing liability policy (which may or may not be triggered by the subsequent litigation), and an ATE Policy, the existence of which is a vital component in the litigation itself. Accordingly, I consider that the traditional approach to the disclosure of liability insurance policies, as summarised by David Steel J in *Total*, is not directly applicable to the disclosure of ATE Insurance Policies. Accordingly, I turn to the CPR to see what general provisions may be relevant to this application.

6.2. *The "Cards on the Table" Approach Behind the CPR*

55. I have already referred to the overriding objective (CPR 1.1) and the court's wide case management powers under CPR Part 3. In a number of the cases which I have cited above, the judges talk of the "cards on the table" approach that lies behind the CPR. In my judgment, pursuant to that approach, the ATE Policy should be disclosed.

56. I reach this conclusion by balancing the parties' respective interests in the litigation, and the effect upon them of the disclosure of the Policy. On the one hand, it is plainly in the defendant's interest to know the terms of the Policy (as per *Henry*), so that it can see what exposure it might have if, at the end of the case, the defendant is successful and seeks to recover its costs. In one sense, that only puts the defendant in the same position as the claimants are in already,

because they can know, by checking the defendant's most recently filed accounts, that the defendant is a large company with more than sufficient assets to meet any costs liability that it may have should it lose these proceedings.

57. I consider therefore that it is just and fair that the defendant is able, at this stage, to identify the risks, if any, inherent in this Group Litigation. I accept, as Gray J accepted in *Henry*, that this can only be done by a sight of the ATE Policy. I consider that it would be unjust and unfair to require the defendant to participate in this Group Litigation knowing that it would have to pay the claimants' costs if it lost, but not knowing that it might not recover any of its own costs if it won, because of some exclusion or limit in the Policy. That would not be a level playing field.

58. On the other hand, the claimants have not been able to identify any prejudice to them if the ATE Policy was disclosed. I accept that things might be different – the balancing of the parties' respective interests might lead to another result – if the claimants had been able to identify some particular detriment or disadvantage to them if the ATE Policy was disclosed (with the amounts of the premiums redacted). But no such detriment has been demonstrated.

59. At one point, Mr Cooksley suggested that, if the ATE Policy was disclosed, the defendant would then seek to exploit its knowledge of the level of cover by running up huge costs bills, thereby forcing the litigation off the road and into the ditch. There are two points to be made about that submission. First, there is absolutely no evidence that the defendant, a large and well-known organisation, would engage in such tactics, and I could not decide the outcome of this application on such a speculative basis. But secondly, and much more importantly, the submission ignores my own wide case management powers as the assigned judge. In the TCC, cases are managed by the same judge from the first CMC all the way through to judgment, which gives the court every opportunity to ensure that the costs are kept down and that all steps and directions are justifiable on costs/benefit grounds. The claimants can rest assured that this Group Litigation, which I will case manage in the usual way, will be tightly controlled, with the result that the costs will always be kept to the lowest possible level in all the circumstances. There will be no question of costs being run up to obstruct the purpose of the Group Litigation.

60. Accordingly, in endeavouring to do justice between the parties,

I am faced with a situation where the defendant would be litigating in the dark without sight of the ATE Policy, whilst the claimants can identify no detriment to them if the terms of the Policy were disclosed. In such circumstances, on a proper application of the court's general case management powers, I would conclude that the Policy should be disclosed. It would be proportionate to the financial position of each party (CPR 1.1(2)(c)(iv)). On that basis, therefore, the only reason why I would not go on and make such an order would be if there was a specific part of the CPR which prevented or prohibited it.

6.3. 44 PD. 19

61. In support of the claimants' position, Mr Cooksley and Mr Cox submitted that, since the claimants had already provided the information identified in 44PD Section 19, they were not obliged under the CPR to provide any further information. Mr Croxford submitted that the information identified in Section 19 was the minimum information required, to be supplied in all cases, but that the provisions there did not prevent a party in the position of the defendant in the present case from seeking disclosure of the entirety of the ATE Policy.

62. In my judgment, Mr Croxford's submissions are correct. There are a number of reasons for this. First, there is nothing within 44 PD Section 19 which stipulates that no information (other than that contained in para 19.4) is ever to be provided. On the contrary, it seems to me that this part of the Practice Direction is stipulating the minimum that must be provided in every case, without any suggestion that, in a particular case where the need has been made out, the Policy itself should not be disclosed.

63. Secondly, it would be an odd outcome if the court were prevented from exercising its wide case management powers pursuant to CPR 1.1 and/or CPR 3 and/or CPR 19 by reference to a list of information buried away in a Costs Practice Direction. That is not how the CPR works. The parties must comply with the applicable Practice Directions; they set out the particular rules and procedures to be followed in any given situation. To that extent, I accept Mr Cox's submission, that para 19.4 is a Code to be followed in cases of this sort. But the court's case management powers apply across the board and, in the absence of express words, cannot be regarded as being

restricted or limited in the way contended for by the claimants and the Intervening Insurers.

64. In my judgment, this approach is confirmed by the introductory words to para 19.4(1) of 44PD ("unless the court otherwise orders..."), set out in para 16 above. Mr Cox was obliged to argue that those words were designed to permit the court only to make an order disallowing the provision of even the minimum information set out in that paragraph, but could not be read as giving the court the power to order the provision of *more* information than that set out there. The basis for that submission was unclear; it seems to me that these words are not to be read in such an artificial and restricted way. On their face, these words allow the court, in appropriate circumstances, to order the provision of either more or less information than that set out in para 19.4. There is nothing to suggest that the power can only be exercised one way.

65. Accordingly, in my judgment, the general application of the court's case management powers (which, for the reasons set out in **Section 6.2**, would lead me to allow the application) are not circumscribed or restricted by 44 PD Section 19.

6.4. *Other Considerations*

66. There are two other matters, canvassed during the course of the submissions, which also seem to me to support my conclusion that I should exercise the court's general case management powers to allow the defendant's application.

67. Despite the absence of clear words in the CPR, an ATE Insurance Policy might well be disclosable in particular circumstances in any event. One example was an application for costs-capping. In a case where a claimant had the advantage of an ATE Policy, and the court is considering making costs-capping order, it is very difficult to see how a sensible order could be made without sight of the ATE Policy. Mr Cox accepted that proposition, (at least insofar as it related to the amount of the premium) despite the fact that the relevant part of the CPR (CPR 44.19 and the associated Practice Direction), do not contain any express reference to disclosure of the ATE Policy.

68. Similarly, a claimant who has the benefit of ATE Insurance may face an application for security of costs. Although CPR 25.12–25.15 do not expressly deal with that topic, the disclosure of the Policy may be necessary in order for the court to arrive at a fair conclusion both

as to the principle of ordering security and, if established, the level of security to be provided. Mr Cox accepted that, in such circumstances, the party concerned may well elect to disclose the Policy to enable the court to reach a sensible conclusion. Both these examples suggest to me that the disclosure (or otherwise) of an ATE Policy will depend on the facts of the particular case and the specific reasons that disclosure is being sought, regardless of the absence of any specific reference to disclosure of the ATE Policy in the relevant Rules.

69. The second matter which, so it seems to me, confirms my approach, is the recent decision of the Court of Appeal in *R (Buglife – The Invertebrate Conservation Trust)* v *Thurrock Thames Gateway Development Corporation* [2008] EWCA Civ 1209. In that case, one of the matters that the court was concerned with was disclosure of the level of the success fee element of a CFA, in the context of a cost-capping order. The provisions of 44 PD do not say in terms that the level of a success fee should be disclosed. However, in the context of an application for a costs capping order, the Court of Appeal had no doubt that this information should be supplied. At para 27 of his judgment, Sir Anthony Clarke MR set out a part of an Appendix to a Report from a Working Group on Access to Environmental Justice (which suggested that the success fee was not to be disclosed) and went on:

> "We do not accept that approach in this context. The agreed success fee is relevant to the likely amount of the liability of the defendant to the claimant if the claimant wins. It is therefore relevant to the amount of any cap on that liability. In our opinion the court should know the true position when deciding what the cap should be."

70. Mr Croxford argues, by analogy, that if, in a particular set of circumstances, the level of the success fee was disclosable, then *a fortiori*, in certain circumstances, the general terms of an ATE Policy must be disclosable too. It all depends on the facts and particular reasons for the application.

71. I accept Mr Croxford's submissions on this issue. It does seem to me that these cases are fact-sensitive, and it is dangerous to draw hard and fast principles from different factual situations. But the cases demonstrate that sensitive matters or documents relating to funding arrangements can be disclosable if they are required in order to allow

the court to dispose justly of the particular disputes between the parties.

6.5. Summary

72. For the reasons set out above, it seems to me that the considerations arising on an application for disclosure of an ATE Insurance Policy may well be different to those that arise in relation to a conventional liability insurance policy, particularly where, as here, the ATE Policy is an integral element of the Group Litigation itself. It seems to me that, on a proper consideration of the court's case management powers under the CPR, the order for disclosure of the Policy in the present case should be allowed. 44PD.19 is not to be read as somehow restricting or preventing the court from exercising those powers in the best way to meet the over-riding objective. Depending on the particular application and its reasons, the terms of an ATE Insurance Policy, and even the level of the success fee, may be matters which are required to be disclosed in order to deal fairly and justly with any given litigation.

73. Taking into account all of the considerations set out in this Section I consider that, on the exercise of court's general case management powers, the defendant is entitled to the disclosure and inspection order sought.

7. Conclusions

74. For the reasons set out in **Section 5** above, I consider that the ATE Insurance policy referred to in the original statement of Ms Evans is a disclosable document pursuant to CPR 31.14. The document is relevant and it is not privileged.

75. For the reasons set out in **Section 6** above, I consider that, pursuant to the court's case management powers, on the material available to me in this particular case, the ATE Policy should be disclosed. That would properly do justice between the parties. 44PD.19 does not prohibit or prevent any such order.

76. For the avoidance of doubt, I should make clear that, if the application for disclosure had been argued at the same time as the application for the GLO (as it would have been, but for the need to accommodate the Intervening Insurers), I would have made the GLO on condition that the ATE Policy was disclosed, but with the amount of the premiums redacted.

77. I will deal with all other matters arising out of the defendant's

application, including all questions of costs, at the handing down of this judgment.

Nigel Cooksley QC and *John Bates* (instructed by Hugh James) appeared for the claimants.

Ian Croxford QC and *Thomas de la Mare* (instructed by Nabarro LLP) appeared for the defendant.

Greg Cox (of Colemans-CTTS LLP) appeared for the intervening insurers.

Case 26
Barr and Others

v

Biffa Waste Services Ltd (No. 2) (Westmill Landfill Group Litigation)

[2010] 3 Costs LR 317

High Court of Justice, Queen's Bench Division, Technology and Construction Court
Neutral Citation Number: [2009] EWHC 2444 (TCC)
2 October 2009

Before:
Coulson J

Headnote

A Group Litigation Order in respect of claims for negligence and nuisance by 163 claimant households alleged to arise out of odour omissions from a site operated by the defendant had been made. The defendant then applied for a costs capping order pursuant to CPR 44.18 seeking to cap the recoverable costs of the claimants should they be successful in the proceedings. The cap sought was the maximum sum due under an ATE policy taken out by the claimants. The court considered the principles relating to costs caps and the application of CPR 44.18, declined to order a cap, but did order that the claimants' eventual recoverable costs be linked to the most recent estimate of their costs.

Judgment

1. Introduction

1. COULSON J: Pursuant to a Group Litigation Order ("GLO") made on 27 March 2009 by Ramsey J, this action comprises claims for negligence and nuisance by 163 claimant households said to arise out of odour emissions from the defendant's Westmill Landfill Site near Ware in Hertfordshire. Other matters of background are set out in my judgment on the defendant's successful application for disclosure of the claimants' ATE insurance policy at [2009] EWHC 1033 (TCC).

2. By an application dated 17 September 2009, the defendant now seeks, pursuant to CPR 44.18, an order capping the recoverable costs of the claimants if, contrary to the defendant's case, the claimants are ultimately successful in these proceedings. The cap sought is by reference to the limit of the claimants' ATE policy. That has recently been increased to £1 million, which is therefore the maximum recoverable by the defendant, if the defendant is ultimately successful in the action. As we shall see, the defendant's application is unusual, because it concentrates on the issue of disproportionality, not by reference to the amount of the claimants' future costs itself – a figure which was in fact unknown to the defendant at the time that the application was made and argued, and which the defendant suggests is in any event too low – but instead by reference to what the defendant says are the significant inequalities inherent in this particular litigation.

3. I summarise the relevant principles of law in **section 2** below. In **section 3**, I identify the particular features of this litigation which lie at the heart of the application. At **section 4**, I then consider the application against the test set out in CPR 44.18 and those principles of law. In **section 5**, I deal with a separate but related point arising out of the claimants' costs estimate and the rules at CPR 44.3. There is a short summary of my conclusions at **section 6**. I am again very grateful to all counsel for their assistance in dealing with this interesting and difficult application.

2. Costs Capping/Relevant Principles of Law

2.1 Pre-April 2009

4. CPR 44.18 came into force in April 2009. It is therefore necessary

to consider, albeit briefly, the pre-April 2009 authorities dealing with costs capping before setting out the new provisions.

5. The starting point for any consideration of costs capping orders is the decision in *Musa King v The Daily Telegraph Group Ltd (Practice Note)* [2005] 1 WLR 2282, in which the court's power to make such orders was affirmed. It was a defamation case in which the claimant's solicitors were working on a CFA with a significant uplift, but there was no ATE cover. In other words, the defendant was faced with what Lord Hoffmann described in *Campbell v MGN Ltd (No. 2)* [2005] 1 WLR 3394 as "the blackmailing effect of defamation litigation conducted under a CFA without ATE insurance". In *King*, the Court of Appeal set out robust general rules relating to the making of costs capping orders.

6. Guidance as to the circumstances in which a costs capping order may be appropriate was provided in *Smart v East Cheshire NHS Trust* [2003] 80 BMLR 175. In that case Gage J (as he then was) said this:

> "In my judgment the court should only consider making a costs cap order in such cases where the applicant shows by evidence that there is a real and substantial risk that, without such an order, costs will be disproportionately or unreasonably incurred, and that this risk may not be managed by conventional case management and a detailed assessment of costs after a trial, and it is just to make such an order. It seems to me that it is unnecessary to ascribe to such a test the general heading of exceptional circumstances. I would expect that, in the run of ordinary actions, it would be rare for this test to be satisfied, but it is impossible to predict all the circumstances in which it may be said to arise. Low value claims will inevitably mean a higher proportion of costs to value than high value claims. Some high value claims will involve greater factual and legal complexities than others."

7. In *Knight v Beyond Properties Pty Ltd* [2007] 1 WLR 625 Mann J applied this test and concluded that, on the facts of that case, no costs capping order was appropriate. That was because, he said, any extravagant costs could be left to detailed assessment post-trial, rather than by way of any application before the costs had actually been incurred. He remarked that "retrospective judgments about such things are likely to be more reliable than prospective judgments". In addition, he rejected the suggestion that *King* was authority for the proposition that costs capping orders would always be made in cases

where there was a CFA and no ATE insurance. On the contrary, he stressed that both *King* and *Campbell* were dealing with "the particular vices of CFAs in defamation actions".

8. The Court of Appeal decision in *Willis* v *Nicolson* [2007] EWCA 199 (Civ) was concerned with a personal injury claim where the damages sought were in the region of £5 million. The defendants sought a cost cap. Although Field J refused an overall cost cap, he ordered that the claimant's prospective costs should not exceed £460,000 (the figure that the claimant's solicitors had estimated), a result that the claimant was in any event quite prepared to accept. The defendant's appeal was rejected. Amongst his general observations Buxton LJ said this:

> "7. In cases where a Group Litigation Order has been made it is well recognised, first, that excessive costs may be a significant problem; and second that the court must for that reason, amongst others, exercise direct and continuing control over the proceedings. Costs capping, or something equivalent to it, is therefore a familiar exercise in that context. ...
>
> 10. But however attractive costs capping orders may be in theory, in practice they present some formidable problems. These can be demonstrated from consideration of the order sought in the present case; and from some more general observations about costs capping that we venture in the last section of the judgment. ...
>
> 24. With all these factors in mind we drafted a comprehensive set of principles to be applied in personal injury cases, which are the most obvious candidates for costs capping; which could also be considered for application to other types of case. However, further discussion with members of the court, including the Master of the Rolls and the Deputy Head of Civil Justice, has demonstrated that, despite the terms in which permission to appeal was granted in this case, and the observations in this court to which attention is drawn in para 8 above, there remain serious doubts as to whether further guidance on costs capping, if it is to be given at all, should emanate from a constitution of the court as opposed to being formulated by the Civil Procedure Rules Committee, after extensive consultation. We are bound to recognise the imperative of that view. We therefore do not pursue the question further. It will be for the Rules Committee to decide whether, and if so with what degree

of urgency, to take up the issues that we have identified earlier in this judgment."

9. The Rules Committee did indeed take up these issues. It is that reference that has led to the new CPR 44.18.

10. Finally, in this short tour of the relevant principles in play before CPR 44.18 came into force, mention should be made of the decision of Akenhead J in the *Corby Group Litigation* [2008] EWHC 619, the only authority that I have been able to find concerning a costs capping order in the TCC in a case where a GLO had been made. There, the parties accepted that the costs on both sides should be capped and the issues before the judge focused on the best way in which the necessary calculations should be carried out. I note that, in a case that might be regarded as rather more complicated than the present one, the costs were capped at £900,000 for the claimants, and £1.25 million for the defendant.

2.2 CPR 44.18

11. CPR 44.18 provides as follows:

"(1) A costs capping order is an order limiting the amount of future costs (including disbursements) which a party may recover pursuant to an order for costs subsequently made.

(2) In this rule, 'future costs' means costs incurred in respect of work done after the date of the costs capping order but excluding the amount of any additional liability. ...

(5) The court may at any stage of proceedings make a costs capping order against all or any of the parties, if –

(a) it is in the interests of justice to do so;

(b) there is a substantial risk that without such an order costs will be disproportionately incurred; and

(c) it is not satisfied that the risk in sub-paragraph (b) can be adequately controlled by –

(i) case management directions or orders made under Part 3; and

(ii) detailed assessment of costs.

(6) In considering whether to exercise its discretion under this rule, the court will consider all the circumstances of the case, including –

(a) whether there is a substantial imbalance between the financial position of the parties;

(b) whether the costs of determining the amount of the cap are likely to be proportionate to the overall costs of the litigation;

(c) the stage which the proceedings have reached; and

(d) the costs which have been incurred to date and the future costs."

12. The reference in subrule (2) to "any additional liability" is a reference to (amongst other things) the percentage uplift within any CFA: see CPR rule 43.2(o). Thus the costs capping order must relate only to the base costs incurred by the solicitors, and not any percentage uplift.

13. It seems to me that, on their face, these provisions reflect closely the words of Gage J in *Smart*. In *Peacock* v *MGN Ltd* [2009] EWHC 769 (QB) Eady J expressed the view the new rules comprised "a more restrictive approach" to costs capping than that favoured by many. He said:

> "8. Thus, it is clear that, at least for the moment, the proactive and interventionist approach recommended by Brooke LJ in *Musa King* is on the wane. The contrasting judicial viewpoint, exemplified by the cautious approach of Gage J (as he then was) in *Smart* v *East Cheshire NHS Trust* ..., is now in the ascendant. Indeed, it is clearly reflected in the wording of the new rules."

14. On the detail of the application in *Peacock*, Eady J reached the same conclusion as Mann J in *Knight*, namely, that the matters raised in support of the making of a costs capping order could be dealt with at the assessment of costs at the end of the case. He did, however, make clear a certain level of unhappiness with this result, saying at para 22:

> "If I had a free hand, and were to follow the guidance offered in *Musa King*, I should be strongly inclined to impose a costs cap and to refer the matter to a costs judge to address hourly rates. I should also recommend that the case was not one in which the costs of leading counsel could reasonably be incurred. At the moment (unlike the situation confronting Gray J in *Henry* v *BBC* [2006] 1 All ER 154) the proceedings are not so far advanced that it would be too late to make a prospective costs capping order. It might be possible thereby to reduce the defendant's exposure by approximately £100,000. On the other hand, consistency in

these matters is important and I do not have a free hand. I am inhibited both by the 'exceptionality' principle and by the fact that I am satisfied that the risk of disproportionality could be adequately controlled by a costs judge at the stage of detailed assessment."

2.3 Summary

15. From these various authorities, I would venture to summarise the law on costs capping orders as follows:

(a) A party seeking a costs capping order will need to demonstrate on the evidence that such an order satisfies the criteria at sub rules 44.18(5) and 44.18(6). Those sub rules mirror the restrictive approach outlined by Gage J in *Smart*.
(b) A case in which these criteria are satisfied is likely to be exceptional: see Eady J in *Peacock*.
(c) The mere fact that the claimant has the benefit of a CFA and no ATE cover will not, as of right, entitle a defendant to a costs capping order: see *Knight*. That position must apply *a fortiori* where there is ATE cover, but it is or may well be insufficient. On the other hand, the fact that there is either no ATE cover, or inadequate ATE cover, must be a relevant fact for the court to take into account in considering all the circumstances of the case.
(d) In cases where a GLO has been made, costs capping orders may be more common: see Buxton LJ in *Willis* and Akenhead J in *Corby Group Litigation*.

16. For what it is worth, I should add that, in my view, the observations of Brooke LJ in *King*, and Lord Hoffmann in *Campbell*, about the potentially blackmailing effect on a defendant, in cases where a claimant has the advantage of a CFA and no ATE cover, are pertinent to all kinds of civil litigation, not just defamation cases. A defendant with no prospect of recovering its costs, even if it successfully defends all the claims made, may well be the effective victim of commercial blackmail, whether the claim is for damage to reputation, damage to property or personal injury.

3. Particular Features of This Litigation

3.1 Introduction

17. I have been provided with a lengthy statement from the defendant's solicitor, Mr Gibson, and a shorter statement from the claimants'

solicitor, Miss Evans. From that evidence and from the other papers in the case, I set out below what I consider to be the particular features of this litigation that are relevant to the defendant's application for a costs capping order.

3.2 *Particular Features of the Claimants' Position*
18. There are 163 claimant households. Their claims are limited to general damages calculated, amongst other things, in accordance with the observations by Lord Hoffmann in *Hunter and Others* v *Canary Wharf Ltd* [1997] 1 AC 655. The claimants suggest that their damages claims are worth about £1 million, which indicates an average recovery of about £6,000 per household. I am bound to say that, on the material available so far, this seems to me to be at the upper end of the range of likely damages recoverable.

19. With a maximum recovery per household of, say, £6,000, and with a real possibility that, even if liability is established, the amount recovered may be less, it will immediately be seen that the making of the GLO in this case was of the greatest importance to the individual claimants. Without it, these claims would almost certainly not have been worth pursuing by the claimants individually. Their own costs, and the risk as to their liability for the defendant's costs if they were unsuccessful, would have been out of all proportion to the likely damages recovered. Furthermore, I note that such GLOs are rare. I am told that there have been about 70 such orders since the relevant legislation was introduced. I am also told that no further GLO has been made by the President of the Queen's Bench Division since the order in the present case in March 2009.

20. It should also be noted that the claimants' solicitors are experienced in the obtaining of GLOs, and the procedure in proceedings such as these. The evidence shows that claims of this kind represent a major element of the claimants' solicitor's business. Given the modest value of the individual claims here, it is inevitable that, as the defendant argued, these proceedings are going to benefit the lawyers on either side just as much as, if not more than, the claimants themselves.

21. The claimants' solicitors are, of course, working on a CFA. It is my understanding that that CFA operates in a relatively standard fashion, namely, that if the action is lost, the claimants' solicitors

recover nothing, and if it is won, they recover 100% uplift on the costs that they have incurred.

22. Unlike in *King*, the claimants here do have the benefit of ATE insurance. That was the policy which I required to be disclosed earlier this year. The limit on that policy was £375,000. That low limit was the subject of complaint by the defendant. A day or so before the CMC last week, the claimants notified the defendant and the court that that limit had been increased to £1 million. Given that the defendant's original application was linked to the total value of the ATE policy, that increase has obviously had an effect on this application.

23. In breach of CPR 43, and para 16.4.1 of the TCC Guide, the claimants attended the CMC without having provided any detail as to their costs, either past or future. They indicated in their answers to the CMC Questionnaire that their costs to date were £500,000, but no breakdown of that figure was provided. The sum for future costs was merely noted "TBA". At the hearing on September 24 I required a proper breakdown to be provided by September 28, so that I could consider the actual figures before reaching a conclusion on the defendant's application. Costs breakdowns were provided in accordance with that order, and I have been helpfully provided with a certain amount of material dealing with those breakdowns. Further short submissions were made on the figures this afternoon.

24. As to the £500,000 said to have been incurred to date, I express some surprise at the size of that figure. I do not under-estimate the organisational effort required to get a GLO off the ground in these circumstances, particularly given the large number of claimants. But as was pointed out during argument, the claimants' pleadings are very short and there is nothing yet prepared by way of expert evidence. The £500,000 therefore appears on its face to be excessive, a point made by the defendant in their written submissions. The skeletal breakdown of the sum provided on September 28 does not provide any information that leads me to modify that view. Of course, the fact that such a large sum has been incurred is largely irrelevant for the purposes of any costs capping exercise, because that can relate to prospective costs only.

25. The future costs to be incurred by the claimants are now said to be £1,471,767 including VAT. This figure is based upon a number of assumptions that may or may not turn out to be accurate. For example, it assumes that there will be one single expert on each side,

as opposed to the defendant's estimate, which is based on there being three experts per side. As things stand, in accordance with the current directions, there will be one expert per party but, depending on the outcome of other directions that I ordered at the CMC, there could be at least one further surveyor expert on each side and possibly – although I have to say that I consider it to be very unlikely – an additional expert in relation to land use and waste disposal policy.

26. I note that the defendant criticises these estimated future costs for being, at least potentially, too low. However, given the assumptions on which they are made, I reject that submission. I consider that in the circumstances they are, if anything, higher than they should be, given the relatively straightforward nature of the issues in this case. However, the estimates mean that in an action which is not, I think, overly complex, and where the likely maximum value of the claim is £1 million, the claimants' overall costs will be £1.471 million for the future and £500,000 already, coming to a total of just under £2 million.

27. The claimants' liability for the defendant's costs, if the defendant is successful will, at least in theory, considerably exceed these figures. The defendant's costs are said to amount to £750,000 so far, with a total estimated at £3.3 million. On the face of it, I am bound to consider that estimate also to be excessive, based as it is on a large amount of expert evidence, some of which I have indicated may well not be necessary, and a 30-day trial, which is also not the period for which the trial has now been fixed. But it may very well be that the claimants' theoretical liability for the defendant's costs will exceed £2 million and could be as high as, say, £2.5 million.

28. There may, however, be significant difficulties in terms of the defendant's ability actually to recover those costs against the claimants. Under the GLO, the claimants are severally liable for the defendant's costs, but they are not jointly liable. Thus, if the defendant is successful and the defendant's costs exceed the amount of the ATE policy, then the defendant will have to commence a number of separate enforcement actions against those individuals, if any, who may have the resources to pay at least their share of the shortfall in the defendant's costs. I accept Mr Croxford's submission that that is, on any view, an unattractive proposition, involving not only further cost, uncertainty of recovery and inconvenience, but also a real commercial dilemma, given the defendant's position as a large local employer.

3.3 Particular Features of the Defendant's Position

29. The very existence of the GLO has created a disadvantage for the defendant, in that, without it, these individual claims may never have been commenced. But that, so it seems to me, cannot now be a source of legitimate complaint. It might be said that this is precisely the sort of situation in which Parliament envisaged that a GLO might give the requisite equality of arms between a large commercial organisation on one side, and individual householders on the other.

30. The defendant also criticises the effects of the particular GLO here. Mr Croxford submits that the defendant is faced with a wholly inadequate ATE limit of £1 million such that, if the defendant was successful, it could only recover £1 million from the insurers by way of costs, and thus be out of pocket to the tune of £2.3 million (on their figures) or between £1 million and £1.5 million (on my figures). There is, of course, the additional problem referred to above of enforcement against the individual claimants.

31. The defendant contrasts that with their potential liability for the claimants' costs if they lose these proceedings. The claimants' current total estimate of costs is, as we have seen, just under £2 million. With 100% uplift, that would mean that the defendant would be faced with a potential costs liability to the claimants of £4 million if they lost (together with their own costs of somewhere between £2 million and £3.3 million). Moreover, all of this – a possible maximum liability of £7.3 million by way of costs alone – would have been spent on proceedings in which the likely damages recovery will not be more than £1 million and may well be less.

32. I should make one further observation on the defendant's own costs (which I consider will be less than the £3.3 million currently estimated). I do understand that the defendant has incurred costs in the region of £750,000 so far, and that at least some of that considerable expenditure can be seen in their extensive pleaded defence, and the defendant's detailed analysis of the issues, in particular their case on the proper operation and running of the Westmill Landfill site. It seems to me this latter topic will lie at the heart of the trial. But, as Mr Croxford has accepted, the defendant, given the nature and size of its business as international waste contractors, sees these proceedings as something of a test case, and I have formed the impression that at least some of these costs may be referable to wider issues, which are not necessarily confined to the Westmill Landfill site. It seems to me that I

must bear that in mind when assessing whether or not a costs capping order is appropriate in the present case.

3.4 *Summary*

33. By reference to the particular features of this Group Litigation, noted in the preceding paragraphs, I am bound to conclude that, in the wider sense, these parties are *not* currently operating on a level commercial playing field. If they win, the defendant is likely to be able to recover only £1 million by way of costs (the maximum sum due under the ATE), because of the difficulties of enforcement noted above. The defendant will therefore be out of pocket to the tune of between £1 million (my lowest figure) and £2.3 million (their figure). And if they lose, the defendant is going to be out of pocket by between £2 million and £3.3 million on its own costs, together with £4 million-odd (including uplift) that will be due to the claimants in respect of their solicitor's costs. To that, of course, must also be added any amount by way of general damages that is awarded.

34. In consequence, it seems to me that the blackmailing effect discussed in the cases noted above is very much present in these proceedings. Whatever the result, the defendant will be out of pocket by a large sum, whilst the claimants' exposure is almost non-existent. But the real issue is whether a costs capping order can or should be made in such circumstances. Can a costs capping order address this underlying inequality? That is therefore the issue to which I now turn.

4. The Application under CPR 44.18

4.1 *The Specific Cap Sought*

35. The cap sought in the original application was £340,000, which was the amount of the ATE insurance limit when the application was made, less the costs incurred on the claimants' unsuccessful attempt not to disclose the ATE policy. In his submissions, Mr Croxford sought to argue that the costs should be capped at the limit of the ATE insurance, now £1 million. He said that this was fair, and created mutuality, because the £1 million was likely to represent in practical terms the maximum that the defendant would be able to recover from the claimants if the defendant was successful. He argued, therefore, that the same figure should be the most that the claimants should be permitted to recover from the defendant if in fact they were successful.

36. Although attractively put, I do not accept the principle that the

amount by way of costs that X may be able to recover against Y, if X is successful in the proceedings, can be equated to the cap to be imposed (pursuant to CPR 44.18) on Y's costs, if it turns out that Y is successful and can recover its costs against X. There is nothing in CPR 44.18 to suggest that that is the right approach; nor do any of the authorities suggest any such connection. Indeed, as I have already noted, in cases where costs caps are imposed on both sides, the amount of the respective caps will often be different: see, for example, the *Corby Group Litigation*. That merely reflects the different levels of costs that might reasonably be incurred by different parties in the same proceedings.

37. In addition, the order sought would have the odd effect of increasing the costs cap (on the costs recoverable by the claimants), whenever the cover was increased by the claimants under the ATE policy, which increase would be solely for the defendant's benefit. We have already seen an increase from £375,000 to £1 million. It seems entirely random to link the amount at which the claimants' costs should be capped to the amount that the defendant can recover against the claimants under the ATE policy, particularly when the latter figure is outside the control of the defendant and, at least directly, outside the control of the court.

38. I therefore reject the submission that the measure of the cap should be the amount of the ATE policy. But I go on to consider whether, as a matter of principle, a costs cap, measured in a different way, should be imposed.

4.2 All the Circumstances of the Case (Sub rule (6))

39. I refer to the analysis set out at section 3 above. For the reasons set out there, I consider that there is a substantial imbalance between the commercial positions of the parties. This is specifically by reference to the commercial risks being run by each side. The claimants will be able to avoid any significant liability, win or lose. The defendant is going to be significantly out of pocket, whatever the result.

40. In the light of the large costs incurred or to be incurred on each side, the costs of determining the cap, if any, are plainly proportionate to the overall costs of the litigation. Indeed, the claimants have not suggested to the contrary. Moreover, the first detailed CMC must be the appropriate time for such orders to be sought and again the claimants have not indicated otherwise.

4.3 The Criteria in Sub rule (5)

(a) Preface

41. It therefore seems to me that what matters for the present application is the criteria set out in sub rule (5). In accordance with that sub rule, I should ask myself the following questions:

(1) Is there a risk that costs will be disproportionately incurred (sub rule (5)(b))?
(2) If so, can that risk be adequately controlled by case management and/or detailed assessment of cost (sub rule (5)(c))?
(3) In all the circumstances, is it in the interests of justice to make a costs capping order?

(b) "Disproportionately Incurred" – Sub rule (5)(b)

42. In truth, the critical issue arising on this application is this: what does "disproportionate" mean? Disproportionate to what? In the reported cases, the costs capping order has been sought by a defendant concerned about the claimant's expenditure on costs which, so it is commonly argued, is disproportionate, either as against the value/worth of the litigation, and/or when measured against the costs that the defendant itself is incurring.

43. Plainly, that second argument is not available to the defendant in the present case because, on any view, it appears that the claimants are going to spend less than the defendant by way of costs. And although the first argument, that is to say measuring costs against the value of the claims themselves, does arise – because the claimants are going to spend £2 million by way of costs on claims which may not be worth more than £1 million and could well be worth less – it may be difficult to say, in all the circumstances, that such costs, even when measured against this likely recovery, are automatically disproportionate in accordance with CPR 44.18(5)(b). After all, both sides anticipate spending much greater sums by way of costs than the amount which the claim is worth.

44. As I indicated at the outset of this judgment, the defendant's argument is a different and novel one. The defendant argues that the costs incurred by the claimants are disproportionate because those costs constitute a major element of the unlevel playing field to which I have referred above, namely, their potential costs liability of £2.3 million (maximum) if they win, and their potential liability of £7.3

million if they lose. It is that essential disproportionality on which the defendant bases the present application.

45. However, that summary position needs to be unpicked in a little more detail. The £2.3 million liability for costs that the defendant may bear, even if successful, is the product of the terms of the ATE and the GLO. The limit of the ATE may be capable of being increased. Further, as Mr Croxford has pointed out this afternoon, the terms of the GLO may also be capable of being modified, if the defendant decides to make an application to that effect. Thus the potential shortfall of £2.3 million allows the defendant at least to raise the possibility of a costs capping order (because of the blackmailing effect, as in *King*), but it seems to me that the shortfall cannot of itself mean that the claimants' costs will be "disproportionately incurred".

46. Moreover, when considering the other side of the equation (namely, the defendant's liability for costs if they lose), CPR 44.18 states plainly that the 100% uplift on the claimants' solicitor's costs has to be ignored. So in reality the only thing that the defendant can truly complain about under this rule is the £2 million base costs to be incurred by the claimants' solicitor, and for the reasons noted above, the defendant cannot say that those costs themselves are disproportionate, because they are going to spend more than that to get through to the end of the trial.

47. I endeavour to test that analysis in this way. If I acceded to the defendant's application I would cap the claimants' recoverable costs at the base cost figure of £1 million. With 100% uplift, that would mean that the defendant, if unsuccessful, would owe the claimants £2 million by way of costs and, say, £1 million maximum by way of damages. That produces a total of £3 million. And if the defendant succeeds then they would have their own unpaid costs liability (which would be unaffected by my order) and which, on their own figures, would be £2.3 million odd. So the order sought, even if granted, would make little overall difference to what I perceive as the unlevel playing field in this case. It would not address the fundamental imbalance in the overall position between the parties. That is because that imbalance is a product, *not* of the future costs to be incurred by the claimants, but the terms of the GLO, the terms of the CFA, and the terms of the ATE policy.

48. Thus, whilst I have considerable sympathy for the defendant's position, it seems to me that it is principally a product of the terms of

the GLO (which may have to be reviewed at some future date); the terms of the ATE (which at least offers some cover and may be increased); and the rule that excludes the 100% uplift from any consideration at all. By contrast with all that, sub rule (5)(a) is designed to focus only on the claimants' base costs and to ask whether those base costs are disproportionate, as against either the value of the claim or the other side's costs. On the evidence, I have concluded that the claimants' costs are not disproportionate when measured in that way.

(c) Case Management/Detailed Assessment – Sub rule (5)(c)
49. As noted, a costs capping order will not be made if the risk of disproportionate costs being incurred (almost always by a claimant) can be contained by case management or a detailed assessment. This sub rule therefore makes clear beyond doubt that what the court is examining on a costs capping application is the claimants' own base costs, and the manner in which they can be controlled by the court, and not the wider considerations contended for by the defendant in the present case.

50. I am unable to say, on the evidence before me, that case management directions and cost assessments could not, between them, control any risk that the claimants' base costs will be disproportionately incurred. There is, I think, no cogent evidence that would allow me to reach a different conclusion. Indeed, I venture to suggest – echoing Mann J in *Knight* and Eady J in *Peacock* – that it would be a very unusual case in which a High Court judge did not feel able to utilise one or both of these tools to control disproportionate costs. That is, after all, what they are there for.

51. Accordingly, I have concluded that the defendant's application does not get over this second hurdle either. It will be apparent from my comments that, in truth, I find it difficult to conceive of any case which could get over this particular hurdle.

(d) Interests of Justice
52. In my view, for the reasons set out in **section 3** above, it would be in the interests of justice to reduce the commercial risks being run by the defendant in this case. But, on my analysis, CPR 44.18 does not provide a route which would allow me to achieve that goal.

5. An Order Under CPR 43

53. Although, for the reasons that I have given, I do not consider that a costs capping order can be made against the claimants in this case, I am concerned about the potential unfairness of the defendant's wider commercial position. As a result, I have raised with the parties the possibility of making an order, similar to the one made by Field J in *Willis*, to the effect that, subject to certain important safeguards, the claimants' eventual cost recovery in respect of future costs will not exceed the amount of their recent cost estimate.

54. Why would such an order be appropriate? Because it would provide for some modest reduction in the burden of risk being faced by the defendant, and because it would provide the defendant with at least an element of certainty: the defendant would know the level of the claimants' costs, if the claimants were successful and the defendant was liable for such costs. In addition, it would be an order that the court was entitled to make, untrammelled by the particular considerations of CPR 44.18. It would be in accordance with the overriding objective; in accordance with CPR 43; and, because of the safeguards to which I shall refer, it would also be in accordance with the decision of the Court of Appeal in *Leigh* v *Michelin Tyre* [2003] EWCA 1766 (Civ).

55. Although in that latter case, Dyson LJ made plain that an order in relation to a costs estimate could *not* be made as if it was the equivalent of a costs capping order, he made plain that costs estimates were an important yardstick as to reasonableness and should be used accordingly. The importance of accurate costs estimates in the TCC, and the adverse consequences of inaccurate costs estimates, was recently dealt with in *Fitzpatrick* v *Tyco (No. 3)* [2009] EWHC 274 (TCC).

56. I consider that an order in these proceedings which seeks to link the claimants' eventual costs recovery with the estimate now put forward, may be a way of ensuring that the claimants act reasonably in this litigation. I have a number of concerns about certain aspects of the claimants' conduct of this action thus far. There was the original refusal, which I considered to be unreasonable, to provide the ATE policy. There has been the failure on the part of the claimants' legal team to address the detailed issues raised by the defendant in their defence as to historic land use and waste policy. In addition there was the very belated increase in the amount of the ATE cover prior to the

CMC; and the failure to provide the estimate of future costs for that CMC. All of those matters, whilst not of themselves overly significant, do seem to me to be matters which would be capable of being controlled in the future (and indeed may not recur at all) if I made an order along the lines indicated.

57. Therefore the proposal that I made to the parties earlier in the week was that:

(a) The claimants' estimate of their future costs (namely, £1,471,767 million) was to be taken as a reasonable estimate of such costs and therefore their likely maximum recovery at the end of the trial, subject to
(b) The claimants having liberty to apply to modify the terms of that order if any of the assumptions made in estimating their costs (such as, for example, having only one expert), was altered or needed to be modified as a result of any of the court's subsequent orders or directions.

58. I was provided with a helpful note by Mr Bates on behalf of the claimants in which he indicated that this was not a course to which they would object. This afternoon (October 2), very helpfully, Mr Bates has confirmed that the claimants consent to an order in those terms, subject to one other safeguard which I shall address in a moment. For that reason I have concluded that this is the direction dealing with the claimants' costs that should be included in the Order arising from the case management conference on September 24.

59. In the course of his submissions this afternoon, Mr Croxford drew attention to the fact that, in the alternative to the imposition of a costs cap, the defendant wished to reserve its right to come back to court to argue for a stay of proceedings until a reasonable level of ATE cover was put in place, and/or to make an application that the terms of the GLO be modified so as, for example, to allow for joint and several liability for common costs. I make plain that the defendant is entitled to come back to the court to raise either of those points subject, of course, to the giving of proper notice. There is a hearing due in March of next year, and it may be that that would be an appropriate time for those matters to be raised again.

60. By the same token, I made plain to Mr Bates that if, by the time of the hearing fixed for March 2010, the claimants have become aware of some significant error or other matter within their present costs

estimate which caused them concern, they could raise that in order for me to consider whether any other modification to the order that I now make as to their costs estimate should be made. Accordingly, those matters too may need to be revisited at the next case management conference. That is the other safeguard to which I referred in para 58 above.

6. Conclusions

61. For the reasons set out in **section 4.1** above, I am not able to make an order capping costs at £375,000 or whatever may be, from time to time, the limit of the ATE insurance.

62. For the reasons set out in **sections 4.2 and 4.3** above, I am not able to make an order capping costs at all under CPR 44.18.

63. For the reasons set out in **sections 3 and 5** above, I will make an order in the terms of para 57 above, linking the claimants' ultimate costs recovery to their recent estimate of future costs, subject to the express safeguards that I have indicated above. It seems to me that all other matters in relation to costs and costs capping should be regarded as open to either party, to be raised at the CMC in March of next year.

Nigel Cooksley QC and *John Bates* (instructed by Hugh James) appeared for the claimants.

Ian Croxford QC and *Thomas De La Mare* (instructed by Nabarro LLP) for the defendant.

Case 27
Shah

v

Ul-Haq and Others

[2010] 3 Costs LR 336

Neutral Citation Number: [2009] EWCA Civ 542
Court of Appeal (Civil Division)
9 June 2009

Before:
Smith, Moses and Toulson LJJ

Headnote

In hearing this second appeal, the Court of Appeal considered whether it was possible under CPR 3.4(2) or at all to strike out a genuine claim on the ground that the claimant had been involved in a fraud upon the court in respect of an associated, false claim.

Judgment

Introduction

1. SMITH LJ: This is an appeal from the decision of Walker J dated 31 July 2008 on appeal from the decision of Mr Recorder Parkes QC sitting in Birmingham County Court on 4 February 2008. This is, therefore, a second appeal. Permission was granted because the appeal raises a point of some general importance, namely whether it is possible, under CPR 3.4(2) or at all, to strike out a genuine claim on the ground that the claimant has been involved in a fraud upon the court in respect of an associated claim.

The Claim

2. The underlying action arose from an apparently simple road accident in May 2006. The defendant, Mrs Anita Shah, negligently drove her Peugeot motor car into the rear of a Rover motor car which was stationary in front of her at traffic lights. The Rover belonged to Mr Wasim Ul-Haq who was driving it at the time. The car sustained minor damage in the collision. Also in the Rover with Mr Ul-Haq were his wife, Mrs Zahida Parveen, and their two children. So much was common ground. When the action was begun, Mrs Shah admitted liability for causing the collision.

3. In addition to Mr Ul-Haq's claim for damage to the car, he and his wife claimed that they had suffered minor whiplash injuries. A claim was also made by Mrs Samara Khatoon, Mr Ul-Haq's mother, who alleged that she too had been in the car and had suffered a whiplash injury. The claims of all three claimants were brought together and Mr Ul-Haq and his wife supported Mrs Khatoon's claim that she had been in the car at the time. Mrs Shah denied that Mrs Khatoon had been in the car at all and also disputed that any claimant had suffered personal injury. She asserted that no claim should be allowed to Mr Ul-Haq and Mrs Parveen because they had been complicit in the fraudulent assertion that Mrs Khatoon had been a passenger.

4. Thus it was that, instead of the claim being settled for a modest sum without a hearing, there was a trial of the issues before the recorder which lasted several days. Mr Ul-Haq and his wife gave evidence of their own injuries and also said that Mrs Khatoon had been a passenger at the time of the collision. Mr Brough on behalf of Mrs Shah submitted that they were lying about their own injuries and about Mrs Khatoon's presence in the car. The recorder should reject all the claims save for the damage to the car. Alternatively, he contended that, even if the recorder were to find that Mr Ul-Haq and his wife had suffered genuine injuries, the recorder should strike out their claims under CPR 3.4(2) on account of their part in the attempted fraud. That rule provides that the court may strike out a statement of case if it appears to the court that the statement of case is an abuse of the process of the court. Mr Brough submitted that their conduct amounted to a serious abuse of the process of the court and that only by striking out their claims could the court mark its profound disapproval.

5. Mr Pitchers, for the claimants, conceded that, if the recorder were to hold that Mr Ul-Haq and his wife had suffered genuine injuries but had conspired to advance Mrs Khatoon's fraudulent claim, there was a discretionary jurisdiction under CPR 3.4(2) to strike out their genuine claims at the end of the trial but urged the recorder not to exercise it.

6. The recorder held that Mrs Khatoon had not been in the car. Mr Ul-Haq and his wife had conspired with Mrs Khatoon to support her fraudulent claim. The fraud was serious; it appeared that within a short time of the accident, Mr Ul-Haq, his wife and mother had all attended the Accident and Emergency Department of their local hospital. The recorder inferred that Mr Ul-Haq had made a rapid decision to encourage his mother to make a false claim. The recorder dismissed Mrs Khatoon's claim with costs on an indemnity basis assessed at £2,666. However, he held that Mr Ul-Haq and Mrs Parveen had genuinely suffered minor personal injuries.

7. After a careful consideration of authority, which I will examine later, the recorder expressed his doubts about the existence of any discretion under that CPR 3.4(2) to strike out a genuine claim at the end of a trial. He was doubtful that that rule was ever intended for such a purpose but, because the point had been conceded, he accepted that he did have the discretion contended for. However, he declined to exercise it. He assessed Mr Ul-Haq's damages at £2,585.38 and his wife's at £2,259.37 and directed that each should pay two thirds of Mrs Shah's costs of defending the claim. Each had to pay £1,777. The net effect of these orders after set off was that Mr Ul-Haq, Mrs Parveen and Mrs Khatoon had, between them, to pay Mrs Shah £1,375.75. Thus, the fraudulent conspiracy had resulted in no benefit; instead a modest deficit.

The First Appeal

8. Mrs Shah then appealed to a High Court judge on the issue of whether the recorder had been right to refuse to strike out the claims of Mr Ul-Haq and his wife. Mr Ul-Haq and his wife did not appear and were not represented. It was contended for Mrs Shah that the recorder had been reluctant to recognise that he had a discretion to strike out the claims under CPR 3.4(2) and that this reluctance had coloured his assessment of the factors affecting the exercise of his discretion. Second, it was contended that, having found Mr Ul-Haq

and his wife to be dishonest, the recorder should not have found that their claims were genuine.

9. Walker J dismissed this second point on the ground that the recorder was quite entitled to conclude that their evidence about their own injuries was truthful. In my view, he was plainly right about that and, although Mrs Shah was given permission to appeal to this court on that ground, it should not have been given. I gave permission due to an oversight. It is not an issue suitable for a second stage appeal and in any event, the point is quite without merit. I shall say no more about that.

10. On the main issue, whether the recorder had been right to refuse to strike out the small but genuine claims of Mr Ul-Haq and his wife, the judge was told that fraudulent claims were becoming a major problem for the courts and for insurance companies. Striking out was the only way in which the court could mark its disapproval and it was in the public interest that such claims should be seen to be counterproductive. He submitted that the recorder had not given sufficient weight to these factors and had also underestimated the seriousness of the fraud in this case.

11. The judge examined all the same authorities as had been considered by the recorder, in particular *Khan, Shah and Mayat* v *Hussein, Ashraf and the MIB* a decision of HH Judge Hawkesworth QC sitting in the Huddersfield County Court in May 2007 and the decision of the Court of Appeal in *Arrow Nominees* v *Blackledge* [2001] BCLC 167. I will discuss those cases below. In addition, he considered two county court cases decided before *Khan* in which the judges had accepted that they had a discretion under CPR 3.4(2) to strike out the otherwise valid claims of parties who had colluded in the bringing of a fraudulent "phantom passenger" claim by a friend or relation. In one, *Ghalib and Ghaffur* v *Hadfield,* HH Judge Phillips, sitting in Preston County Court in 2004, had propounded what he considered to be the appropriate test for the exercise of the discretion. He said that the judge must consider two questions: (1) to what extent had the claimant failed to help the court to further the overriding objective, taking into account the definition of that objective in CPR 1.1; and (2) whether in the light of the conclusion under (1) the discretion should be exercised to strike out the claim under CPR 3.4(2). In *Ghalib,* Judge Phillips weighed the factors which pointed towards and against striking out the claim and, in the event, declined

to do so. In the second such phantom passenger case, *Patel and Others v Ali,* Mr Recorder Wilby directed himself according to Judge Phillips's test and, after conducting a balancing exercise, concluded that the first claimant's claim, which was in itself valid, should be struck out.

12. From his consideration of authority, Walker J was satisfied that there was a discretion under CPR 3.4(2) to strike out a genuine claim even at the end of the hearing. He accepted that the recorder's approach to his task had been coloured by his doubts as to the existence of this power and decided to exercise the discretion afresh. He approved the approach suggested by Judge Phillips in *Ghalib* and then carried out the balancing exercise suggested by that case. He concluded that, although the fraud was serious, it was not of the most serious kind and declined to strike out the claims. He dismissed the appeal.

The Appeal to This Court

13. Mr Ul-Haq and his wife did not appear on the appeal. Mrs Shah was represented by Mr Ralph Lewis QC. At the outset, Mr Lewis sought to impress upon the court the gravity of the situation which faces insurance companies who have to contend with false claims. I myself was already aware of the general nature of the problem. It was graphically described in the following way by His Honour Judge Hawkesworth QC in a county court case to which I will refer later:

> "Unhappily such fraudulent claims are now legion. They occupy the court time of district judges and circuit judges in West Yorkshire literally week in and week out. My own judicial experience reflects, I have no doubt, that of many of my brethren throughout the country. Just about every variant of a fraudulent claim comes before the court, including deliberately staged collisions, damage caused to vehicles which have never been in collision at all, claims deriving from the most trivial touching of vehicles, and claims in which a driver will assert that his car was carrying other members of his family including his children, when in fact none were present but all of whom have reported to a hospital or their General Practitioner that they have been injured, and who are then able to produce an apparently independent expert's report confirming the fact of such injury. The cost to the insurance industry and to other honest policy holders must be very substantial. In addition, and of more relevance to these proceedings, the cost in court time in trying such cases is very high, with the added knock-on effect of casting suspicion onto

many genuine claims so that claimants are put to proof of their legitimate and genuine claims for compensation when in other circumstances they might not have been called upon to do so."

Mr Lewis told us that the insurance company involved in the present case had successfully challenged no fewer than 157 phantom passenger cases in the last twelve months; that was in addition to claims involving staged accidents. He urged this court to hold that the judge should have struck out the genuine claims of Mr Ul-Haq and his wife and thereby to make it plain to the perpetrators of frauds such as this that, if they were found out, not only would the fraudulent claims be dismissed but the other associated claims would be struck out, even if genuine.

14. Mr Lewis submitted that CPR 3.4(2) provided the jurisdictional basis for the remedy he sought. He relied on the same authorities as had been considered below. He submitted that the judge had rightly accepted that there was jurisdiction to strike out these genuine claims but had wrongly refused to do so. He had failed to give proper weight to the gravity of the fraud in this case and to the public interest need for such frauds to be stamped out.

15. We were in a similar position to the recorder and the judge in that there was no forensic opposition to the submission in respect of CPR 3.4(2). Like the recorder and the judge, we will have to consider whether that rule does provide a basis on which the court can strike out a genuine claim on the ground that the claimant has abused the process of the court in respect of a collateral claim.

16. However, before considering whether CPR 3.4(2) provides a procedural peg on which to hang a decision to strike out a genuine claim by reason of collateral dishonesty, I first wish to discuss the more fundamental question of whether it is right to do so as a matter of substantive law. My preliminary reaction to the suggestion that this might be appropriate was one of surprise. I had thought that the only circumstances in which a genuine claim would be dismissed on account of dishonest exaggeration were where the claim was based on an insurance contract: see *Axa General Insurance Ltd* v *Gottlieb and Gottleib* [2005] EWCA Civ 112, in particular Mance LJ's discussion of authority at paras 17 *et seq*. There is a well established common law rule that if a genuine claim made under an insurance contract is dishonestly exaggerated, the whole claim will be dismissed; further, if

money has already been paid pursuant to a claim under such a contract before the fraud is discovered, all the sums paid under that claim will be recoverable by the insurer, including any sum referable to the genuine part of the claim. However, this rule is limited to claims brought under insurance contracts, which are, of course, contracts of good faith. If there were a general rule of law, whether in contract or tort, that the dishonest exaggeration of a genuine claim would result in the dismissal of the whole claim, there would be no need for a special rule applying to contracts of insurance.

17. I am satisfied that there is no such general rule of law. I am unaware of any reported case in which a judge has dismissed the whole of a claim because he has found that the claim has been dishonestly exaggerated. The invariable rule is that, in those circumstances, the judge awards the limited damages which are appropriate to his findings. Of course, a claimant's credibility may be so damaged that he fails to prove any part of his loss, but if he proves some loss, he recovers that even though he has fraudulently attempted to recover far more. Not only am I unaware of any reported case in which this rule has not been followed, my own long experience of personal injury work at the Bar and on the bench confirms this view. I have, I regret to say, considerable experience of exaggerated claims. Of course, not all exaggerated claims entail dishonesty; sometimes exaggeration can be innocent, resulting from a subconscious preoccupation, even obsession, with the injury. Judges are always careful to take account of such effects when assessing damages. But there are some cases where the exaggeration is plainly dishonest. In nearly 40 years' experience, I have never known a judge refuse to award damages for a genuine injury on the ground that the claimant had dishonestly sought to exaggerate the injury and its effects.

18. The only suggestion that it might be possible to refuse to award any damages at all where the claim has been exaggerated came in the *obiter dicta* remarks of Laws LJ in *Molloy* v *Shell UK Ltd* [2001] EWCA Civ 1271. That was an appeal against the costs order made by the judge below following an assessment of damages in a personal injury case. The claimant had been injured and liability was admitted. He claimed a grossly exaggerated sum for loss of earnings based upon the contention that he was now unable to work as a scaffolder. In fact he was working as such. The truth came out and the judge awarded general damages for the injury and a modest sum for loss of earnings.

I interpose to say that the judge thereby did what judges always do. The claimant just failed to beat a Part 36 offer made well before trial. The judge ordered the defendant to pay the claimant's costs up to the date of the Part 36 offer and ordered the claimant to pay 75% of the defendant's costs thereafter. He declined to give the defendant all its costs on the ground that the claimant had failed to better the Part 36 offer by only a narrow margin. The defendant appealed, contending that, in the light of the claimant's dishonesty, the judge should have awarded it the whole of its post-Part 36 costs. The Court of Appeal (Mummery and Laws LJJ) allowed the appeal. Laws LJ observed that, from the time when his claim was filed until he was found out, the claimant's approach had been "nothing short of a cynical and dishonest abuse of the court's process". He continued:

> "For my part I entertain considerable qualms as to whether, faced with manipulation of the civil justice system on so grand a scale, the court should, once it knows the facts, entertain the case at all save to make the dishonest claimant pay the defendant's costs. However, all that that is sought here is an order for 100% of the appellant's instead of 75%, the costs in question being only those incurred after the date of the Part 36 payment. The appeal certainly cannot be resisted on that basis."

Thus, when seen in context, all Laws LJ was saying that, where a genuine claim was dishonestly exaggerated on a grand scale, maybe the court should dismiss the whole claim. He did not consider whether there was power to do that or whether such a course would be consistent with existing authority or practice. In my respectful view, this was little more than wishful thinking by Laws LJ.

19. In *Churchill Car Insurance v Kelly* [2006] EWHC 18 (QB) Gibbs J was invited to deprive a claimant of the genuine part of his claim because he had been found out in a blatant attempt to inflate his claim. No authority was cited to him to support the insurer's submission, save for *Molloy*. The judge expressed some sympathy with Laws LJ's view but held that he could not accede to the submission. He noted the limited rule relating to insurance contracts. In my view, he was unquestionably right.

20. In my judgment, it is well established that a claimant will not be deprived of damages to which he is entitled because he has fraudulently attempted to obtain more than his entitlement. Should the position be different where the claimant's attempted fraud consists of

lying to support the claim of another person rather than lying to enhance the claimant's own claim? I can see no logical justification for suggesting that the claimant who lies about another person's claim should be treated more severely than the claimant who lies about his own claim. Both behave disgracefully; both commit the criminal offences of attempting to pervert the course of justice and attempting to obtain property by deception or attempting to obtain a pecuniary advantage by deception. Yet the policy of the law has not been to shut them out from justice altogether – save where the claim relates to an insurance contract.

21. It may be that that policy is wrong and the law should be changed. Indeed, like Laws LJ and Gibbs J, I have some sympathy with the view that fraudulently exaggerated claims should be struck out in their entirety. However, I do not think that such a change would necessarily solve the problems of insurance companies; their real problem with phantom passengers and staged accidents is detecting the frauds in the first place. But in any event, I consider that the law is so well-established that I would not think it right to change it by judicial intervention. In my view, such a change would have to be a matter for Parliament.

22. In the light of that conclusion, consideration of CPR 3.4(2) becomes a side issue. If the common law permits the court to deprive a claimant of the fruits of a genuine claim because he has lied either in exaggeration of his own claim or in support of another claim, then it would not, in my view, be necessary to find a procedural peg on which to hang the decision. The judge would just dismiss the claim.

23. However, out of respect for the decisions of Walker J and the circuit judges who have concluded that CPR 3.4(2) provides a discretionary power to strike out the whole of a claim as a response to dishonest conduct, I will deal with the question.

24. CPR Part 3 is headed: The Court's Case Management Powers. It deals with a wide range of powers by which the court can control the process of litigation. CPR 3.4 is headed: Power to strike out a statement of case. Rule 3.4(2) provides:

"The court may strike out a statement of case if it appears to the court –

(a) that the statement of case discloses no reasonable grounds for bringing or defending the claim;

(b) that the statement of case is an abuse of the court's process or is otherwise likely to obstruct the just disposal of the proceedings; or

(c) that there has been a failure to comply with a rule, practice direction or court order."

25. All three judges who have held that this rule provides a discretionary power to strike out a genuine claim (Walker J, HH Judge Phillips and HH Judge Hawkesworth QC) were strongly influenced by the judgments of this court in *Arrow Nominees*.

26. In that case the respondents to a petition for relief under s 459 of the Companies Act 1985 applied to strike it out before the trial on the basis that the petitioners had forged and disclosed documents so that a fair trial would not be possible. That application was refused but renewed at trial on the basis that it was now clear that the petitioner had lied about the circumstances of the previously admitted forgeries and there was a danger that other documents had been forged. The judge again refused to strike out the petition, saying that a fair trial was still possible. On appeal, the Court of Appeal held that the judge should have struck out the petition at the time of the second application for two reasons. First, once the judge had accepted that documents had been forged and it would no longer be possible to have a fair trial of certain issues, the judge should have struck out the petition because there was no other evidence which was capable of supporting the relief claimed. However, Chadwick LJ gave a second reason for his conclusion. At para 54 he said:

"But for my part, I would allow that appeal on a second and additional ground. I adopt, as a general principle, the observations of Millett J in *Logicrose Ltd v Southend United Football Club Ltd* (1988) *The Times*, March 5, that the object of the rules as to discovery is to secure the fair trial of the action in accordance with the due process of the court; and that, accordingly, a party is not to be deprived of his right to a proper trial as a penalty for disobedience of those rules, even if such disobedience amounts to contempt for or defiance of the court, if that object is ultimately secured, by (for example) the late production of a document which has been withheld. But where a litigant's conduct puts the fairness of the trial in jeopardy, where it is such that any judgment in favour of the litigant would have to be regarded as unsafe, or where it amounts to such an abuse of the process of the court as to render further proceedings unsatisfactory and to prevent the court from doing justice, the court is entitled, indeed, I would hold bound, to refuse to allow that litigant to take further part in the proceedings and (where appropriate) to determine the proceedings against him. The reason, as it seems to me is that it is no part of the court's function to proceed to trial if to do so would give rise to substantial risk of injustice. The function of the court is to do justice between the parties; not to allow its process to be used as a means of achieving injustice. A litigant who has demonstrated that he is determined to pursue proceedings with the object of preventing a fair trial has forfeited his right to take part in that trial. His object is inimical to the process which he purports to invoke.

55. Further, in this context, a fair trial is a trial which is conducted without an undue expenditure of time and money; and with a proper regard to the demands of other litigants upon the finite resources of the court. The court does not do justice to the other parties to the proceedings in question if it allows its process to be abused so that the real point in issue becomes subordinated to an investigation into the effect which the admittedly fraudulent conduct of one party in connection with process of litigation has had on the fairness of the trial itself. That, as it seems to me is what happened in the present case. The trial was 'hijacked' by the need to investigate which documents were false and what documents had been destroyed."

Chadwick LJ then considered the facts of that case and held that the judge, on considering those facts, ought to have held that it was not fair to the respondents or in the interests of justice generally to allow the trial to continue. He concluded:

"A decision to stop the trial in those circumstances is not based on the court's desire (or any perceived need) to punish the party concerned: rather it is a proper and necessary response where a party has shown that his object is not to the fair trial which it is court's function to conduct, but to have a trial the fairness of which he has attempted (and continues to attempt) to compromise."

27. Ward LJ agreed with Chadwick LJ but added an additional reason for reaching the same conclusion. He observed that the court's powers of case management are to be exercised so as to further the overriding objective. The overriding objective of the CPR is to enable the court to deal with cases justly. Dealing with a case justly included, so far as

practicable, ensuring that the parties were on an equal footing. Ward LJ was of the view that the attempt to pervert the course of justice which had occurred in this case was the very antithesis of the parties coming to the court on an equal footing. The judge below had erred in failing to take this additional factor into account. The petition should have been struck at the second application part way through the hearing.

28. In so far as Walker J, Judge Hawkesworth and Judge Phillips regarded *Arrow Nominees* as support for the proposition that CPR 3.4(2) provides a power to strike out a claim at the end of a hearing where there is no suggestion that it has not been possible to hold a fair hearing, in my respectful view, they are mistaken. Everything that was said in *Arrow Nominees* related to the situation which arose in the course of the trial, once it had become apparent that the petitioner's dishonesty was such that a fair trial had become impossible. The case does not support the proposition that, where, as here, the trial has taken place and the recorder has been able to reach reliable findings, it is open to him to strike a genuine claim out. In those circumstances, the judge must give effect to his findings. He can mark his disapproval of the way in which the court's time and the parties' money has been wasted by an order for costs. But he cannot, in my judgment, mark his disapproval by depriving the claimant of that which the claimant has proved to be his entitlement.

29. I would add that the expression "strike out" has a time-honoured use and is not apt to describe the decision that a judge makes at the end of the trial. At that stage, the judge either upholds the claim or dismisses it. He does not strike it out. The rule, as it appears to me, is primarily designed to permit a judge to strike out a claim before or at the beginning of the trial. The rule focuses on the statement of case – *viz* the particulars of claim or defence – in other words a pleading. The main objective seems to be to allow the court to deal summarily with a bad claim or defence before the expense of a trial is incurred. I can see that, in the kind of circumstances as arose in *Arrow Nominees*, the power to strike out may be deployed during a hearing where it becomes apparent either that it will not be possible to have a fair trial or because, without some corrupted evidence, which has to be disregarded, the claim cannot succeed. There again, the objective is to cut matters short so that further costs will not be wasted. I prefer to offer no view as to whether it would be appropriate for the judge to

strike out the claim (as opposed to dismissing it) if, at the end of the evidence he concluded that he had been unable to conduct a fair trial, on account of one of the parties' conduct. The point is academic anyway because strike out at that stage would have the same effect as dismissal. But in the present case, there was no suggestion of an unfair trial. There was a great deal of wasted time and money, caused by the claimants' dishonesty but the recorder saw through that dishonesty and reached what are accepted to have been entirely proper findings.

30. For the reasons I have given, I would dismiss this appeal. However, my conclusion that the respondents should not be deprived of their modest damages is based on quite different reasoning from that by which the judge below reached the same conclusion.

31. MOSES LJ: I agree.

32. TOULSON LJ: I also agree.

33. A person with a valid claim may try to deceive the other party or the court in different ways. Dishonest exaggeration of the amount of the damage suffered; the concoction of lies, or production of false documents, in support of the claim; the destruction or falsification of evidence which might tend to weaken the claim; these are all examples. So too a defendant who has a valid defence to all or part of a claim may use dishonest means in order to defeat or reduce the amount of the claim, but we are concerned with dishonesty by claimants.

34. In this case Mr Ul-Haq and his wife (the first and third claimants) were guilty of dishonesty, but of a more remote kind. It had nothing to do with their own claims, which arose from being respectively the driver of, and a passenger in, a car involved in a minor accident caused by the defendant's negligence. It had to do with a false claim by Mr Ul-Haq's mother (the second claimant), supported by the first and third claimants, that she too had been a passenger in Mr Ul-Haq's car and had suffered injury. For convenience the three claims were brought in a single action, but the alleged causes of action were several and not joint. In the cases of the first and third claimants, only damages were in dispute at the trial. In the case of the second defendant, the principal issue was whether she had been a passenger in the car. Mr Recorder Parkes QC found that she had not.

35. The question at issue is whether at the end of the trial the judge ought to have "struck out" the claims of the first and third claimants

as an abuse of the court because they had conspired to support the second claimant's false claim in the same proceedings.

36. As a matter of substantive law, I did not understand it to be suggested that the dishonest behaviour of the first and third claimants affected their separate causes of action. As Smith LJ has explained, such a suggestion would be novel and contrary to well established practice. It would also present conceptual and practical problems.

37. There is a special rule of insurance law that an insured cannot recover in respect of any part of a claim in a case where the claim has been fraudulently exaggerated or where a genuine claim has been supported by dishonest devices: *Manifest Shipping Co Ltd v Ini-Polaris Co Ltd (The Star Sea)* [2001] UKHL 1; [2003] AC 469; *Agapitos v Agnew* [2002] EWCA Civ 247, [2003] QB 556; *Axa General Insurance Ltd v Gottlieb* [2005] EWCA Civ 112. Different views have been advanced to explain the jurisprudential basis of the rule, but it is unnecessary to consider them because it is clear that the principle (whatever its foundation) is special to fraudulent insurance claims: see *Axa* para 31, per Mance LJ. Moreover, the operation of the principle is restricted to the period prior to the issue of proceedings: *Agapitos v Agnew* paras 47 to 53.

38. The first and third claimants' causes of action accrued at the time of the accident. There is no legal basis for treating their dishonest support for the second claimant's bogus claim as extinguishing their own right to damages. To change the law because of the problem of fraudulent claims referred to by Smith LJ in para 13 would be a radical step. Any suggested change would have to be thought through with care and in detail, not only as to its general desirability but as to its form and limits, and would be a matter for Parliament.

39. With those points in mind I turn to the argument advanced by Mr Ralph Lewis QC under CPR 3.4(2). As Smith LJ has observed, part 3 of the CPR is headed "The Court's Case Management Powers". The purpose of the court's management powers is to assist it to arrive at a determination of the parties' legal rights and obligations in a way which is just and expeditious: see CPR 1.1 (the overriding objective) and CPR 1.4 (the court's duty to further the overriding objective by its case management).

40. With that end in view, CPR 3.4 gives to the court the power to strike out a statement of case or part of a statement of case, thereby avoiding the time and costs of a full trial of the case or part of it, in

cases where, in summary, the statement of case is hopeless on its face (ground (a)), or it is an abuse of process or otherwise likely to obstruct the just disposal of the proceedings (ground (b)) or there has been some breach of a rule or order meriting the draconian step of a strike out (ground (c)).

41. In the present case, the action proceeded to trial and the judge was able on the evidence to determine the parties' respective rights. At that stage his proper course was to give judgment on the various claims, as he did.

42. Mr Lewis submitted that he should not have proceeded to give judgment on the claims, but could and should have struck out the entire action as an abuse of the process of the court under CPR 3.4(2)(b).

43. I do not accept that argument.

44. The term "abuse of the court's process" in ground (b) is not defined, and the categories of abuse are not closed. Whilst in a sense the making of a fictitious claim is of course an abuse of the court's process, I am doubtful whether CPR 3.4(2)(b) is intended to cover the situation where the issue is whether the claim is true or false, because CPR 24.2 makes provision for a court to give summary judgment against a claimant on the whole of a claim or a particular issue if it considers that the claimant has no real prospect of succeeding on the claim or issue. If the court were satisfied that a claim was fictitious, without a full hearing, the natural course would be to give judgment against the claimant on the claim.

45. However, that is not my reason for rejecting Mr Lewis' argument, because I recognise that there is a potential overlap between the power of the court under CPR 3.4(2)(a) to strike out a statement of case on the grounds that it discloses no reasonable cause of action and its power under CPR 24.2 to give summary against the claimant on the claim; and I accept that the better view may be that there is a similar potential overlap between CPR 3.4(2)(b) and CPR 24.2.

46. Nonetheless, where a statement of case contains a mixture of false and genuine claims (whether by the same claimant or by two or more claimants), I cannot see that the inclusion of a false claim would or could of itself turn a genuine claim (or genuine part of a claim) into being an abuse of the court's process, so as to warrant the court striking it out under CPR 3.4(2)(b). To hold otherwise would be to deprive a claimant of his substantive rights in respect of an accrued

cause of action as a mark of the court's disapproval of his conduct in advancing, or supporting, a false claim made by himself or another in the same proceedings, which in my judgment the court has no power to do.

47. I have said that I cannot see that the inclusion of a false claim would "of itself" turn a genuine claim into being an abuse of the process of the court. I use the words "of itself" because there could be a case, to quote from Chadwick LJ's judgment in *Arrow Nominees Inc v Blackledge* [2000] EWCA Civ 200, [2000] 2 BCLC 167, para 54,

> "where a litigant's conduct puts the fairness of the trial in jeopardy, where it is such that any judgment in favour of the litigant would have to be regarded as unsafe, or where it amounts to such an abuse of the court as to render further proceedings unsatisfactory and to prevent the court from doing justice..."

48. In such a case the proceedings would fall to be struck out, as Chadwick LJ said, for the reason

> "...that it is no part of the court's function to proceed to trial if to do so would give rise to a substantial risk of injustice."

49. However, that is not this case. This was never a case in which it was suggested, or could plausibly have been suggested, that there could not be a fair trial of the first and third claimants' claims (where the only contested issues concerned damages); or, for that matter, that there could not be a fair trial of the claim by the second claimant, which the judge heard and dismissed.

50. That brings me back to a point which I have already made. Where, as in this case, there has been a full trial, the proper course for the judge is to give judgment on the issues which have been tried. To have struck out the claims of the first and third claimants would have been to invoke a case management power not for a legitimate case management purpose (in other words, for the purpose of achieving a just and expeditious determination of the parties' rights, or avoiding an unjust determination where a party's conduct had made a safe determination impossible), but for the very different purpose of depriving those parties of their legal right to damages by way of punishment for their complicity in the second claimant's fraudulent claim, which in my judgment he had no power to do. It was open to

him to impose costs sanctions on the first and third claimants, which he did, but that is a different matter.

51. As a postscript, I would add that everyone knows that fraud is a scourge of our time. On the judge's findings the claimants were guilty of serious criminal offences, including conspiracy to defraud and conspiracy to pervert the course of justice. If, as has been suggested, such fraudulent claims have reached epidemic proportions, it may be that prosecutions are needed as a deterrent to others.

Ralph Lewis QC and *Alasdair Brough* (instructed by Morris Orman Hearle) appeared for the appellant.

The respondents were neither represented nor present at the hearing of the appeal.

Case 28
Widlake

v

BAA Ltd

[2010] 3 Costs LR 353

Neutral Citation Number: [2009] EWCA Civ 1256
Court of Appeal (Civil Division)
23 November 2009

Before:
Ward, Smith and Wilson LJJ

Headnote

This appeal against an award of costs against a successful claimant on the grounds that she had deliberately misled her own medical experts with regard to her previous medical history, resulted in a helpful review of cases involving exaggerated or dishonest claims and their affect upon the award of costs.

Judgment

1. WARD LJ: On 28 November 2008 His Honour Judge Seymour QC, sitting as a judge of the High Court, assessed the claimant's damages for personal injuries in the sum of £5,522.38 plus interest agreed at £355.33 but he nonetheless ordered the claimant to pay the defendant's costs of the action to be assessed on the standard basis if not agreed. The claimant now appeals against the award of costs against her.

2. The claimant, Miss Martine Widlake, was employed by BAA Ltd, the defendant, as a security guard at Stansted Airport. On 12 July

2004 she was undertaking a foot patrol in the baggage reclaim area of the airport and began to descend a staircase leading to an emergency exit when she lost her footing and fell twelve or thirteen steps down the staircase. It was common ground that what caused her to lose her footing was a loose rider immediately below the top step. She brought a claim for damages for personal injury and liability was not disputed.

3. As a result of that fall she sustained bruising to her back, her buttocks, her legs and thighs, knees and elbow. The bruising to her arm settled within about a week of the accident. The bruising to the shin and ankles caused some discomfort on walking for about a week after the accident but resolved uneventfully. The right thigh was "black and blue" for about six weeks after the accident and caused her discomfort and disturbance of her sleep which persisted for about two months. The bruising to her back resolved itself but she contended that she continued to suffer low back pain.

4. There was a lively dispute about the consequences of that injury. The defendant accepted that the claimant had suffered aggravation for about twelve months of pain in her lower back referable to degenerative changes which existed prior to the accident. It was contended on behalf of the defendant that the appropriate compensation for pain and suffering and loss of amenity in respect of the injuries which BAA accepted was £3,250. Her case, on the contrary, was initially that she had sustained continuing pain to her right sacroiliac joint solely as a result of that fall. By the time of the commencement of the trial, her case was that the deterioration in the condition of her lower back, which it was by then accepted was inevitable even without the supervening accident, had been brought forward by five years as a result of the fall. She contended that the pain she was experiencing by the acceleration of the pre-existing degenerative changes justified an award of £11,000 for pain and suffering and loss of amenity.

5. There was also an issue as to the level of special damages. On her case, as set out in her third schedule of loss dated 16 October 2008, she had lost £23,906.40 but, on the defendant's case, the value of that claim was only £2,022.38.

6. Thus the judge identified the issues as follows:

"11. The important issues for determination at the trial were thus, first, whether the effect of the accident on Miss Widlake's back was simply to aggravate the pain resulting from pre-existing degenerative changes for about twelve months or to advance the inevitable deterioration in the pre-existing low back problem by about five years; and, second, the extent of the pain which Miss Widlake actually suffered between the days of her accident and the end of the period which I find is that over which the pain in the back was aggravated or by which the inevitable deterioration in her condition was advanced."

7. As is to be expected, there was considerable attention devoted at the trial to the extent of the claimant's suffering. The experts, Mr Macfarlane for the claimant, and Mr Karpinski for the defendant, were agreed that "the claimant had a significant pre-accident history of lumbar symptoms. The medical records refer to severe back pain radiating to the right leg in 1999. There is a reference to right lumbar back in 2001, and sacroiliac joint pain in 2003." The unusual feature of the case lies in the fact that Mr Macfarlane was not the first consultant to have been retained on behalf of Miss Widlake in connection with her claim for compensation for these injuries. The first consultant was Miss Porter, who saw her on two occasions and prepared two reports and wrote two letters relevant to the case, all of which material was relied on in the particulars of claim and put in evidence. In her first report dated 15 March 2005 Miss Porter recorded that:

"She reports no past history of low back pain and this is confirmed by review of the records. There is no other relevant past history."

In her second report dated 8 February 2006, she confirmed that:

"Ms Widlake's past medical history was covered in my previous report. She tells me she has had no medical problems other than those relating to the accident since my last examination."

Even when the claimant saw Mr Macfarlane on 23 January 2008 he was told:

"There was no low back problem prior to the index accident."

8. As one would expect, Miss Widlake was cross-examined, and, having admitted that Mr Macfarlane has accurately recorded her recollection, she proffered the explanation that she had forgotten that she had had lower back pain previously.

9. When she was seen by Mr Karpinski on 7 December 2007 she

gave him a broadly similar account of her symptoms as she was to give Mr Macfarlane on 23 January 2008. Both surgeons addressed the possibility of "illness behaviour", that is a patient describing symptoms for the presenting condition for which there is no organic cause in the condition in question and they tested that by the presence of the so-called "Waddell's signs". Mr Karpinski found none, but Mr Macfarlane did find evidence of illness behaviour. Mr Karpinski's conclusion was:

> "I therefore believe that Miss Widlake's injuries from a jarring of the lower back would have largely settled over a period of some twelve months post-injury."

Mr Macfarlane's conclusions were:

> "Chronic pain is a debilitating condition and, in my opinion, there is evidence of illness behaviour although it is difficult to exclude malingering on the basis of a single consultation, I think she does have genuine symptoms emanating from the sacroiliac joint and any exaggeration is likely to be unintentional ... Whilst accepting that there is no scientific basis upon which to base such estimations [as to when she would have suffered a relapse of her previous problems], I think a reasonable estimate would be an acceleration period of around five years."

10. In April 2008 the claimant was covertly filmed on behalf of the defendant and it seemed to the judge that "during all these activities ... Miss Widlake was acting completely normally, as if she had no pain or disability".

11. The experts agreed that the surveillance video did not show any evidence of overt disability. Her explanation was that she took painkillers on a daily basis 4–5 times a day and had taken them shortly before she was filmed. The experts were not entirely agreed as to whether the claimant was deliberately exaggerating her disability as Mr Karpinski suggested or whether the difference in mobility could be accounted for by her having taken analgesics.

12. Miss Widlake's own evidence shifted. In her first witness statement prepared for the purposes of the action on 4 October 2004, she did not say much about the effects of her fall slightly less than three months earlier saying that the pain interfered with her keep fit exercises, and that she found it difficult to bend and therefore to do

her work properly. That account indicated consequences considerably less serious than those later reported to Mr Karpinski and Mr Macfarlane. What the judge described as a "rather more dramatic account" was given by her in her second statement dated 14 December 2007 which recorded permanent feelings of cramp and stabbing pains every few minutes with resultant considerable interference with her daily life.

13. The shape of her claim also altered. In the first schedule of loss compiled on her behalf dated 6 June 2007 and in the second dated 16 August 2007 claims were made for loss of earnings as a security guard for the rest of her working life, that loss being put at £148,878.02. That claim was, however, modified in her third schedule dated 16 October 2008 to reflect the medical opinion and to claim a loss for a period of five years from the accident assessed at £23,906.40 as I have already set out.

14. The defendant paid £4,500 into court pursuant to CPR Part 36. The payment was made on 2 July 2008, by which time the covert surveillance had been conducted, and the experts were in between their two meetings to reach their common ground which they did on 5 August 2008. The trial took place on 6, 7 and 10 November 2008. No further payment in was made. No counter-offer was forthcoming.

15. The judge made these findings:

"52. I was not impressed by Miss Widlake as a witness. I considered her explanations offered in cross-examination on the important issues of why she had not disclosed to Miss Porter and Mr Macfarlane the previous history of her back problems and why she appeared to be acting perfectly normally in the extracts from the film which were put to her to be implausible. The truth of the matter, as I find, is that, while she did injure her back in a fall on 12 July 2004, the consequences were comparatively minor, as indicated by the first account contained in her witness statement dated 4 October 2004, which contain no reference to the sort of pain later described, made no reference to taking any drugs at all, and seemed to limit the consequences of the injury which endured to interference with keep fit exercises, the inability to use her cross-trainer, and not being able to bend at work to carry out body searches. I find that Miss Widlake, who was obviously a person of reasonable intelligence, deliberately concealed the previous history of her back from Miss Porter and then from Mr Macfarlane, in the hope of increasing the amount of compensation which she would recover in respect of her injuries in the accident on 12 July 2004. ..."

16. The judge also said that whilst he was very impressed with Mr Macfarlane as a witness, in the end he did not feel able to accept his opinion as to the consequences for Miss Widlake of her injury because he differed from him on a matter which was uniquely within his [the judge's] province, namely the assessment of the evidence of Miss Widlake.

17. In the result, on the basis that the injuries would have resolved within twelve months of the accident, he assessed the quantum of damages for pain and suffering and loss of amenity at £3,500 and her loss of earnings, about there was no dispute, at £2,022.38. He was not satisfied she had suffered any other loss.

18. The judge then had to deal with the costs of the action. He repeated his findings that Miss Widlake had deliberately concealed her history of low back pain from Miss Porter and also from Mr Macfarlane "in the hope of increasing the amount of compensation which she would recover". He said that he had "in effect ... accepted the position adopted by the defendant in the counter-schedule as to what it is that Miss Widlake is entitled to compensation for". He took account of the fact that the defendant had paid £4,500 into court and added that "obviously Miss Widlake has succeeded in obtaining judgment for a sum in excess of that". He recorded that it was "a feature of this case that Miss Widlake did not make any counter proposals to the Part 36 payment, and indeed she made no attempt ... to negotiate in relation to the settlement of the claim, notwithstanding that liability was never in issue". He referred to decisions of this court in *Molloy v Shell UK Ltd* [2001] EWCA Civ 1272 and to *Painting v University of Oxford* [2005] EWCA Civ 161 and concluded:

"13. It is plain, in my judgment, that the real winner of the trial before me was the defendant. The issues were whether Ms Widlake suffered the back pain of which she complains to the extent to which she complained, and whether, as a result of suffering from such back pain, she had been disabled in the way that she complained and had the consequences of her low back pain brought forward for the period of five years, which I have mentioned. Ms Widlake's case, in my judgment, is a rather more serious case than it appears that either of the cases of *Molloy* or *Painting* were, because in Ms Widlake's case, it is plain, on the evidence, and I have found, that Ms Widlake set out first of all to mislead her own medical experts. So it was not a case in which she was complaining merely of symptoms which were exaggerated. She deliberately withheld from her own medical experts material information as to her previous medical history. This case, in my judgment, is material because it amounts to an attempt – taking the words of Laws LJ in *Molloy* – to manipulate the civil justice system. Not only that, but Ms Widlake, in my judgment, who plainly knew at all material times what the effects upon her back of falling down the stairs had been, exaggerated them grossly in order to project a case of having suffered symptoms which, even on her latest revised case, were being brought forward by some five years, but which in fact, on my findings, as I have explained in my judgment, amounted to very little and resolved itself almost certainly within a few weeks of the date of the accident.

14. Although the figures in this case have been smaller than the figures which the Court of Appeal had to consider in the case of *Molloy*, and indeed smaller than the figures which the Court of Appeal had to consider in the case of *Painting*, the approach, in my judgment, has been to seek, so far as Ms Widlake is concerned, to manipulate the civil justice system on a grand scale, and although it appears that there has not so far been any decision – certainly my attention has not been drawn to any decision – in which the suggestion of Laws LJ in *Molloy* has been adopted, in this case it seems to me that it is appropriate to adopt that suggestion and the consequence of setting out, as I find, to abuse the court's process, in the cynical and dishonest fashion which I have found Ms Widlake did, should have the consequence, notwithstanding that she has recovered damages in excess of the amount which was paid into court on behalf of the defendant, that contrary to her recovering her costs she should pay the costs of the defendant."

19. The Civil Procedure Rules are by now well enough known. The overriding objective is to deal with cases justly. The court encourages parties to settle the whole or part of the case. Part 36 contains the rules about offers to settle and the consequences where an offer to settle is made in accordance with that Part. Relevantly for our case, if a claimant fails to obtain a judgment more advantageous than the defendant's Part 36 offer, then the court will, unless it is unjust to do so, order that the defendant is entitled to his costs and interest on those costs: CPR 36.14(2). Interestingly, and quite clearly as an

encouragement to the claimant to make a Part 36 offer, he can recover interest up to 10% above base rate on any sum of money awarded to him, costs on the indemnity basis and interest on those costs not exceeding 10% above base rate if the judgment against the defendant is at least as advantageous to the claimant as the proposals in the claimant's Part 36 offer: CPR 36.14(3).

20. The general rule about costs is contained in Part 44 and CPR 44.3 sets out the circumstances to be taken into account when the court is exercising its discretion as to costs. The general rule is that the unsuccessful party pays the costs of the successful party but the court may make a different order in deciding what order (if any) to make: CPR 44.3(2). The court has regard to all the circumstances including conduct, success even on part of the case, and any payment into court or admissible offer to settle even if not an offer to which the costs consequences under Part 36 apply: CPR 44.3(4). Conduct includes conduct before as well as during the proceedings, whether it was reasonable to raise, pursue or contest a particular allegation or issue, the manner in which that was done and, relevantly for this case, "whether a claimant who has succeeded in his claim, in whole or in part, exaggerated his claim": CPR 44.3(5). The orders the court can make are, among others, that a party pays but a proportion of the other's costs or a stated amount of those costs or costs from or until a certain date only or costs relating to particular steps or distinct parts of the proceedings: CPR 44.3(6).

21. It is obvious from the moment one sees that all the circumstances of the case must be taken into account when the court exercises its discretion as to costs that every case will depend upon its own facts and that a close analysis of the facts of decided cases may not be very enlightening. But some points of principle may emerge. Judge Seymour was much influenced by *Molloy v Shell UK Ltd* [2001] EWCA Civ 1272 decided on 6 July 2001. That was a claim for damages for personal injury. Liability had been conceded. The defendant appealed against the order that it should recover 75% of its costs incurred after the date of a Part 36 payment made by it. In his schedule of loss the claimant claimed some £68,000 for past losses and some £232,000 for future loss of earnings from his employment working on the oil rigs. But a few days before the trial the defendant discovered that the claimant had indeed returned to work as scaffolder on the oil platforms some three years previously. It was "entirely plain

that the claim had been grossly and deliberately exaggerated by him", and "his particulars of claim were spectacularly dishonest", per Laws LJ giving the judgment with which Mummery LJ agreed.

22. It seemed to Laws LJ obvious that the claimant did not better the payment into court but even if that was wrong there was only one way in which the judge's discretion as to costs could properly have been exercised and that was to award the defendant its costs. But he added obiter:

> "The judge was obliged by Part 44.3(5) as I have said, to consider the whole of the party's conduct. It does appear that he may have considered the respondent's conduct only after the date of the Part 36 payment. If that is so he fell into error. At least since the particulars of claim filed on 20 September 1999 and until he was found out the respondent's approach to this action has been nothing short of a cynical and dishonest abuse of the court's process. For my part I entertain considerable qualms as to whether, faced with the manipulation of the civil justice system on so grand a scale, the court should once it knows the facts, entertain the case at all save to make the dishonest claimant pay the defendant's costs."

23. *Molloy* must, however, be read in the light of *Shah* v *Wassim Ul-Haq* [2009] EWCA Civ 542 decided on 9 June 2009. There the issue was whether it was appropriate to strike out a genuine claim on the ground that the claimant had been involved in a fraud on the court in respect of an associated claim. The defendant Mrs Shah had negligently driven her motor car into the rear of Mr Ul-Haq's vehicle. He claimed for the damage to his car and he and his wife claimed that they had suffered minor whiplash injuries. But his mother also alleged that she had been in his car and had suffered a whiplash injury. The recorder held that was simply untrue. Mr Ul-Haq and his wife had conspired with his mother to support her fraudulent claim. Her claim was accordingly dismissed with costs awarded on an indemnity basis. At the end of the trial the recorder was invited to strike out Mr Ul-Haq's claim but declined to do so. He awarded him and his wife damages and directed that each should pay two thirds of Mrs Shah's costs of defending the claim. Mrs Shah appealed against the refusal to strike out the claim, impressing upon the court the gravity of the situation which faces insurance companies who have to contend with false claims. Smith LJ gave the leading judgment. She said:

"17. I am satisfied that there is no such general rule of law [that the dishonest exaggeration of a genuine claim would result in the dismissal of the whole claim]. I am unaware of any reported case in which a judge has dismissed the whole of a claim because he has found that the claim has been dishonestly exaggerated. The invariable rule is that, in those circumstances, the judge awards the limited damages which are appropriate to his findings. Of course, a claimant's credibility may be so damaged that he fails to prove any part of his loss, but if he proves some loss, he recovers that even though he has fraudulently attempted to recover far more. Not only am I unaware of any reported case in which this rule has not been followed, my own long experience of personal injury work at the Bar and on the bench confirms this view. I have, I regret to say, considerable experience of exaggerated claims. Of course, not all exaggerated claims entail dishonesty; sometimes exaggeration can be innocent, resulting from a subconscious preoccupation, even obsession, with the injury. Judges are always careful to take account of such effects when assessing damages. But there are some cases where the exaggeration is plainly dishonest. In nearly 40 years' experience, I have never known a judge refuse to award damages for a genuine injury on the ground that the claimant had dishonestly sought to exaggerate the injury and its effects.

18. The only suggestion that it might be possible to refuse to award any damages at all where the claim has been exaggerated came in the *obiter dicta* remarks of Laws LJ in *Molloy* v *Shell UK Ltd* [2001] EWCA Civ 1271."

My Lady then gave a résumé of *Molloy* and set out the paragraph in that judgment cited above at para 22. She then continued:

"Thus, when seen in context, all Laws LJ was saying was that, where a genuine claim was dishonestly exaggerated on a grand scale, maybe the court should dismiss the whole claim. He did not consider whether there was power to do that or whether such a course would be consistent with existing authority or practice. In my respectful view, this was little more than wishful thinking by Laws LJ."

She had some sympathy for the insurance companies, observing that "their real problem with phantom passengers and staged accidents is detecting the frauds in the first place". The law was, however, too well-settled to change it by judicial intervention. In his concurring judgment

Toulson LJ suggested that if fraudulent claims have reached epidemic proportions, it may be that prosecutions are needed as a deterrent to others.

24. The other case to which Judge Seymour referred was *Painting* v *University of Oxford* decided on 3 February 2005. This was another personal injuries claim in which the defendant admitted liability and admitted 80% responsibility for the accident. The claimant put the value of her claim at £500,000 which, less the 20% contributory negligence, would have given her judgment for £400,000. In fact, she only recovered some £32,000 less 20%, i.e. just over £25,000. The defendant had originally paid into court the sum of £184,000 but on seeing video surveillance evidence which undermined her claim, that payment was reduced with leave of the court to £10,000. So the claimant beat the relevant payment in and although the defendant contended that the claim was exaggerated, the recorder ordered the defendant to pay all the costs. The University appealed. The recorder was satisfied that the claimant had exaggerated her injuries and the Court of Appeal was satisfied he had taken that into account. Maurice Kay LJ was of the view that the two day hearing was concerned overwhelmingly with the issue of exaggeration and the University won on that issue. Moreover, two further points called for the affording of considerable weight by the recorder which he had not given:

> "The first is the strong likelihood that, but for exaggeration, the claim would have been settled at an early stage and with modest costs. The second is that at no stage did Mrs Painting manifest any willingness to negotiate or put forward a counter-proposal to the Part 36 payment. No-one can compel a claimant to take such steps. However, to contest and lose an issue of exaggeration without ever having made a counter proposal is a matter of some significance in this kind of litigation but must not be assumed beating a Part 36 payment is conclusive. It is a factor and will often be conclusive but one has to have regard to all the circumstances of the case."

25. He did however also make this observation:

> "What the University chose to do was to make a Part 36 payment which amounted to a rock-bottom figure even on the basis that it established exaggeration to the maximum extent. If it had chosen to do so, it could

have pitched the payment higher without for a moment weakening its position on the central issue in the case."

26. In his concurring judgment Longmore LJ considered that a distinction should be drawn between intentional exaggeration and unintentional exaggeration. The fact that the exaggeration was intended and fraudulent was a very important element which needed to be addressed in any assessment of costs. But he too agreed that it was relevant that the claimant had made no attempt to negotiate, made no offer of her own and made no response to the offers of the University.

> "That would not have mattered in pre-CPR days, but to my mind, that now matters very much. Negotiation is supposed to be a two-way street and the claimant who makes no attempt to negotiate can expect, and should expect, the courts to take that into account when making the appropriate order as to costs."

In the event the appeal was allowed and the claimant was ordered to pay the defendant's costs on the standard basis up to the date of the reduced payment in and on an indemnity basis thereafter.

27. Counsel placed a number of other authorities before us. The next in point of time was *Jackson* v *Ministry of Defence* [2006] EWCA Civ 46 decided on 12 January 2006. In that personal injury claim £150,000 was paid into court but the claimant recovered £155,000 and the judge ordered the defendant to pay 75% of the claimant's costs. The defendant appealed. The judge had decided that when the claimant gave his evidence there was a significant degree of exaggeration. There the attempt was made on the defendant's behalf to contend that, as in *Painting*, the defendant was the successful party because the whole trial was about whether the claimant had exaggerated his claim. Tuckey LJ with whom Keene and Wilson LJJ agreed, held:

> "15. Persuasively and persistently though these submissions were put, I do not accept them. The claimant was successful in the sense that he established a claim for substantial damages and beat the payment into court, albeit by a small margin. The defendant was perfectly able to protect itself against the fact that it faced an exaggerated claim. As most defendants do in such circumstances, it had access to experienced lawyers and, if necessary, experts to evaluate the strength of the claim it

faced. It could with the benefit of such advice – and perhaps with the benefit of hindsight in this case should have – made an earlier Part 36 payment into court, and certainly could have increased that payment into court by making a further payment after the unsuccessful settlement meeting. The judge took into account the fact that the claimant had only just beaten the payment in which had been made, as I have already said. What is more, the judge made it clear that it was open to the defendant to challenge specific items relating to the abandoned claims, such as the costs of the experts which were not relied on at trial, at the detailed assessment, where of course the claimant will only be able to recover costs which were reasonably incurred. ...

16. The reduction which the judge made – and the reduction which we can anticipate the costs judge is likely to make – must act as a considerable disincentive to claimants and their advisers against making exaggerated claims. The case of *Painting* is, as Miss Griffiths accepted, an exceptional case where the claimant persisted in a claim for £400,000 at trial and was awarded about £25,000 at the end of the process."

The appeal was dismissed.

28. In *Hall and Others v Stone* [2007] EWCA Civ 1354, dated 18 December 2007, the claimants recovered damages for personal injuries suffered after a road traffic accident. The judge awarded them only 60% of their costs and they appealed submitting that there was no reason why they should not get 100%. The judge had acquitted the claimants of dishonesty and found that they had suffered injuries caused by the accident but found some exaggeration in that the injuries were much less serious than the claimants were alleging. Smith LJ, with whose judgment Lloyd LJ agreed, Waller LJ dissenting, held that the claimant was the successful party, having recovered damages in the face of a defence which asserted they were not entitled to a penny. There was no Part 36 offer. It was not a case such as *Painting* in which a defendant could claim to have won on such an important issue that he could properly regard himself as the victor even though the claimant had beaten the Part 36 offer. In *Painting*:

> "the issue of exaggeration had been central to the case and the claimant had lost. Here the central issue of dishonest fabrication of symptoms had been resolved in the appellants' favour. The question of whether they had exaggerated (as opposed to fabricated) their symptoms was

secondary. In any event the appellants were acquitted not only of dishonest fabrication but also of conscious exaggeration."

She did not think that a judge could cut down the costs of a successful party merely because he has not done quite as well as he had hoped. She added:

> "73. What amounts to partial success will be a matter of fact and degree and will be case-sensitive. The focus should be on the partial success of the losing party on an issue with costs consequences. The mere fact that the defendant has succeeded in keeping the damages down below the sum claimed by the claimant will not necessarily make him the victor or even a partial victor. Of course, where, as in *Painting*, the main issue in the case was whether the claimant had grossly exaggerated the claim and that issue had important costs consequences, it will be open to the judge to hold that the defendant was the victor. But if the claimant's exaggeration was no more than to put his case rather high, it does not seem to me that a defendant who has not made an effective and admissible offer can be regarded as the victor. I would accept that exaggeration by a claimant may be taken into account as 'conduct' under CPR 44.3(4)(a). However, for a defendant to regard himself as a winner or even partial winner on an issue of exaggeration, the exaggeration must be an important feature of the claim with costs consequences. ...
>
> 77. However, even if there were either a finding or an irresistible inference that the claimants had lied or exaggerated their symptoms to the first set of doctors, whether consciously or unconsciously, I do not think that would warrant any abatement of their costs. ...
>
> 79. Nor does it appear to me that the initial exaggeration of the claims had any real effect on the costs of the action. The early medical reports were abandoned – so the claimants ought not in any event be entitled to recover the costs of obtaining them – but they were replaced by Mr Older's reports and would not have played any part in the hearing had the respondent's counsel not chosen to use them against the claimants on issues of credibility."

Exercising discretion afresh, Smith LJ ordered the defendant to pay all the costs with the exception of the costs attributable to the first set of medical reports.

29. In *Straker* v *Tudor Rose* [2007] EWCA Civ 368, dated 25 April

2007, the defendants had made a Part 36 offer before the commencement of the proceedings and soon after the commencement had paid £9,000 into court under Part 36. The judge awarded over £11,000 and £2,000 of accrued interest. Despite beating the payment in the claimant was only given costs limited to pre-action costs and no costs thereafter. The claimant's appeal was allowed and he was awarded 60% of his costs. Waller LJ did not gain much assistance from the authorities cited to him, save in so far as they laid down clear principles and urged that it was to the rules that one should go. He agreed with what Longmore LJ had said in *Barnes v Time Talk UK Ltd* [2003] EWCA Civ 402 para 28 that "the most important thing is to identify the party who is to pay money to the other". But in considering whether factors militating against the general rule apply, clear findings are necessary to show for example that the successful party unreasonably pursued an allegation so as to deprive that party of what would normally be an order for costs in his favour. Unreasonableness or dishonesty, like exaggeration, can very properly lead to punitive orders though on the facts of that case, that was not established. The Court of Appeal awarded the claimant his costs but marked its disapproval of the claimant's failure to comply with the pre-action protocol by reducing his costs by 40%.

30. Bearing in mind Waller LJ's strictures in *Straker* that not much assistance can be gained from fact-sensitive decisions absent point of principle, I do not gain any assistance from *Morgan v UPS* [2008] EWCA Civ 1476 dated 11 November 2008.

31. The seminal textbook on costs is, of course, *Cook on Costs* and His Honour makes this useful observation in para 11 of 11.12 of the 2009 edition:

> "Although exaggeration of a claim cannot of itself deprive the claimant of his entitlement to costs, it is relevant to consider whether the exaggeration has caused costs to be incurred which would not have been incurred had there been a more realistic evaluation of the claim. 'A claimant should be *prima facie* entitled to his full costs of preparing and presenting his claim. The Board of Assessment's discretion to reduce the award from the payment of full costs should be exercised judicially. If it holds that the claim was grossly excessive it is necessary for the Board then to enquire whether the exaggeration gave rise to an obvious and substantial escalation in the costs over and above those which it was

reasonable for the claimant to incur. If it is satisfied that this was the case, then it is open to the Board to exercise its discretion to deprive the claimant of part of his costs. The amount of departure from full payment of the plaintiff's costs shall be proportionate, having regard to the waste of time and costs properly attributable to the claimant's acts or omissions': *Blakes Estates Ltd v Government of Montserrat* [2005] UKPC 46, [2006] 1 WLR 297."

32. I can broadly summarise the submissions made to us in this way. For the appellant, Mr Guy Sims submits that the judge was wrong to rely on *Molloy*; in so far as the claim was exaggerated, costs should be disallowed only in so far as they were attributable to the exaggeration; the defendant should have protected itself by using Part 36 to make a better offer than the judgment which the claimant could have obtained at trial; the effect of the order is to penalise the claimant disproportionately, bearing in mind she had, and was entitled to bring, a genuine claim for damages and, at least at the trial, had presented her case realistically. Thus he contends that the defendant should pay the costs because the claimant recovered more than had been offered and that any exaggeration should be reflected in a reduction of the proportion of costs she should be entitled to recover. Mr Alex Glassbrook, for the respondent, submits that the claimant's exaggeration permeated both the question of whether there was acceleration of back pain by five years or an aggravation of the pre-existing degeneration in the back by twelve months and the extent of the pain which she had suffered during the material period; this was deliberate exaggeration which justified a punitive order for costs; since the claim was not reduced until three weeks before the trial, the costs consequences of the exaggeration endured throughout and, bearing in mind there was no offer to settle, the court should mark its disapproval as the judge did. We should not interfere with that exercise of discretion.

Discussion

33. Costs being at the discretion of the judge, this court will not interfere unless the judge has misdirected himself and was guilty of an error of principle or he has taken into account, or failed to take into account, a fact which should not, or should, have been taken into account or he was plainly wrong in the sense that he has exceeded the

generous ambit within which there is reasonable room for disagreement.

34. Here I am satisfied that Judge Seymour did misdirect himself in finding that this case is "a rather more serious case" than *Molloy*. Mr Molloy was claiming a loss of earnings when for three years or more prior to the trial he had been fully employed on the oil rigs and there was, therefore, every reason to find that he was "spectacularly dishonest". Here Miss Widlake lied to Miss Porter and to Mr Macfarlane. Mr Macfarlane was not taken in by the lie because he had access to her medical records as did Mr Karpinski. So although the claim was advanced in August 2007 on the basis of Miss Porter's report, the defendant knew the truth from December 2007 on receipt of Mr Karpinski's report. Thereafter there was disagreement between the medical experts as to the consequences of the injury and no criticism was made of Mr Macfarlane for holding his obviously honest professional opinion that there was five years' acceleration even if the judge found against him because he did not accept the claimant's evidence. This case does not approach the scale of Mr Molloy's dishonesty. The judge erred in characterising the claimant's actions as an attempt to manipulate the civil justice system on a grand scale tantamount to an abuse of the court's process. Furthermore, the views of Laws LJ in *Molloy* have been doubted in *Shah* v *Ul-Haq* and henceforth *Molloy* should be treated with considerable caution. To be fair to Judge Seymour, I must point out that *Shah* was decided after he had given his judgment. Since *Molloy* was considered to be a "useful" illustration in *Painting*, it may have had some influence on that decision. Be that as it may, I am satisfied that the judge misdirected himself and for that reason alone, I would allow the appeal. It is, therefore, necessary for this court to exercise its own discretion.

35. I agree with Waller LJ in *Straker* that one must go to the rules and apply the approach which the rules prescribe.

36. Thus the first question is to determine which was the unsuccessful party. There may appear to be some difference in the approach of this court if one compares *Painting* with *Jackson* or *Hall* and I hope I can reconcile those differences. I prefer the approach of Tuckey, Keene and Wilson LJJ in *Jackson* that the claimant was successful in the sense that he had established a claim for damages and beaten the payment into court. Although it was a case set in a commercial context, Waller LJ was surely right in *Straker* to endorse

Longmore LJ's views that the most important thing is to identify the party who is to pay money to the other even in a case of personal injury. The claimant had to come to court to establish her claim, a genuine claim, because she had suffered an injury through the admitted negligence of the defendant. The judgment in her favour is a vindication of her stance.

37. The authorities which I have analysed deal with exaggeration as an "issue" in the case. I do not for a moment suggest that the question of exaggeration was not a proper and important consideration for the court in the exercise of its discretion and, having been given a steer in this direction by Waller LJ in *Straker*, I find it useful to look at the rules to see how it fits into the analysis offered by the rules. The umbrella to cover it may be CPR 44.3(4)(a). That requires the court to have particular regard to the conduct of the parties and conduct is defined at 44.3(5) so as to include, at (b):

"whether it was reasonable for a party to raise, pursue or contest a particular allegation or issue."

The rules draw a distinction between an "allegation" and an "issue" which I confess had not struck me until I read Waller LJ's judgment. At the risk of being pedantic, I think the cases can be reconciled by treating exaggeration as "an allegation" relevant to "the issue" of the quantum of damages.

38. So viewed, there may be no need to determine who has been the "winner" of a particular "issue". All the court needs to do is establish whether it was *unreasonable* for the claimant to pursue her allegation that she had suffered such pain (a) that it justified her case that her pre-existing condition was accelerated by 5 years and (b) that it was of the severity she described in support of her claim for general damages for pain and suffering. If it was unreasonable then that was conduct which the court had to take into account.

39. The way in which regard is to be had to that conduct is principally to enquire into its causative effect: to what extent did her lies and gross exaggeration cause the incurring or wasting of costs? It is obvious that she should recover nothing in respect of the reports she obtained from Miss Porter and the costs judge would disallow anything arising from that. On the other side of the balance sheet the defendant should have some compensation for the wasted costs incurred by having to consider those reports and to deal with the case

on the basis that they formed part of the pleaded claim which it had to meet. The lie was short-lived: on receipt of its own medical report in January 2007 the defendant knew of the pre-existing injury and was able to judge how to run its own case. The defendant was able to protect itself by making a proper Part 36 offer. Nevertheless the schedule of loss before the court, and thus the case the defendant still had to meet, on paper at least, was one valued by the claimant in the sum of about £160,000. The defendant was entitled to protect itself against a claim of that magnitude or even a claim of some £35,000, which it became three weeks before the trial. The claimant was not treating it as a claim which should be measured at about £5,000. Small claims are not worth contesting, are not worth engaging enquiry agents to carry out covert surveillance and small claims are often not worth fighting and so are much more likely to settle. Here the defendant was put to expense arising out of the manner in which the case was unreasonably being conducted, certainly up until the final schedule of loss was served in October. Some compensation for the defendant put to the expense of defending such an exaggerated claim should be entered on the notional balance sheet.

40. Similar costs consequences apply if one considers the case under umbrella of CPR 44.3(5)(d) which is obviously the most appropriate rule in play. The court simply asks:

> "whether a claimant who has succeeded in his claim, in whole or in part, exaggerated his claim."

Here there was gross exaggeration as the judge found. That was, therefore, conduct to take into account in disapplying the general rule.

41. In addition to looking at it in terms of costs consequences, the court is entitled in an appropriate case to say that the misconduct is so egregious that a penalty should be imposed upon the offending party. One can, therefore, deprive a party of costs by way of punitive sanction. Given the judge's findings of dishonesty in this case, that may be appropriate here. I sound a word of caution: lies are told in litigation every day up and down the country and quite rightly do not lead to a penalty being imposed in respect of them. There is a considerable difference between a concocted claim and an exaggerated claim and judges must be astute to measure how reprehensible the conduct is.

42. Defendants are, therefore, used to having to cope with false or

exaggerated claims. Defendants have a means of protecting themselves. Part 36 is that shield. The court may not now always attach the same significance to a defendant's failure to beat his payment into court as applied in the days before the CPR. Coming close can now sometimes have an impact on costs. But the rule remains that a defendant has this ability to win outright by making an offer which the claimant fails to beat and where, as here, the facts were well-known to this defendant from the time of Mr Karpinski's report, the fact that it did not make a sufficiently high Part 36 offer counts against it. The basic rule is that the claimant gets his (or her) costs if the defendant fails to make a good enough Part 36 offer so that goes to the claimant's credit on the balance sheet.

43. Part 36 now also affects a claimant. Whilst not obliged to make a counter-offer, in this day and age of encouraging settlement, claimants who do not do so run the risk that their refusal will impact upon the costs they may otherwise be entitled to recover. Here there was no attempt to negotiate and that counts against the claimant.

44. Having tried to represent these considerations in a balance sheet, where does the balance lie? I start with the claimant getting her costs because she beat the payment in and was the successful party. That is the starting point. Those costs should not include costs related to Miss Porter's reporting and the costs judge must be directed to exclude those matters. Pursuing her claim in the exaggerated way she did had the result that this became heavily contested litigation whereas it might have settled. The defendant has been put to unnecessary expense. But an order for costs against the claimant is less justified where, as here, the defendant failed to alleviate its predicament by making a proper Part 36 offer and so lost the opportunity provided by the rules of recovering those costs from the claimant. The claimant's dishonesty must be penalised. The claimant's failure to negotiate a claim which was clearly capable of being settled must also be recognised. When I balance those factors, and attempt to do justice to both parties and to be fair to them, I conclude that the right order in this case is that there be no order for costs.

45. I would therefore allow the appeal, set aside the judge's order and make no order for the costs below.

46. SMITH LJ: I agree.

47. WILSON LJ: I also agree.

Guy Sims (instructed by Ward Gethin) appeared for the appellant.

Alex Glassbrook (instructed by Vizards Wyeth) appeared for the respondent.

Case 29
MasterCigars Direct Ltd
v
Withers LLP

[2010] 3 Costs LR 374

Neutral Citation Number: [2009] EWCA Civ 1526
Court of Appeal (Civil Division)
7 December 2009

Before:
Master of the Rolls (Lord Neuberger), and
Maurice Kay and Stanley Burnton LJJ

Headnote

The Court of Appeal has given its reasons for refusing to hear appeals from the decisions of Morgan J reported at [2008] 1 Costs LR 72 and [2009] 3 Costs LR 393.

Judgment

1. LORD NEUBERGER: There are before the court four applications for permission to appeal against three decisions of Morgan J in relation to the assessment of costs as between a solicitor and a client arising out of trademarks.

2. The applications were considered on the papers in the usual way by Mummery LJ. Having considered the three judgments of Morgan J and the 60-page, 185-paragraph skeleton argument on behalf of the applicant, MasterCigars Direct Ltd ("MasterCigars"), Mummery LJ was "unconvinced" that any of the applications should be granted, as he thought that the issues raised on the prospective appeal turned on the application to the particular facts of the case of the law, relating to

the assessment of solicitors' costs which are disputed by a client who had been given an estimate. However, he directed that the applications be adjourned to be heard by a three-judge court which should proceed immediately to hear any appeal if all or any of the applications were granted.

3. The background to the applications is as follows. In around May 2004 Withers LLP ("Withers") were instructed by MasterCigars to act for them in connection with a trademark and parallel import dispute with Corporacion Habanos SA of Havana and Hunter and Franker Ltd. The dispute led the proceedings in the Chancery Division.

4. In March 2005 Withers sent a letter to MasterCigars which amounted to an estimate of costs ("the estimate"). The relevant part of the letter was in these terms:

> "The costs of litigating this matter will depend on a number of circumstances. The most important will be whether the matter settles prior to a trial or whether it will be necessary to have a trial of the issues and one must also take into account the hearing or hearings relating to the determination of the preliminary point. It seems clear that the hearing of the preliminary point will go ahead although it is possible that there may be settlement prior to full trial. Should the matter go to trial, I would estimate that it will last for 3 to 4 days depending on the number of witnesses required on each side and could be longer. I have set out in a schedule details of costs and disbursements to the end of January and thereafter my estimate of costs up to and including a trial. I have made a number of assumptions in this assessment. If for example there were further hearings prior to the trial or disclosure was much more extensive or there are more witnesses – or expert witnesses – than I have anticipated then the costs will increase. Conversely, if matters turn out to be more straightforward than I have anticipated, then the costs will be less. I will update this cost estimate from time to time as events develop. I should add that, as claimant, it would be most unlikely that you would instruct us to continue this litigation up to and including a trial unless you considered that the risks, including those in relation to costs, were commercially justifiable."

5. Included with the estimate were the terms of business of Withers, which included in para 4 the following:

> "When you instruct us we will do our best to tell you the likely level of

our fees. Unless we tell you otherwise, this will be an estimate only, not a fixed quotation. If you asked for a fixed quotation, we will try to provide one. However, it may not be possible to predict the amount of time we will need to deal with the matter. You may set an upper limit on costs. We will not do any work that will take our fees over this limit without your permission. If we provide a fixed quotation, this will only apply to the work we agree in writing, at the time. If you then ask us to do extra work, we will charge you for the extra work."

6. The schedule attached to the estimate indicated that the accrued costs and disbursements up to the date of the estimate were around £150,000 and the anticipated costs and disbursements up to and including the trial were a further £206,500 odd. Withers were duly instructed and the proceedings were issued.

7. A little later, on 6 May 2005, there was a discussion about revised estimates, and Withers sent an email on 6 May 2005 to MasterCigars which included this:

"So far as our own fees are concerned, there are some unknowns in the sense that we really do not have an idea of how much disclosure they will produce (I suspect too little requiring the prising out of the balance, especially at the Habanos end) nor do we have any accurate idea what they will produce in the way of witness evidence. One of the things that was said at the outset was that although the basic framework is relatively simple and clear, the twists and turns of evidence, interim applications and so forth can change the scene out of all proportion very quickly."

8. The proceedings, once they got under way, involved a number of disputed interlocutory hearings, and culminated in a trial before HHJ Michael Fysh QC, which lasted 16 days over July, September and October of 2005 and led to a reserved judgment on 10 March 2006, now reported at [2006] RPC 805. MasterCigars failed on the parallel input issue, but they successfully appealed that aspect of the decision to the Court of Appeal see [2007] EWCA Civ 176. By the time of the hearing of the appeal they had parted company with Withers.

9. Various bills of costs were prepared by Withers and presented to MasterCigars in connection with the proceedings and the total of the bills appears to have been in the region of £1.05 million. These bills have been hotly contested; there have been thirteen applications to the costs judge and five appeals to the High Court.

10. The first and second of the instant applications relate to the first decision of Morgan J on appeal from Costs Judge Rogers. Morgan J's decision was given on 23 November 2007 [2007] EWHC 2733 (Ch) and it is reported at [2008] 3 AER 417. By that judgment (the first judgment), Morgan J allowed Withers' appeal from the costs judge given after a two-day hearing on 25 April 2007. The costs judge decided in effect to cut Withers' costs up to the fourth day of the trial to the levels detailed in the estimate, and, in respect of the remaining eleven days, he only allowed them what MasterCigars conceded, namely payment at the daily rate set out in the estimate and the fees of counsel; and he allowed Withers nothing in respect of the work done in connection with the appeal.

11. The appeal before Morgan J, which he heard with Costs Judge Campbell and Mr Carter, lasted four days, and Morgan J gave a full and careful judgment. So far as is relevant, in paras 69 to 106 he discussed "the effect of an estimate", and during the course of his discussions he cited a number of authorities on the topic. Because he proceeded in the first decision to deal with this question by reference to a number of authorities, the most convenient summary of his reasoning in that first judgment is to be found in para 54 of a second judgment which was in these terms:

> "In my judgment, the legal process involved in a case where a client contends that its reliance on an estimate should be taken into account in determining the figure which it is reasonable for the client to pay is as follows. The court should determine whether the client did rely on the estimate. The court should determine how the client relied on the estimate. The court should try to determine the above without conducting an elaborate and detailed investigation. The court should decide whether the costs claimed should be reduced by reason of its findings as to reliance and, if so, in what way and by how much. Whether there should be a reduction, and if so to what extent, is a matter of judgment. Specific deductions can be made from the costs otherwise recoverable to reflect the impact which an erroneous and uncorrected estimate had on the conduct of the client. Such an approach requires the court to form an assessment of the impact of the estimate on the conduct of the client. The court should consider the deductions which are needed in order to do justice between the parties. It is not the proper function of the court to punish the solicitor for providing a

wrong estimate or for failing to keep it up to date as events unfolded. In terms of the sequence of the decisions to be made by the court, it has been suggested that the court should determine whether, and if so how, it will reflect the estimate in the detailed assessment before carrying out the detailed assessment. The suggestion as to the sequence of decision making may not always be appropriate. The suggestion is put forward as practical guidance rather than as a legal imperative. The ultimate question is as to the sum which it is reasonable for the client to pay, having regard to the estimate and any other relevant matter."

Morgan J referred to this as being the summary of his reasoning in his first decision.

12. At paras 107 to 111 of the first judgment Morgan J discussed and rejected MasterCigars' contention that there was an implied term in Withers' retainer that they would comply with the Solicitors' Costs Information and Client Care Code and that failure to do so would prevent them from claiming any costs which complied with their obligations thereunder.

13. He then discussed "the effect of the estimate and the retainer" and reached his conclusion in paras 112 to 129. His main reason for allowing the appeal was set out in paras 112–113, and he dealt with a passage in *Cook on Costs* in that paragraph, where he said this:

"112. MasterCigars also made submissions as to the scope of the solicitors' retainer. As I understood the submissions, it is necessary for me to deal with two particular aspects of them. The first aspect is the contention that Withers were retained to do the work in the estimate and no other work. If Withers did other work then it was outside the retainer and they were not entitled to be paid for it. A second aspect is the contention that the client only agreed to pay the costs in the estimate and was not liable to pay anything beyond the estimate unless it was asked to, and expressly agreed, to do so. I reject both these contentions. As to the second, it is clear from Withers' standard terms of business that the estimate was not placing an upper limit on costs and much less was it placing a definition on the work required of Withers. As regards the first contention, I hold that the estimate did not define the extent of the work to be done. Withers were instructed to do what was reasonably necessary on behalf of the client in the litigation as it evolved. Further, there was no suggestion from MasterCigars that any of the items of work which were done by Withers on its behalf were not within Withers' retainer in the sense that they were unauthorised and should not have been done. It follows that Withers is entitled to a reasonable fee for work within the retainer and the estimate does not define the work for which a charge may be made.

Applying the Above Reasoning to the Third Appeal

113. The next step is to apply the above reasoning to this particular case. In para 66 of his judgment, the costs judge stated that in agreement with Mr Brown's closing submissions for MasterCigars, the case really turned on the true contractual position as set out in the documents. The closing submissions were recorded by the costs judge at paras 59 and 60 of his judgment, which included the reference to *Cook on Costs*, 2007 Edition, page 15. The passage in *Cook on Costs* stated that unless the client was notified of the further sums payable, preferably before they were incurred, then the solicitor would be unable to recover costs in excess of the estimated amount. In my judgment, that passage does not correctly state the law. It seems to me that on a fair reading of the judgment, the costs judge was relying on this passage in *Cook on Costs*. In so far as the costs judge relied upon that passage in *Cook on Costs*, he was led into error in making his finding as to the contractual position. The contractual position is that the solicitors are entitled to a reasonable fee and in the present case, in respect of certain bills, that fee is to be the subject of a detailed assessment. At the stage of the detailed assessment, the estimate has the relevance which I have described above as a yardstick and in respect of any case raised by the client as to reliance on the estimate. Although the costs judge referred in para 67 to 'all the evidence, oral and documentary', it seems to me that I must inevitably find that his reasoning is based on his analysis of the contractual position, which for the reasons I have given was incorrect. It follows that I must allow the third appeal and in particular the appeal against para 1 of the order of 25 April 2007, which held that Withers were bound by the sum set out in the estimate of 6 May 2005."

14. As a result of allowing the appeal Morgan J decided to remit the case to a different costs judge. Meanwhile MasterCigars applied to the Court of Appeal for permission to appeal the first decision of Morgan J, that application came before Lloyd LJ who rejected it on 23 April 2008. While accepting that some of the points [that] were to be raised on any appeal were of importance, he thought that MasterCigars had

no "reasonable prospect of success" and that "the judge's reasoning [was] compelling". He also made the point that as it was only a preliminary judgment it would in any event be more appropriate for an appeal if any to be considered at a later stage.

15. Although MasterCigars renewed their application to the extent of seeking a hearing of the application for permission to appeal, they abandoned it on receiving the remission decision of Costs Judge Simons who, after a two-day hearing, gave the judgment on 11 July 2008. Costs Judge Simons found that MasterCigars had relied on the estimate, and the proper way to give effect to their reliance was to limit the profit costs chargeable by Withers on the two sample bills before him to the amount of the estimate plus a margin of 20% for the period covered by the estimate. Subsequently, on 14 November 2008, at a further hearing Costs Judge Simons effectively gave effect to that decision in relation to (inaudible) bills.

16. Withers appealed against those two decisions of Costs Judge Simons and the hearing was directed, very sensibly, by Peter Smith J to be heard by Morgan J on the ground that he had given the first judgment. Morgan J heard the appeal with Senior Costs Judge Hurst and Mr Carter as assessors over two days and gave a judgment on 30 March 2009 – see [2009] EWHC 651 Chancery.

17. In para 23 of his judgment (the second judgment) he referred to earlier decisions where the courts had expressed concern at the danger of satellite litigation and the relevance of an estimate when it came to a detailed assessment of costs. He said:

> "It is clear that the present case is a bad example of satellite litigation which has gone beyond the proper bounds. The sums directly involved in the present dispute are not insignificant, but in the context of the total fees claimed by Withers they are comparatively modest. I was told at the hearing that the significance of the disputes has now gone beyond the sums nominally at issue. That is because the parties have incurred very considerable costs in relation to the detailed assessment and the outcome of these appeals may have a bearing on who ultimately will bear those costs."

18. In para 43 of the second judgment, Morgan J summarised the findings made by the costs judge on the issues of reliance in these terms:

"He held that MasterCigars had used the estimate of 6 May 2005 to approach funders; he held that it had arranged funding by reference to the estimate; he held that if the estimate of 6 May 2005 had been at a level approaching the figures in later bills from the relevant period then MasterCigars would have instructed other solicitors in place of Withers. Beyond those findings, in my judgment, the Master did not clearly go."

19. Morgan J then went on to consider various arguments raised by Withers as to why the costs judge was wrong to find that MasterCigars had relied on the estimate and rejected all those arguments. In relation to reliance he said this in para 47 of his judgment:

"Further, in *Leigh* v *Michelin Tyre plc* at [31], Dyson LJ suggested that the question as to how the client relied on the estimate should be determined 'without conducting an elaborate and detailed investigation'. Accordingly, in my judgment, it is not necessary for the client to prove detriment in the sense of showing on the balance of probabilities that it would have acted in a different way, which would have turned out to be more advantageous to the client. In a case where the client satisfies the court that the inaccurate estimate deprived the client of an opportunity of acting differently, that is a relevant matter which can be assessed by the court when determining the regard which should be had to the estimate when assessing costs. Of course, if a client does prove the fact of detriment, and in particular substantial detriment, that will weigh more heavily with the court as compared with the case where the client contends that the inaccurate estimate deprived the client of an opportunity to act differently and where the matter is wholly speculative as to how the client might have acted."

20. After the passage I have already quoted from para 54 of the second judgment Morgan J said this in relation to the approach adopted by Costs Judge Simons:

"56. My own understanding, based on my discussions with my assessors, when I dealt with the earlier appeals in this case, and again with my assessors in connection with the present appeal, is that the margin approach is very much favoured by costs judges. Costs judges have tended to adopt the margin approach, certainly ever since the decision in *Wong* v *Vizards* [1997] 2 Costs LR 46. As I attempted to explain in my earlier judgment, *Wong* v *Vizards* does not say that the margin approach is the correct approach as a matter of legal principle.

Indeed, on the facts of *Wong* v *Vizards*, that case does not provide very much support for the adoption of a margin approach. I am happy to find that I am not alone in reacting in this way to the decision in *Wong* v *Vizards*. I refer to the discussion of the point in *Reynolds* v *Stone Rowe Brewer* [2008] EWHC 497 (QB) at [72], per Tugendhat J.

57. Of course, the adoption of a margin approach greatly simplifies the steps which a costs judge needs to take when carrying out a detailed assessment of a bill, which has been preceded by a lower estimate. When I considered my earlier judgment, and when I reviewed the decision of Master Simons in this case, I very carefully considered whether I was able to support the adoption of a margin approach in many, if not all, cases. The incentive to do so was considerable. If the margin approach became the permissible conventional approach then the costs of the detailed assessment could be reduced and the outcome would be more predictable. However, it is obvious, at least to me, that the adoption of a margin approach as the conventional approach in the majority of cases pays scant, if any, attention to the legal process which I attempted to describe in my earlier judgment and have now restated in para 54 above. Conversely, I have not previously said, and do not now say, that a conclusion by a court, having followed the appropriate legal process, to express itself by reference to a margin, doing the best it can to quantify the costs payable, can never be right. It may be that the court is constrained to express itself by the use of a margin, because no other method is available which better expresses the result of the legal process which I have described."

21. Morgan J then turned to consider "the costs judge's findings as to the effect of relevance" at paras 58 to 70 where he discussed the argument before him on the effect of reliance. In paras 71 to 86 he discussed the reasoning of the costs judge and came to the conclusion that he could not accept his finding of the 20% margin, saying this in paras 80 and 81:

"80. Notwithstanding the reasons why I should be cautious about criticising [85] of the decision, my conclusion is that the decision is inadequate as a statement of reasons for the selection of a 20% margin. The figure of 20% has all the appearance of being arbitrary rather than calculated. The costs judge plainly felt that the selection of the margin should be influenced by some of the factors in paras 121 to 125 of my earlier judgment. If so, it was necessary, in order to give proper reasons for the conclusion, for the costs judge to identify which factors could be taken into account and which should be left out of account. In the case of these factors, it was also necessary for the Master to give brief reasons as to why a factor was taken into account, or left out, as the case may be.

81. At the hearing of these appeals, I was shown various calculations relating to the costs claimed for the matters referred to in paras 121 to 125 of my judgment. Following the hearing, both parties made a series of further submissions which included submissions on these figures. It is simply not possible to tell from the costs judge's reasons how he arrived at the figure of 20% and what contribution to that 20% was made by which of the matters in question. On the information before me, it seems very difficult to justify a margin of 20% unless one disallowed the majority of those matters and, in that event, it was incumbent on the costs judge to say which matters he disallowed, with his reasons for that conclusion."

22. It is right to say that Morgan J also considered that the costs judge had wrongly taken certain matters into account that he ought not to have done (see para 69) and had wrongly rejected two other possible approaches as not open to him as a matter of law (see para 76).

23. The result, as explained in paras 87 to 89 of the second judgment, was that Morgan J concluded Costs Judge Simons' decision could not stand and was overturned.

24. In paras 90 to 92 of his second judgment Morgan J then turned to the question of how matters should proceed from there. He decided that, rather than remitting the matter yet again to another costs judge, he would ask a senior costs judge, under CPR 35.15(3A), to prepare a report on "any matter at issue in the proceedings" in order to "enable the court to decide the final outcome of the questions which are outstanding". In other words, Morgan J decided that he would resolve any outstanding issue of costs, but that he would only do so after he had been provided with the report from the Senior Costs Judge.

25. When the second judgment was handed down MasterCigars objected to that procedure, and Morgan J permitted them to argue against it at a further hearing on 22 April 2009. At that hearing Morgan J gave an extemporary judgment and decided to stick to his

view as to how matters should proceed. At para 15 he directed the four questions which were to be the subject of termination:

"1) What is a reasonable sum that the work can be done [for] by Withers, the subject of the two contested bills?

2) What work was done during the estimated periods which was not covered by the estimate?

3) What is the impact of MasterCigars' reliance on the estimate?

4) In light of the impact referred to above and any other material considerations, what sum is reasonable to MasterCigars to pay?"

26. Shortly after that, in para 18 of his judgment, Morgan J turned to the question of what he called "the impact of MasterCigars' reliance on the estimate" and he said this:

"The parties are not entitled to have a second go or a third or fourth go to retrieve their respective cases on this question of reliance on MasterCigars. The parties are to be bound by Master Simons' findings of fact on the fact of reliance"

I have already identified these, I need not read more.

27. As I have mentioned, there are four applications rather than three before this court, although only three judgments of Morgan J are sought to be appealed. The reasons there are four applications is that, in relation to the first judgment, there are two effectively identical applications, although the first has been amended. The first application was that which was before Lloyd LJ and is now sought to be restored. In the alternative, and no doubt to protect themselves, MasterCigars have issued a second application out of time. I will treat those first two applications as a single application when considering the various grounds of appeal. The second application relates to the second judgment and third application to the third judgment.

28. Having summarised the relevant factual background relating to these applications and the content of the judgments which it sought to appeal, I now turn to the central question of whether, at least in my view, permission to appeal should be granted in respect of any of the issues raised. In that connection I have reached the clear conclusion that we should refuse MasterCigars permission to appeal on any of the many issues covered in their various applications. My reasons for that conclusion may usefully be considered in two sections.

29. The first section involves simply concentrating on the specific issue which MasterCigars seek to raise on the projected appeals and explaining why they are not appropriate for an appeal. The second section comprises other factors, which particularly, when taken together, provide to put it at its lowest – powerful support for the notion that permission to appeal should be refused.

30. Most of the points which MasterCigars seek to raise in their notice of appeal – and it is only fair to Mr Simon Brown of counsel who appears on their behalf on this application to record that they were not points which he pressed in oral argument – relate to the particular facts of the case, and, while they may at least in some circumstances be of significance to the parties, they cannot possibly be said to be of wider relevance and therefore they do not cross the hurdle requisite for a second appeal. This consideration alone is enough to dispose, in my view, of grounds 1 and 5, parts of ground 2 and of ground 4 in the first application; grounds 1, 3, 4 and 6 and most of grounds 2, 5, 7 and 8 of the second application; and grounds A1, A2, A3, A5, A7 and A8 and the whole of grounds B and C in the third application. Quite apart from this, most of the issues raised in the third application concern case management decisions or costs orders and are therefore inappropriate for this court.

31. I can see that there is a fairly powerful argument for saying that, if there is a real *prima facie* case to suggest that a judge has made a series of errors which have led to an unjust result, then, even though the appeal would be a second appeal, it could be right in some cases to grant permission. This is not the occasion to consider the correctness or scope of such an argument, but in my clear view, far from there appearing to be any error on the part of the judge in relation to any of the matters raised in the grounds to which I have so far referred, he was very probably, indeed in most cases plainly, right or at least entitled to come to the conclusion that he did.

32. I accept that in relation to the third application it can be said that it would not really raise a second appeal as it largely concerns Morgan J's decision as to how to proceed with the resolution of the costs issue before him. However, those decisions were, as I have mentioned, case management decisions upon which this court would be very slow to grant permission to appeal, even where it is a first appeal, and in any event they were, to put it at its lowest, decisions to which the judge was entitled to come. In particular, he was entitled to

say on the reliance issue, which involved evidence including cross-examination, [that it] should be regarded as concluded by the findings of Costs Judge Simons which Withers had unsuccessfully appealed and which MasterCigars had not even sought to challenge. He was also entitled to limit the issues and permit them to extend to the four points he identified in para 15 of his third judgment. It was, to put it at its lowest, a proper use of his case management powers to identify the issues on which he wanted to receive argument, and it seems to me that it was a legitimate and proper implementation of that power to limit the issues and permit them to extend to those four items, reflecting as it did the need to keep the issues as limited as possible to expedite the outcome, and minimise the costs, of these proceedings, while at the same time giving the parties a proper opportunity of making submissions to the very tribunal which was going to determine, hopefully finally, the outcome of this long drawn out matter.

33. Having said all that, I readily accept that the applications also raise points of law of potentially wider significance. In my opinion, however, while at least some of these points can be said to be of sufficient importance to cross the second appeal threshold, there is no real prospect of this court holding Morgan J's conclusions to be wrong. In this connection it seems to me that there are four points of principle. First, there is Morgan J's summary in para 54 of his second judgment, accurately reflecting what he said more fully in his first judgment as to the effect of an estimate on the assessment of costs. It seems to me that what the judge said in those passages was correct and, despite submissions to the contrary on the part of MasterCigars, quite consistent with principle and with the previous authority.

34. The argument that the estimate of May 2005 was binding on Withers in the sense that it could not be exceeded appears to me unsustainable. First, it is inconsistent with the 20% margin uplift which Costs Judge Simons potentially awarded Withers, and which MasterCigars had accepted as correct. Secondly, it is inconsistent with the concept of an estimate, particularly one worded in the way in which the estimate of 6 May 2005 was worded. Thirdly, as pointed out by my Lord, Stanley Burnton LJ, it is inconsistent with para 4 of Withers' terms of business accompanying the estimate. Fourthly, it produces a potential windfall result for a client who, for instance, as pointed out again by my Lord, may not have relied on the estimate or

would have proceeded with the action but with other solicitors. Why should they not pay at least a reasonable sum reflecting that?

35. Furthermore, the suggestion that the decision of Toulson J in *Wong* v *Vizards* [1997] 2 HLR 46 is consistent with the view that an uplift is appropriate has a number of problems. First, at most it could be said to be consistent with the view that an uplift margin is appropriate; it certainly could not, on the most generous reading, suggest that it is the only way of achieving a result. Secondly, it does not undermine the point that in this case the judge was entitled to conclude that there was no basis for awarding a general 20% uplift. Thirdly, this was a much more complicated case than *Wong* v *Vizards* and very different on the facts. Fourthly, in *Wong* v *Vizards* the solicitors sent a letter which confirmed that the estimate was "hopefully" setting out "the fullest extent of the liability". Indeed, *Wong* v *Vizards* was referred to in *Garbutt* v *Edwards* [2006] 1 WLR 2907 by Arden LJ, giving the only judgment of the court in para 44, and she regarded it as authority to the fact that:

"... in determining what is a reasonable amount for [the client] to pay for the work done, regard should be had to the level of costs which he had been led to believe represented a worst case assessment of his potential liability."

In other words, entirely consistent with Morgan J's approach, it was something to be taken into account. That disposes of ground 6 and 7 and what remains of grounds 4 in the first application and the remainder of grounds 2 in the second application.

36. Secondly, there is Morgan J's rejection of the argument, that there is to be implied into a retainer that solicitors will comply with the Solicitor's Costs and Information and Client Care Code, as discussed in paras 107 to 111 of the first judgment. The rejection of that argument seems also to me to be unassailable. That disposes of what remains of grounds 2 and of ground 3 of the first application.

37. Thirdly, there is the question of whether the judge was right about what he said in relation to the margin approach in paras 56 and 57 of his judgment, and his rejection of Costs Judge Simons' application of the 20% margin in paras 81 to 83 of his judgment. In my opinion, that was a view the judge was entitled to form.

38. In the first place, Morgan J was not saying that it was never appropriate to apply a margin or uplift. Secondly, although it is true

that the margin approach has been frequently applied, as the judge himself said, there is nothing in any authority, to suggest that it is prescribed by the law. Thirdly, the problems that the margin approach seems to involve are, on the face of it, well identified by Morgan J Fourthly, the margin approach appears, from what we are told, to have been based on the decision on *Wong* v *Vizards*, to which I have referred, where it is said that the 15% margin approach was adopted. But if one looks at what was said by Toulson J on page 50 it appears to me, in common with Morgan J, that all he was saying was that the figure he arrived at happened to represent a 15% margin.

39. It is interesting to note that in the subsequent case of *Reynolds* v *Stone Rowe Brewer* [2008] EWHC 497 (QB) Tugendhat J and the counsel before him all appear to have accepted the correctness of Morgan J's approach in this connection (see para 48). That deals with what remains of ground 5 in the second application.

40. Finally there is the question whether the judge had power to order in his second judgment and to confirm in his third judgment, that the outstanding questions relating to costs should be dealt with him following a report by the senior costs master in further submissions from the parties. In my view he plainly did (see CPR 35.15(3A) already referred to, 52.10 and 52.11; and, in relation to the receipt of further evidence, *Irwin* v *Liverpool City Council* [2005] 1 WLR 2557). That appears to me to dispose of the remainder of ground 7 and 8 of the second application and ground A4 of the third application.

41. That leaves ground A6 of the third application, where it is alleged that Morgan J's "observations and indications in the course of argument" on 22 April 2009 served to:

"give the appearance that the learned judge is unfairly disposed [towards MasterCigars and its case and] make it inappropriate that the learned judge continued to hear this case"

42. This is said in MasterCigars' skeleton argument to arise from what they call "the strong indication" that the finding of reliance made by Costs Judge Simons "will probably have little effect on the detailed assessment". Provided they do so fairly and moderately, judges are entitled to express preliminary views, and, by 22 April 2009, in the sorry history of these proceedings, it was certainly no bad thing for the judge to have done so. There has been no particularisation of

MasterCigars' allegation, and in my view it is not sustainable. Morgan J has given three careful impressive judgments, dealing with matters in a balanced way, showing no conceivable bias in either party's favour, and, for the very reason Peter Smith J directed that the appeal which resulted in the second judgment be heard by Morgan J, it seems to me that it is clearly appropriate for him to hear this matter if it is to come to a High Court judge.

43. I mentioned that there are other reasons for refusing permission to appeal. I think there are three. First, even if one confines oneself to the issues considered in the five judgments so far discussed, namely the two judgments of the cost judges and the three judgments of Morgan J, eleven days of court time, ignoring the handing down of reserved judgments and ignoring today's hearing and ignoring the time before Lloyd LJ on paper, have been devoted to arguing the costs issues. There have been, we are told, other hearings on the costs issue. I have already quoted what Morgan J said in para 23 of his first judgment and I wholly agree with it. I leave open the question of whether or not that is a good enough reason on its own to refuse permission to mount a second appeal or even a first appeal, but it is a certainly a very powerful factor which supports the decision to refuse permission to appeal, especially a second appeal, in relation to costs.

44. Secondly, in relation to the issues arising out of the first judgment, the first application for permission was made in time but it was withdrawn some time in the summer of 2008 after Lloyd LJ refused permission, and it was revived some eight months later when Costs Judge Simons' decision was overturned. The second application was made more than 16 months out of time. It is true that Lloyd LJ included as part of his reason the fact that the application could be premature, but he also refused permission on the merits. Mr Brown frankly accepted, no letter was written by MasterCigars indicating that the application should be adjourned or that it might be renewed. In my view, bearing in mind the issues and history in this matter, it would be inappropriate to allow this application to be restored or renewed way out of time when matters had proceeded for many months on the basis that the first judgment of Morgan J was not being appealed. This is an important point as I consider that, of the various issues of principle which [one] can identify as being raised by these applications, the more significant really arise out [of] Morgan J's first judgment.

45. Thirdly, the very sensible procedure which Morgan J proposed

at the end of his second judgment and confirmed in his third judgment, means that many of the issues sought to have been raised on these appeals may either turn out to be irrelevant or can still be raised and argued pursuant to the directions proposed by the judge in his April 22 judgment. It is not for me at this stage to go through all the issues and say which, if any, can be so raised or might be relevant, but it is clear that this is an additional reason to my mind for refusing permission.

46. Finally, in fairness to the judge and indeed to the parties, I should like to add that the judge's intention to grasp the costs issue himself with the assistance of a report from the Senior Costs Judge seems to me not merely to have been a course which was open to him, but is a course which was an eminently sensible way of dealing with and disposing of this particular costs dispute in the light of its lamentable history. The dispute has gone on far, far too long; it has taken up far, far too much court time, and it has involved the parties in far, far too much expense. It is a prime example of satellite litigation which has got completely out of hand and which I am bound to say reflects discredit on our legal system.

47. Accordingly, for my part, I would dismiss these four applications.

48. MAURICE KAY LJ: I too would commend Morgan J for the clarity of his three judgments. I agree that the applications for permission to appeal should be refused for the reasons given by my Lord.

49. STANLEY BURNTON LJ: I agree.

ORDER: Applications refused.

Simon Brown (instructed by Crane and Staples) appeared on behalf of the appellant.

Jeremy Morgan QC (instructed by Withers LLP) appeared on behalf of the respondent.

Case 30
Sulaman

v

Axa Insurance plc and Another

[2010] 3 Costs LR 391

Neutral Citation Number: [2009] EWCA Civ 1331
Court of Appeal (Civil Division)
11 December 2009

Before:
Sedley, Longmore and Aikens LJJ

Headnote

The Court of Appeal considered the decision of the court below to award the successful claimant only one-third of her costs due principally to the fact that she had lied to the court on two occasions.

Judgment

1. LONGMORE LJ: This appeal on costs arises from a fraud practised on Axa and other insurers by a number of persons who insured genuine cars against Third Party Fire and Theft. An initial instalment premium was paid and a direct debit system set up but soon after the inception of the insurance, the fraudsters claimed that the car had been involved in an accident for which the owner was to blame. There was therefore an innocent (but usually fictitious) victim who had a claim which was bound to succeed against the driver, who was himself sometimes fictitious and sometimes genuine but unaware that proceedings were to be taken against him. Claims for repairs, hire charges and such like would be made by a claims management firm and those claims would

be paid by the insurers to the claims management firm or as that firm directed. Considerable sums thus found their way into the pockets of the fraudsters. The fraud which was considerably more complex than I have described can be seen in all its glory in an extremely detailed and lucid judgment of His Honour Judge Edward Bailey, handed down in the Central London County Court.

2. When Axa realised what was happening they refused to pay further claims; the persons whose cars had been supposedly insured began to bring actions to recover sums for which the car owners were supposedly liable. Axa and other insurers were parties to those proceedings and rather than pay up they decided that those they believed to be the originators of and main participants in the fraud should themselves be joined as Part 20 defendants. The police were apparently uninterested in prosecuting although a prosecution did take place in relation to an allied fraud. In the civil proceedings Axa and the other insurers joined six persons including the main fraudster Mohammad Essa Sulaman and his sister Sughra Sulaman.

3. Insurers set themselves a high hurdle. They sought to recover all the sums they paid out in consequence of the false claims and accepted (for the purposes of, at any rate, their primary case) that for that purpose they had to prove that the Part 20 defendants participated in a joint design to defraud insurers or (in some cases) a design limited to specific policies under which payments had been made. After a long and expensive trial which lasted from January to March 2008 they succeeded triumphantly against most of the Part 20 defendants but failed to prove the common design they asserted as against Sughra Sulaman. All the Part 20 defendants were on legal aid. Sughra Sulaman's costs alone are in the region of £450,000. In November 2007 she had made a Part 36 offer in the sum of £7,600 plus costs to date. Not unnaturally after her "victory" she applied for her costs up to 6 December 2007 on a standard basis and on an indemnity basis thereafter but the judge only awarded her one third of her costs (albeit on both the standard and indemnity basis for the respective periods) because he was satisfied that she had lied to him in two respects in her evidence at the trial. She now appeals to this court with the permission of Moore-Bick LJ.

4. The first lie centred round a Mazda car which was insured in Sughra Sulaman's name. When it had supposedly been in an accident, she telephoned Axa's predecessors in title. If that was for the purpose

of notifying the claim that might be evidence of her participation in the common design, although that appears never to have been specifically alleged by the insurers. Alternatively if it was a genuine inquiry as to why her account was being debited when she had never insured the car, the evidence of a second telephone call in which she said she wanted to continue the policy might show she was part of a dishonest conspiracy with her brother as from that time. She claimed, however, in her second witness statement that it was prompted by a bank statement or a letter concerned with her account at Abbey National. When it turned out that that could not be correct because of a confusion over the number of the account, she changed her evidence and, in the course of her oral testimony, she said that it must have been a letter from her insurers that triggered the telephone call. That the judge did not believe. She further claimed that in the course of a second telephone call she asked for the insurance to be cancelled. The judge was sceptical about that also, partly because between the two calls she had spoken on the telephone to her brother and the judge did not believe that her brother would have been happy to allow the insurance to be cancelled and partly because Axa's own note of the call was that she had asked for the policy to be left running.

5. The second lie centred round a cheque made out to Sughra Sulaman for the sum of £5,733.89 which she cashed and then paid the proceeds to her brother. She said at trial that she thought it was money due to Essa from a friend of his but the judge described that as inconceivable and he concluded that she must have known that the cheque represented money which was itself the result of Essa's fraudulent activity.

6. In spite of these lies and in spite of his conclusion that Sughra Sulaman was giving knowing assistance to her fraudster brother, the judge decided that he could not conclude that Ms Sulaman was part of the common fraudulent design to which he found that Essa was a party or that she was otherwise a party to any deceit practised on insurers.

7. But when he came to make his judgment on costs he attached great importance to those lies. Relying on (among other things) a note in the White Book which referred to the costs decision of Mance LJ in the *Grupo Torras* litigation he awarded Ms Sulaman only one third of her costs.

8. Mr Kuldip Singh QC represented Ms Sulaman at the trial, at the

costs application and in this appeal against the costs order. He accepted that he could not realistically challenge the judge's findings that Ms Sulaman had lied to the court about the two matters which I have mentioned but submitted:

i) the lies which Ms Sulaman told were not greatly consequential to the case as a whole or even to the individual case against Ms Sulaman which, after all, she had won;
ii) it was, therefore, too harsh to deprive Ms Sulaman of two-thirds of her costs for those reasons;
iii) the judge had not satisfactorily enunciated any other reason for his order save that he relied on a White Book reference to and his own recollection of the *Grupo Torras* litigation both of which failed accurately to state the true position in that case;
iv) to the extent that the judge intended to say either that Ms Sulaman's lies increased the length of the trial or that she should be penalised for the lies she had told, he did not keep those concepts separate or give proper particulars as to the extent that the trial had increased or proper reasons for the penal consequences that he imposed;
v) the judge had ignored the Part 36 offer made by Ms Sulaman which the insurers failed to beat;
vi) the exercise of discretion was, therefore, flawed and we should exercise a fresh discretion which would lead to the consequence that Ms Sulaman should recover all her costs;
vii) the judge failed to make any order that some of the costs should be recoverable from a date earlier than the date of his order of December 12 together with interest running from that date; indeed he failed to make any order for the costs to carry interest at all.

9. Mr Marven (who had not appeared for the insurers at the trial or on the costs application below) contested all these points and invited the court to read paras 352 and 361 of the judgment as containing general criticism of the way in which Ms Sulaman conducted herself in relation to the proceedings, which went wider than lies she had told on the two specific topics I have identified.

General Approach

10. This court is always in a difficult and, indeed, invidious position when an appeal is made on costs after a lengthy trial. This judge was

intimately involved with the entire case against six Part 20 defendants over a number of months. He must have taken time to read into the case before the trial which was itself spread over three months and he then took two months to consider his judgment before sending the initial draft to the parties. This court just dips its toe into the case for one day, although it was a long day preceded by such reading time as the exigencies of our lists permit. In spite of all the help counsel gave us we cannot begin to have the same feel for the case as the judge and before we interfere we must be satisfied that something has gone very seriously wrong. That is a high hurdle for any appellant to surmount.

11. For my part I am most reluctant to accede to any submission that a decision on costs after a long trial is insufficiently reasoned. The initial judgment speaks for itself and does not have to be extensively referred to in the costs judgment. The part of the original judgment which deals with Ms Sulaman consists of 47 closely reasoned paragraphs (paras 315–362); the costs judgment has 14 paragraphs relating to Ms Sulaman (paras 35–48). It is easy enough to understand why the judge did what he did; elaborate judgments on costs are to be strongly discouraged.

12. I would also deprecate excessive reliance on authorities. We were provided with about 20 authorities but each of these turned on their own facts. Occasionally one can find a useful statement of principle but it is not permissible to conclude that because a defendant lied in one case and forfeited some of his costs, so it should happen in another. Some of the notes in the White Book do give useful guidance on questions of principle but I would respectfully regard the reference to the *Grupo Torras* case in 44.3.2 as unfortunate. The judgment is unreported and given before the current computerised system applicable to judgments of the Commercial Court came into place. It could not be placed before the judge on the costs application and there is force in Mr Singh's submissions that the judge was not entirely accurate in his own recollection of the case and that the notes in the White Book to some extent understate the true nature of the defendants' conduct. The main point, however, is that it is not usually helpful to compare factual details in one case with factual details in another.

Ms Sulaman's Lies

13. These are set out in detail in the original judgment and I have

already attempted to summarise them. The truth of the matter is that Ms Sulaman told lies about both the first telephone call and the second telephone call. In relation to the first call the judge said (para 348):

> "Whatever triggered the phone call Sughra Sulaman has been caught out giving detailed evidence as if from recollection which cannot be correct. It ill lies in Sughra Sulaman's mouth to complain that the insurers have misled her about her own bank account or that they have failed to investigate the matter thoroughly so as to prevent her falling into error by closely following documents when preparing her statements."

In relation to the second call the judge said (paras 350–351):

> "On the face of the note of the second call Essa persuaded Sughra Sulaman to allow the policy to keep running, and so she rang back and told A Quote that the insurance should be maintained in operation. In the course of cross-examination insurers suggested to Sughra Sulaman that she was persuaded by Essa to become a party to the common design between these two telephone calls.
>
> Sughra Sulaman's evidence however is rather different to what might be supposed on the face of the note. At para 23.12 of her second statement (see above) Sughra Sulaman says that she explained the effect of her telephone calls to Essa who 'then said that the insurance should have been cancelled and, if it had not, then I should cancel it'. Notwithstanding her concern about having money coming out of her account, and Essa saying that the policy should have been cancelled all along, Sughra Sulaman then proceeded to keep the policy alive. This because she was concerned that her card might be cancelled. There is some irony here given that the card used was her sister's not hers. In oral evidence however Sughra Sulaman contradicted her statement. She said that she did want to get across to the A Quote employee where she says that she asked the lady to cancel the insurance during the first call, she said that this was during the second call."

14. Then in para 352 the judge said:

> "There is no question that Sughra Sulaman has got herself into a terrible tangle here. The insurers' accusation that, in effect, she is prepared to give false evidence to fit in whatever factual material presents itself for comment is not misplaced ... Sughra Sulaman is, I regret to say, a witness

who is prepared to be untruthful when she thinks that in doing so she will assist her brother Essa."

Although these comments of the judge are made in relation to the Mazda part of the case and cannot be treated an entirely general, they do relate to more than just a single inconsequential lie. The whole Mazda area of the case (confused as it was) was made much more confused by the fact that Ms Sulaman said things in relation to both telephone conversations which could not possibly be true.

15. In relation to the cheque the judge disbelieved her account that she thought it was money due to Essa from a friend. He then in his para 361 headed "conclusion" said:

"Reaching my overall findings on Sughra Sulaman has not been straightforward. She has done herself no credit in the witness box. Her loyalty to Essa has become somewhat frayed at the edges, but she still remains ready to be untruthful on his behalf. I am quite satisfied that she was aware when she paid in the Axa cheque that this had not been honestly come by; she was giving knowing assistance to a fraudster."

Mr Singh said that this conclusion related only to the cheque but I do not read it that way because he talks of his "overall findings" and, again, I think Mr Marvin is justified in saying that the comment applies to both the Mazda and the cheque parts of the case and, although confined to those parts of the case, are of general import in that context.

16. In the light of these lies it seems to me that the judge was entitled to make an order depriving Ms Sulaman of some part of the costs she would otherwise recover. The only question can be how much.

17. The complaint that there was insufficient calculation by the judge of the time and expense taken up by these lies is misconceived. Any such calculation is bound to be speculative. It is not sufficient to say (as Mr Singh does) that the question in these matters only took 35 minutes or even any particular time. Lies maintained and repeated in a complex case are insidious. If Ms Sulaman had said from the beginning of the trial that she could not recall the circumstances in which she made the telephone calls to the insurers but (in accordance with insurers' note) that she finally did ask them to carry on with the policy and she accepted she was dishonestly assisting Essa to obtain money to which he was not entitled in relation to the cheque, the case

against her might well have taken a completely different course. So indeed might the case against Essa. But it is incontrovertible that the litigation was made more difficult and the judge's task more intractable as a result of Ms Sulaman's lies.

18. When one adds to that that the judge was undoubtedly entitled to express his disapproval of Ms Sulaman's lies, quite apart from their precise effect on the trial process, it becomes even more difficult to attack his discretion. The fact that the judge is so entitled is recognised in the recent case of *Widlake* v *BAA* [2009] EWCA Civ 1256. Indeed it would be odd if the judge in charge of the trial process could not express his disapproval in this way. There is, in my judgment, no need for the judge to apportion different parts of his order between lies which prolong the trial process and lies of which he merely disapproves.

Part 36 Offer

19. Mr Singh complains that the judge's order has, in effect, ignored the offer made by Ms Sulaman of £7,600 which was in fact the amount of the cheque together with interest made in November 2007. It is not, of course, true to say the judge has actually ignored it because the costs order he did make in Ms Sulaman's favour (one third of her costs) is to be one third of her standard costs up to 6 December 2007 and one third of her indemnity costs thereafter. The question is whether that is a sufficient recognition.

20. It is true that insurers did not reply to or negotiate around that offer. That will often count against a litigant as it did against the fraudulent claimant in *Painting* v *University of Oxford* [2005] EWCA Civ 161. But this is a very different case. Here insurers were bringing what was inevitably a loss-making action in order to establish the principle that fraudsters cannot assume they can get away with their frauds because it will be too expensive and time-consuming to prove the frauds to the satisfaction of a judge. It would be wrong to assume that the case could settle if Ms Sulaman's offer was accepted. Moreover it was she that was the liar not an honest person making an offer. She never said that she accepted liability because she knew that cheque was a dishonest cheque; the insurers' case could, moreover, never be helped by the acceptance of what was evidently a tactical (without admission of liability) offer. Although the judge did not formulate these reasons for only taking the offer into account in the

way he did, one can well understand why he did not take it into account to any great extent.

Reliance on Grupo Torras

21. Mr Singh submitted that the judge ought to have stated his preliminary conclusion about costs, and then, if necessary, seen whether authority supported that conclusion. Instead he stated that Mance LJ had deprived a liar of two thirds of his costs and so he mechanistically decided to do the same.

22. Although the form of the judgment on costs lends some credence to these submissions, it is, I think, an unfair attack on the judge. I have already said that judges should be careful about relying on the facts of one case to come to the same conclusion in another case on different facts. That is not what the judge did. He was entitled to take his previous judgment as read without repeating the detail of his fact finding. He made clear in para 43 of the costs judgment the basis on which he was coming to his conclusion namely the knowing assistance, the untrue witness statements and the untrue oral evidence. His comparison with individuals in the *Grupo Torras* case may have been misplaced but was not so misplaced as to vitiate his discretion.

23. In these circumstances I do not consider that the judge's decision to award Ms Sulaman only one-third of her costs was outside the wide area of his discretion. One notes that in *Widlake v BAA* (of course, on different facts) the court deprived the lying claimant of the whole of her costs even though she had beaten the payment-in. I would dismiss the appeal on costs.

24. As to Mr Singh's seventh submission, I see no reason why interest on costs should be payable from any date earlier than the order. They carry interest automatically at the judgment rate which is beneficial to Ms Sulaman since at 8% it is higher than any current rate. I would not disturb the judge's order in this respect because, even though it does not say so in terms, interest at 8% will be payable in any event pursuant to s 17 of the Judgments Act 1838 (as amended) and CPR 40.8.

Post-Script

25. We asked Mr Singh in whose interest this appeal was being brought. Ms Sulaman had the benefit of legal aid and is now living in Canada and is at no personal risk of paying the costs of her own

litigation out of her own pocket. Mr Singh responded that, although he was acting for Ms Sulaman, he was really protecting the interest of the Commission for Legal Services and of the taxpayer. It was explained that the Legal Services Commission had made contracts (in normal form) with solicitors and counsel for Ms Sulaman which provided for standard fees (and disbursements) in the event of recovery from the claimants but "reduced" fees to the extent that no recovery could be made from the claimants. It seems therefore that the persons who stand to benefit from the appeal if it succeeds are Mr Singh and his solicitors. They thus have a direct interest in the outcome of this appeal. That makes the task of this court all the more distasteful, since Mr Singh has argued this appeal with both ability and moderation. But it is axiomatic that all appeals have to be decided as if the Legal Services Commission were not involved and as if it was only Ms Sulaman's interests that are affected by the outcome of the appeal. That is, of course, what I have sought to do.

26. AIKENS LJ: I agree.

27. SEDLEY LJ: I agree with the judgment of Longmore LJ in every respect save one. I consider that the decision to deprive the appellant of two thirds of her costs was unjustified either by the facts or by the judge's reasoning and was disproportionate.

28. Taking it shortly, since Longmore LJ has set out with care all the base material, one starts from the proposition that, other things being equal, the appellant was entitled to her costs. The reduction was on the face of it considerably greater than was warranted by the two untruths, told under pressure of events, including a confusing mistake made by Axa's lawyers, and of a misplaced sense of family loyalty (or possibly fear). The judge was entitled to hold these nevertheless against Ms Sulaman. But they had not appreciably prolonged the trial – certainly not to an extent commensurate with the reduction. The reduction was punitive in character, and while this is permissible, it still has to bear some proportion to the issues as a whole.

29. Secondly, the judge's explanation not only fails, in my respectful view, to justify the reduction but comes closer than is appropriate to translating or transposing the facts of one decided case into those of another. It would be an error to suppose (and counsel for Axa does not invite us to suppose) that an outcome which commended itself to one judge in one particular case has somehow set a benchmark for other

cases. Far from allaying the concern that the reduction of two thirds was far too high, the judge's reasons seem to me to increase it.

30. For these reasons I would for my part allow the appeal to the extent of increasing the award of costs to the appellant from one third to two thirds.

Kuldip Singh QC (instructed by West London Law Solicitors) appeared for the appellant.

Rob Marven (instructed by Keoghs LLP) appeared for the respondent.

Case 31
Pankhurst
v
White and Another

[2010] 3 Costs LR 402

Neutral Citation Number: *[2010] EWHC 311 (QB)*
High Court of Justice, Queen's Bench Division
18 February 2010

Before:
MacDuff J

Headnote

Another case which considered the operation of Part 36 of the Civil Procedure Rules where there were changes to the rules between the date of the earliest offers and the trial.

Judgment

1. **MACDUFF J:** This judgment addresses issues arising out of the operation of Part 36 of the Civil Procedure Rules.

2. In June 2009, following a trial of the issue of quantum in this case, I made an award of damages in favour of the claimant. I awarded damages together with conventional interest, as well as making an order (agreed by the parties) for periodic payments. On a conventional basis, the award (if one capitalises the periodic payments) amounted to approximately £6.1 million. At the end of the trial, I reserved judgment. When I handed down judgment (as I say in June 2009) I was told that there were significant arguments to be advanced upon the issue of costs, and that a day should be set aside for those arguments.

I heard the parties' submissions upon costs on 21 September 2009 and reserved this judgment, which I am handing down today.

3. As stated, the issues arise out of Part 36 offers, and involve consideration of that rule. There is the additional potential complication arising out of the fact that there have been changes made to Part 36 between the date of the earliest offers and the trial.

4. I must deal with the relevant background facts. I need to go back to the spring of 2006. At that time, there had been an order for a split trial on liability, with quantum to follow later. Thus, at that time, the expert evidence upon quantum issues – or most of it – had not yet been obtained. In fact, liability had already been established, but there remained a real issue as to whether the claimant had been guilty of contributory negligence. Although Mr Methuen, on behalf of the defendant had contended (in his skeleton argument for the liability trial) that contributory negligence might be assessed at 50%, he conceded to me that realistically, he had been hoping for a reduction of 25% or, at best, 33%.

5. On April 12 and 8 May 2006 the defendant made Part 36 offers which the claimant rejected. Those are now of no more than passing interest.

6. On 23 May 2006, the claimant himself made a Part 36 offer of settlement to the defendant. He made alternative offers: a conventional lump sum of £3.4 million, alternatively a lesser lump sum plus periodical payments. (It is common ground, as one might imagine, that the second offer, when capitalised, was of similar value to the first.) I will refer to this as the May 2006 offer.

7. This was an offer to settle the whole case, not just the liability issue. It was an offer which, at a relatively early stage, amounted to a genuine attempt to compromise everything – it took account of the risks inherent in the first trial (contributory negligence), as well as the uncertainties of quantification. At that early stage, (before much of the expert evidence had been obtained) it was impossible for the parties to have any real handle on individual heads of damage. They could only approach the likely assessment of damages with a broad brush. This was a genuine attempt at overall compromise, with a concomitant large saving of costs, at a time when there were many unknowns.

8. Within a very short time (on 31 May 2006) the defendant's representatives rejected that offer. They did so in a telephone

conversation. That rejection was then reported in a letter of the same date from the claimant's solicitor.

9. On 26 and 27 June 2006 the first part of the case came on for trial before Wilkie J, who gave judgment for the claimant, for damages to be assessed, with no reduction for contributory negligence.

10. On 3 July 2006, Messrs Stewarts, on behalf of the claimant, wrote a letter to the defendants.

> "Whilst you have indicated your client's rejection of the claimant's Part 36 offer of 23 May 2006, in addition to which the 21 day time period for acceptance has expired, for the avoidance of doubt on the issue, we would like to clarify that whilst the claimant was prepared to settle on those terms during the 21 day acceptance period, he is no longer prepared to do so, now that we have the judgment of Mr Justice Wilkie, confirming there is to be no deduction for contributory negligence, the claimant believes that he is likely to recover a higher settlement figure ...
>
> ... We put you on notice that the claimants will continue to rely on his Part 36 offer in relation to his entitlement to interest and costs. That offer was genuine, and, had it been accepted within the 21 days, would have concluded the court proceedings at that stage, avoiding all further costs. Therefore, the claimant will, if he recovers damages in excess of the two alternatives he proposed in that letter, be seeking to recover interest on those damages at 10% above the base rate, interest on costs, and an indemnity costs order ..."

11. In support of the assertion that he would continue to rely upon the offer, the claimant referred in the letter to the case of *Stokes Pension Fund* v *Western Power Distribution* [2005] 1 WLR 3595.

12. It is the second paragraph of the letter which encapsulates the principal dispute between the parties. The claimant now seeks an indemnity costs order, from the date of that offer, as well as additional interest. It is the defendant's case that, the offer having been withdrawn (or otherwise not available) there is no such entitlement.

13. Before I consider the argument on that point, I need to complete the narrative. Over the next 18 months or so, the parties prepared for a trial on quantum. I have been provided with a helpful chronology, as an appendix to the defendant's skeleton argument. I do not need to repeat the detail, except to note, *en passant*, that, (i) at no time did the defendant make any application, either formal or informal to accept

the May 2006 offer. It was well understood between the parties that such an application would have been resisted, and that any formal application would have been doomed to failure. Mr Methuen, in submission, suggested that such an application would have been a charade; (ii) on 24 July 2006 the claimant's solicitor wrote, "We would not want to actively engage in a discussion concerning the current value of the claim until we have obtained an updating report from the claimant's lead medical expert ..." and (iii) the defendant made a further Part 36 offer (on 29 August 2006), which was rejected. In fact, this offer almost exactly reproduced the claimant's pre-trial offer, and, in one sense, could be viewed as an attempt (albeit via a different route) to accept that which had been offered before the trial, i.e. the May 2006 offer.

14. It is of some interest that, following that last offer (the August 2006 offer), the claimant's solicitors wrote, noting that the offer was no better than the May 2006 offer and "consequently the court would be highly likely to exercise its discretion to award indemnity costs, interest on costs and it is arguable that may even extend to interest on damages as well... Would you please clarify whether the second defendant is prepared to revise the terms of this offer to reflect the fact that it will not have beaten the one made by the claimant on 23 May 2006". The defendant made some concessions (in a letter of 9 October 2006) but was unwilling to revise its offer in relation to costs.

15. I can move forward, to 28 May 2008, shortly before the trial on quantum. The defendant made a Part 36 offer (the May 2008 offer). It was an offer to pay a lump sum of £3 million, plus annual periodical payments of £260,000, indexed to Ashe 6115. It is common ground that, in capital terms, that was the equivalent of a total offer of around £6.8 million. The offer was rejected by the claimant.

16. At trial, the claimant presented a schedule of loss amounting to approximately £7.9 million, in capital terms. The defendant's counter schedule amounted to the capital equivalent of around £5.9 million. Most heads of damage were agreed. However, there remained a gap of approximately £2 million. (In fact, the schedule and counter schedule were both expressed as a part lump sum, with substantial periodic payments.)

17. After a trial lasting several days, I awarded the agreed periodic payments of £260,000 per annum (appropriately indexed), plus a lump sum of £2.317 million. This represented an equivalent capital

value of around £6.1 million. It followed, to use the phraseology of Part 36, that the claimant had obtained a judgment which was more advantageous than the May 2006 offer, but that he had failed to obtain a judgment more advantageous than the May 2008 offer.

18. It is agreed between the parties that the defendant should have its costs from the date upon which the May 2008 offer should have been accepted, that is to say the 21st day after 28 May 2008. There is a small point as to whether that date should be moved on by a few days to take account of a request for clarification. And there is also an argument as to whether, if the claimant succeeds upon the principal argument (see below) his total award may become "more advantageous" than the sum offered by the defendant. If so, it is suggested that the defendant would not then be entitled to its costs from that date.

19. However, the first and principal issue is concerned with the effect of the May 2006 offer. It is necessary to consider the rule. Since the offer was made, the terms of the rule have changed. The main purpose of the change was to dispense with payments into court. Now, in broad terms, Part 36 offers are made in the same way, whether made by claimants or by defendants. But there were other changes also, which may need to be considered. For the moment, it is sufficient to note that the May 2006 offer was made under the old regime; the quantum trial took place under the new.

20. The relevant parts of CPR 36, as in force in 2006, may be summarised as follows:

- Part 36.5 dealt with the form and content of a Part 36 offer. The offer had to be in writing and expressed to remain open for 21 days from the date on which it was made. It also made provision for acceptance after the conclusion of the 21 day period or after the start of a trial. Of particular note for present purposes, Part 36.5(8) provided that "If a Part 36 offer is withdrawn it will not have the consequences set out in this Part".
- Rule 36.21 prescribed the "costs and other consequences where the claimant does better than he proposed in his Part 36 offer". It applied only after the "advantageous" judgment was given after "a trial". (This provision has been amended in the new rule; nothing turns on this change.)

- (Parts 36.5 and 36.21 have been replaced in somewhat modified form by the new Parts 36.2 and 36.14)

21. Where (as in this case) the claimant obtains a more advantageous judgment than the proposals in his Part 36 offer, Part 36.21(2) provides that "the court may order interest on the whole or part of an sum of money (excluding interest) awarded to the claimant at a rate not exceeding 10% above base rate for some or all of the period starting with the latest date on which the defendant could have accepted the offer without needing the permission of the court". By Part 36.21(3)(a) and (b) "the court may also order that the claimant be entitled to his costs on the indemnity basis from the latest date when the defendant could have accepted the offer without needing the permission of the court and interest on those costs at a rate not exceeding 10% above base rate". (I will hereafter refer to these "costs and other consequences" as "enhanced consequences".)

22. By Part 36.21(4) "where this rule applies, the court will make the (enhanced consequences) orders ... unless it considers it unjust to do so".

23. Part 36.21(5) provided that, in considering whether it would be unjust, the court must take into account all the circumstances of the case, including the circumstances which were thereafter set out.

24. Thus a step by step approach is required:

- First, the court must consider whether the enhanced consequences provisions apply. This depends entirely upon whether the May 2006 offer had been withdrawn, within the meaning of Part 36.5(8).
- Secondly, if it were not withdrawn, the court must consider whether or not it would be unjust to make an enhanced consequences order, having regard to all the circumstances of the case, including those specified in 36.21(5).
- Thirdly, if it would be just to do so, the court must exercise its discretion as to several further matters: (i) whether to award interest upon the whole or only part (and if so which part) of money awarded to the claimant, (ii) the appropriate rate of interest up to a maximum of 10% above base rate; (iii) whether to award interest upon those sums and at that rate for a whole or only part of the period (and what part of the period); (iv) similar questions as to the period for the award of indemnity costs; and (v) similar

questions as to rate of interest upon the indemnity costs. This third step, discretionary as it clearly is, also requires a consideration of what would be just.

25. I must consider the first step; whether the court is empowered to make an enhanced consequences order; whether CPR 36.21 is engaged. (In fact, to make the matter clear, the transitional provisions provide that for this part of the exercise, the operative rule is the new CPR 36.14. The question is thus whether CPR 36.14 is engaged.) This question depends entirely upon whether the May 2006 offer was withdrawn by the letter of 3 July 2006. The claimant's argument is that, by that date, there was no extant offer remaining. The offer had been made, and it had been expressly rejected. The ordinary principles of contract apply, and (notwithstanding that the offer had been made within the context of Part 36) there was nothing to withdraw.

26. Here reliance is placed upon the words of Dyson J, as he then was, in *Pitchmastic* v *Birse Construction*, unreported, 19 May 2000:

> "I do not accept ... that there are special principles for deciding whether a contract of compromise has been made in the context of existing litigation. The question falls to be decided by the application of the ordinary rules of offer and acceptance ... The offer of March 6 was terminated upon its rejection the same day ... if the offer terminated upon its rejection, and if it was not subsequently revived ... I do not see how new life can be breathed into the offer merely because it was relied on when it came to the question of costs. The relevance of the offer at the stage of the arguments as to costs was that the offer had been made and rejected. That was a historical fact and Birse was entitled to rely on it in arguing issues about costs."

27. Reviewing an earlier decision of the Court of Appeal, *Bristol and West Building Society* v *Evans Bullock and Co*, unreported, 5 February 1996, he noted that a *Calderbank* offer had been made and subsequently withdrawn. It was held that the offer should have been accepted:

> "The question that arose was how that impacted on the question of costs. It was held that, although the offer was no longer operative in the sense of being available for acceptance, the effect of the letter still remained in relation to costs. So too here. Although the offer of March

6 was not withdrawn, it ceased to be capable of acceptance once it had been rejected by Pitchmastic."

28. These observations were clearly obiter. The issue before the court was whether or not the action had been compromised. Moreover, the remarks were not dealing with whether an offer had been withdrawn by the offeror, but solely with where it had been rejected by the offeree. And I must remind myself that it is Mr Methuen's submission that, although the May 2006 offer had been rejected (as in *Pitchmastic*) it had also been subsequently withdrawn (notwithstanding the normal law of contract). It is also clear that the practices surrounding *Calderbank* offers, and the small branch of jurisprudence which had developed in that area pre CPR, have many significant differences from the regime created by Part 36.

29. The potential significance of the remarks of Dyson J can be stated in two propositions:

- That contract law governs offers under Part 36 and rejection sees the death of the offer, so that there was no offer to withdraw at the date of the letter of 3 July 2006.
- That, notwithstanding that the offer was no longer available for acceptance, it was a "historical fact" which should be capable of consideration on costs arguments; even to the point where the offer had two independent lives – one for acceptance by the other party, and one for the purpose of Part 36. That the first was dead did not mean that the second died with it.

30. Mr McDermott also relies upon *Scammell* v *Dicker* [2001] 1 WLR 631 to support this part of his argument. This case was also concerned with whether or not an action had been compromised. An offer had been made under CPR 36 (by a defendant). The offer was expressed to remain open for 21 days (as it had to do to comply with Part 36). However, some four days later, the defendant withdrew the offer. The claimant sought to accept the offer within the 21 days. The judge at first instance held that the offer could not be withdrawn unilaterally within the 21 days. He relied upon the fact that it was expressed to be a Part 36 offer, open for 21 days. However, the Court of Appeal found otherwise. Part 36 was there to enable a party to obtain the advantages provided by the rules. It did not seek to exclude the general law of

contract and an offer could thus be withdrawn at any time prior to acceptance.

31. Mr McDermott relies upon this case to support what was said by Dyson J in *Pitchmastic*. The normal rules of contract apply. Thus, if an offer has been rejected, there can be no question of its subsequently being withdrawn. Although *Scammell* might be decided differently today under the revised Part 36, the fact remained that the Court of Appeal held that, when looking at offers made under Part 36, the normal rules of contract apply.

32. In his judgment, Aldous LJ touched upon the very issue which I have to determine:

> "Our attention was drawn to the judgment of Dyson J in *Pitchmastic* v *Birse*, in which it was held that an offer once rejected could not be accepted. Of course, that reflected the established law of contract. However, the judge went on to express a view as to the effect of Part 36. Insofar as he did so, it appears to me that his observations were obiter. I prefer to express no view on the effect of rejection of a Part 36 offer – in particular whether ... the offeror can keep the advantages of having made a Part 36 offer while at the same time treating it as at an end due to its rejection." (*per* Aldous LJ [2001] 1 WLR at pages 637–8)

That, of course, is the very issue upon which I am required to express a view.

33. It is common ground between the parties that the offer was in fact rejected. But Mr McDermott advanced his argument upon a second alternative front, which did not rely upon what one might call the contract rejection point. Even if there had been no rejection, the offer would have lapsed – overtaken by the liability trial. It was no longer available for acceptance. The offer was expressed to be open for 21 days. Thereafter, it could only be accepted with permission from the claimant or by order of the court. Certainly, there could be no question of acceptance once the draft judgment on liability had been given to the parties. In that sense, an offer would always be "withdrawn"; the offeror would no longer allow the offeree to accept it. The offer was only available for unilateral acceptance for 21 days, and no court would order that it could be accepted, once there had been a judgment on contributory negligence and a consequent shift in the landscape. At that stage, an application by the defendant to accept the offer would have been refused by the court. Thus, it was not available for

acceptance. But it had not been "withdrawn" within the meaning of the rule. It retained its potency in relation to costs, although it was no longer on the table as an available offer.

34. This analysis is further supported by the submission that the whole purpose of making the offer was (a) to try to achieve an early settlement acceptable to all parties notwithstanding (at that time) the many unknowns (including the risks of a finding of contributory negligence) and (b) to take advantage of the enhanced consequences provisions, if the offer was not accepted. If, as soon as liability had been determined, and the offer was no longer capable of acceptance, the claimant were to lose the benefit of the offer which he had made only a few weeks earlier, the whole purpose of making the offer in the first place would have been lost.

35. This, it seems to me, is a powerful argument. The defendant argues that there would be injustice in allowing an offer, which is no longer available for acceptance, to sit in the background operating against him. It may be fair to penalise him (if penalise be the right word) for the short period between the offer and the judgment on contributory negligence, but not for any longer period.

36. There is a superficial attraction to that argument. How can it be fair to require him to pay enhanced costs and interest over a period when he could not accept the offer, as it was no longer available for acceptance? The answer, as Mr McDermott suggested, is (i) that he should have accepted the offer when it was available; (ii) that he was on notice for those 21 days of the risk he would take if he failed to take the offer; and (iii) having failed to do so, he could and should have appreciated his costs risk at the conclusion of the contributory negligence trial, and taken protective steps, by making a realistic Part 36 offer himself.

37. The case of *Stokes Pension Fund* v *Western Power Distribution* [2005] 1 WLR 3595, to which the claimant had referred in the letter of 3 July 2006 was principally concerned with a failure to make a payment into court by a defendant who made a Part 36 offer (an issue which can no longer arise in view of the changes to the rule). However, there is a wider significance. In that case, long before the matter came to trial, the offer had been withdrawn (or at least unavailable for acceptance). Nevertheless, the court held that the offer should have been accepted in the 21 days available, and the defendant was entitled

to its costs of the whole action from the date by which the claimant should have accepted.

38. That, of course, was a different case in that the offer was made by a defendant (not a claimant) and the court was concerned with simple costs and not with the enhanced consequences provisions. It is, however authority for the proposition that an offer which is no longer available for acceptance may remain alive for costs purposes.

39. If *Stokes Pension Fund* was a case where the offer had come from a defendant, *Capital Bank* v *Stickland* [2004] EWCA Civ 1677 was concerned with a claimant's offer and the enhanced consequences provisions. In that case, several months before trial, the claimant made a Part 36 offer which was expressed to be open for 21 days. The letter giving the offer expressly indicated that it was made "provided it is accepted by your client by no later than 31 December 2003". The offer was not accepted. Two days prior to trial the defendant purported to accept the offer but was told that it was no longer available, and that any application to the judge would be opposed. The judge refused to allow the offer to be accepted. At the trial, which followed, the claimant obtained a "more advantageous" judgment and applied for what I have called an enhanced consequences order. The judge awarded indemnity costs and interest upon them for the whole of the period from the date upon which the offer should have been accepted (31 December 2003). This decision was upheld in the Court of Appeal.

40. That authority also demonstrates that an offer which is no longer available for acceptance may, nevertheless, retain its costs potency.

41. I return to the words of Part 36.5(8): "If a Part 36 offer is withdrawn it will not have the consequences set out in this Part". What is the meaning of "withdrawn"? Where, after the end of the 21 day period, the offeror is put in a stronger position (than when the offer was made) by some change in circumstances, he is entitled to refuse an application to accept. I cannot conceive that it was intended that this should be a "withdrawal", removing the costs potency of the offer. Where there has been a material change in circumstances, and the 21 day period has expired, the offer has not been "withdrawn" for the purpose of the rule. It may have lapsed; it may be no longer available for acceptance; the offeror may inform the offeree that it is no longer on the table. But it retains its costs potency.

42. In my judgment, it is only where the offer is unilaterally

withdrawn at a time where the offeree could have accepted it, whether within the 21 day period or later with the leave of the court, that rule 36.5(8) applies.

43. It will be appreciated that this judgment is concerned with the rule in force in 2006. The re-drafted rule bears consideration. Now, the offer cannot be withdrawn (or made less advantageous to the offeree) during the 21 day period without the court's permission; CPR 36.3(5). After 21 days, the offeror may withdraw the offer or change its terms by serving written notice of the withdrawal/change; rule 36.3(6) and (7). Costs consequences (including what I have called the enhanced consequences) do not apply where the offer has been withdrawn or made less advantageous and the offeree has beaten the less advantageous offer; Rule 36.14(6). However, in those cases, the court is required to consider the offer in its historical context and have regard to rule 44.3 (see particularly rule 44.3(4)(c)).

44. I mention the new rule only because, as it seems to me, the matter is even clearer now. It reinforces the view that I have reached: that the May 2006 offer was not withdrawn within the meaning of the old rule 36.5(8). It matters not, in my judgment whether, as here, it had been rejected, or had merely been left in place until judgment in the contributory negligence trial. Once the trial had taken place, the offer had plainly lapsed for acceptance purposes. But it retained its costs potency.

45. In reaching this conclusion, I should also say that I have considered the wider scheme of the cost provisions, within the context of the Overriding Objective. I have read carefully the judgment of Lord Woolf MR, as he then was, in the case of *Petrotrade* v *Texaco*, unreported, 23 May 2000, CA. I have paid particular attention to the early paragraphs of the judgment where he gave an overview of the provisions of Part 36 with particular reference to offers made by claimants and the enhanced consequences provisions.

46. If I were to accept the submissions made by Mr Methuen on behalf of the defendant, it would mean that the claimant would have benefited not at all from making the May 2006 offer. If I limited my order to the short period up to the end of the liability trial (Mr Methuen's secondary position) the claimant would be seriously short changed. His was not just an offer to deal with liability (an offer, say, to accept 10% contributory negligence against the risk of a finding of 25%) in which case the enhanced consequences would have applied

only up to the end of the liability trial. The offer, as previously stated, took into account all possible future contingencies, and, if it had been accepted, would have resulted in a full and final settlement and a huge saving in time and costs. The claimant should have the benefit.

47. I have also considered what the defendant could have done to protect himself, after the end of the liability trial. Mr Methuen asks rhetorically: what could he have done? He could not have been expected at that early stage to offer the sum of more than £6 million, which he eventually needed to do. He had no proper schedule and no sufficient information. However, an offer of, say, £4 million or a little more, would have given him a strong platform from which to resist this application. That would have been a genuine attempt to duplicate the claimant's earlier offer, against the new landscape. It would have been an acknowledgement of the fact that the contributory negligence argument had been lost. It would not have provided the defendant with costs protection for his own costs in view of the eventual award. But it would have provided a strong argument, two years later, to resist an application for an enhanced consequences order.

48. It follows that rule 36.21 (as it was in 2006) is engaged and that, the "court will make (an enhanced consequences order) unless it considers it unjust to do so"; Part 36.21 (4).

49. I now move on to deal with the second stage, and ask myself whether or not it would be unjust to make the order. This is a question which effectively answers itself. It would be unjust, for the reasons set out above, if the claimant were to be deprived of the benefits of his offer. There is no injustice to the defendant. Those arguments advanced by Mr Methuen (set out in his written submissions, and developed in oral argument) are little to the point on the broad question to be considered at stage two. They come into their own at stage three, when I have to consider the extent and nature of the enhanced consequences order. Provided that the order is proportionate and fair to both parties, it is entirely just for an order to be made.

50. The third stage. What order should I make? The potential range of orders is enormous. There are two parts to it:

- enhanced interest on damages;
- indemnity costs with or without enhanced interest

51. As to interest on damages, there are four decisions to be made:

- Whether to award enhanced interest; if so
- The period over which the interest is to be awarded
- The part of the award which should attract the enhanced interest
- The rate of interest to be awarded up to a maximum of 10% above base rate.

52. As to the costs:

- Whether to award indemnity costs
- The period over which the claimant should have his indemnity costs
- Whether to award interest on those costs
- If so, the rate of interest, up to a maximum of 10% above base rate.

53. At this stage, it is necessary to consider the arguments advanced on behalf of the defendant as to the justice of the case, as well as looking at general principles. In summary, Mr Methuen submits:

- At the date of the claimant's May 2006 offer, the claim appeared to be very much smaller (to both parties) than it later turned out to be. Of more significance, the pleaded schedule of loss was significantly smaller than it was in its final form some two years later. For example the annual claim for care was £122,000; less than one half of the final agreed figure. It was thus difficult if not impossible at that stage for the defendant to make its own offer – and impossible to judge the level of offer needed to provide adequate protection.
- No further signed schedule was forthcoming from the claimant until May 2008, some two years later. It was not until then that the defendant was able to appreciate how the pleaded case had increased in value. Moreover, the schedule was served late (in breach of an order requiring it to be served by February 2008). As soon as it had the schedule, the defendant made its own offer (the May 2008 offer) which turned out to be an adequate one.
- There was significant delay in moving to the trial on quantum, caused by the claimant's purchase and rebuilding of Archers Post, a course of action which the court subsequently held to be unreasonable. This delay enabled the claimant to formulate a much larger claim than had first appeared in his original schedule. It caused some of the experts' reports to be delayed, as well as

delaying the production of a final schedule. It also delayed the trial. During this period, it would be unfair to the defendant to be required to pay the enhanced interest for the whole period, when the defendant had no control over the timetable or the claimant's actions. The longer the claimant delayed, the higher the award would be; it cannot be fair and proportionate to require the defendant to pay additional interest at high rates for the whole of this period. It cannot be fair that the claimant's lawyers are able to recover indemnity costs (for example) at a time when, the longer they take to get the case to trial, the more they are likely to recover.

54. Mr Methuen's submissions incorporate, at least in part, the matters listed in CPR 36.21 (reproduced in the new Part 36.14) – for example that the court should have regard to the information available to the parties at the time when the offer was made; see Part 36.21(5)(c). Also, Part 36.21(5)(d) may have some relevance. There is force in Mr Methuen's submissions. The submissions were designed to resist the application in its entirety; to persuade me that it would be unjust to make the order. They are relevant to the wider question – what order should I make? As I have already noted, there is a wide range of options available to me within rule 36.14 (formerly rule 36.21). My aim should be to make an order that is proportionate and just to both parties.

Interest on Damages
55. I have no doubt that it is just to make an order that the defendant should pay enhanced interest upon at least part of the damages.

The Period
56. Over what period should enhanced interest be awarded? It seems clear that the starting date should be the date by which the May 2006 offer should have been accepted; that is to say the 21st day after the making of the offer. *Prima facie*, the period should end at the time when the May 2008 offer should have been accepted by the claimant. In broad terms that would be a period of two years. On any view, the making of an adequate offer by the defendant should bring to an end his liability to pay enhanced interest.

57. However, there is a case for reducing this period to some extent having regard to the defendants' submissions that the case could and should have been more fully particularised at a somewhat earlier stage,

and/or brought more speedily to trial. In my judgment, there is some strength in this argument, although the delay, such as it was, was not great. I have decided to reduce the period to one of 21 months (1.75 years).

The Part of the Award

58. Upon which part or parts of the award should the enhanced interest be granted? Although the rule provides that the court may order interest to be paid at an enhanced rate upon "a whole or part of any sum of money awarded" I have reached the conclusion that it would be wrong to make any award of interest, enhanced or otherwise, in respect of those damages which were awarded for future losses and future expenditure, that is to say those damages which would not attract interest in the normal way. There is some authority to support this conclusion. In *Petrotrade* itself, Lord Woolf envisaged that, where the court would otherwise award interest, it could, where these provisions applied, order the interest to be paid at "more than the going rate". Upon damages for future losses, where interest is not awarded, there can be no "going rate". In a case (for example) of breach of contract, where the damages all represent past loss, it would be normal to award interest on the full amount of the award. If Part 36.21 (now Part 36.14) applied, it might be appropriate to award that interest at higher than the "going rate" on the whole of the award. But not where interest would not normally be awarded at all. This was the view of the Court of Appeal in respect of libel damages in *McPhilemy v Times Newspapers* [2001] EWCA Civ 933: "Given that, in a defamation action, it would generally be unjust to award interest upon the damages, *let alone at an enhanced rate*, it becomes more important that a Part 36.21 order is made as to costs ..." (my emphasis); per Lord Justice Simon Brown, as he then was, at para 28. This was also expressed by Eady J in *Jones v Associated Newspapers* [2007] EWCA 1489 (QB). Where interest would not normally be awarded upon damages, it would be inappropriate to award enhanced (or any interest) upon those damages under the old Part 36.21 (now 36.14). Accordingly, I have decided that it would be appropriate to award enhanced interest upon past losses only, and not upon future losses.

The Rate of Interest

59. What of the rate at which interest on past losses should be

awarded, noting, as I do, that the total rate of interest is not to exceed 10% above base rate; see 36.21(6) (now 36.14(5)). I clearly have a very wide discretion. There is little or no guidance, certainly not in the Rules, upon how the rate of interest should be selected. Of course, it is necessary to remind myself that the provision is not intended to be penal; it is to provide the claimant with more generous compensation, taking account of the fact that he made an offer which should have been accepted and that he has been caused the added stress of more prolonged proceedings, and to wait longer for his compensation, albeit that in this case there have been substantial interim payments. He should be rewarded (proportionately) for his successful offer.

60. Although there is no help as to how the rate of interest should be divined, I should remind myself that Lord Woolf envisaged that the court would award something above "the going rate". It seems to me that the starting point (for determining the rate of interest to award under the enhanced consequences provisions) will depend upon the nature of the case and the basis upon which interest would normally be awarded. There are widely different interest rates in different types of case (see para 7.0.17 in the current White Book). The rates of interest normally given in commercial cases, debt recovery cases, and personal injury cases (for example) will be different. And the approach may need to be modified depending upon the availability and cost of money at the relevant time, and the rate of return which could be obtained.

61. It seems to me that the starting point should be to use the approach mentioned by Lord Woolf, and to award interest at something more than the "going rate". Although the rule provides that the maximum should be no more than 10% *above base rate*, there is nothing to say that the court has to express the rate with reference to the base rate. In some commercial cases, interest is awarded with reference to base rate. But for past losses in personal injury cases, the award is normally made for special damages using the special account rate. In other cases interest is calculated by reference to the commercial rate, the judgment debt rate and so on.

62. In my judgment, the starting points are these. Damages for past losses (special damages if you like) are calculated at special account rate, which, although it may vary from time to time, was in fact stationary at 6% for the whole of the relevant period. Interest on general damages for pain suffering and loss of amenity is fixed at 2%.

I propose to make awards in respect of those two heads of damages at a couple or more percentage points above those going rates. Of course, this encompasses the interest which has already been awarded. When I handed down my judgment, I was presented with agreed figures of £16,775 and £9,690 for interest upon special damages and general damages respectively. Those, I think, are incorporated into an Order which has already been made. I was not privy to the calculations, but I can set out my understanding of how the calculation would have been made. The calculation for special damages is intended to award 6% interest upon every item of loss or expenditure from the time that the loss occurred or the expenditure was incurred to the date of judgment. (If the losses are spread broadly across the time frame, the interest is usually calculated at half rate for the full period.) The calculation also takes account of interim payments, so that interest is only calculated for the period when the claimant was kept out of his money. That, I assume, is how the interest was computed in the present case. Although past losses amounted to almost £900,000, the interest was agreed at £16,775.

63. My intention is this. For a period of 21 months (1.75 years) I propose to revisit the award of interest upon special damages and award interest at 4% above the going rate, that is to say an overall rate of 10%. Thus for that period, the claimant is entitled to an additional 4% over and above that which has already been awarded. It will also take account of interim payments. Rather than ask the parties to perform a detailed recalculation, I will do this now with a broad brush. The starting point is to take the £16,775 and apply a factor of 4/6. That produces an additional sum of £11,183. I then have to discount to take account of the fact that the original amount was awarded as interest from the date when the loss or expenditure occurred (going back to the date of the accident) until the date of judgment. The extra interest is only payable for a period of 1.75 years, ending in June 2008. My broad brush produces an award of an additional £9,000 after discounting. I have kept in mind that, during the relevant period, base rate varied between 4.5% and 5.75% an average of, say around 5%. Thus I am effectively awarding interest at approximately 5% above base rate upon the special damages.

64. So far as interest upon general damages is concerned, I propose to award interest at double the "going" rate for the period of 1.75 years. Thus the claimant is entitled to an extra 2% on £225,000. The

extra interest is thus £225,000 × 2% × 1.75 = £7875. I will round this up to £8,000. Thus the total additional award of interest will be £17,000.

65. Finally, costs. I award the claimant his costs on a standard basis up to the 21st day after the May 2006 offer. Thereafter the claimant should have his costs on the indemnity basis up to the 21st day after the making of the May 2008 offer. I do not extend the 21 day period – as I was asked to do – on the basis of the request for clarification. I note that, regardless of that request, the claimant expressly rejected the offer well within the 21 days. Thereafter, the defendant should have its costs on a standard basis.

66. I do not award any enhanced interest upon those indemnity costs. The order itself, together with the additional interest awarded upon the damages, is reward enough. I remind myself that the award must be proportionate, and must be fair. An order for additional interest of £17,000 with indemnity costs for two years is, it seems to me, a just and proportionate order, particularly as there is a conditional fee arrangement in place. Additionally, I award the indemnity costs for the whole two year period (not the period of 21 months).

Gerard Mcdermott QC (instructed by Stewarts Law LPP) appeared for the claimant.

Richard Methuen QC and *Harry Steinberg* (instructed by Berrymans Lace Mawer) appeared for the second defendant (the Motor Insurers Bureau).

Case 32
Richard Buxton (Solicitors)

v

Mills-Owens and The Law Society

[2010] 3 Costs LR 421

Neutral Citation Number: *[2010] EWCA Civ 122*
Court of Appeal (Civil Division)
23 February 2010

Before:
The President of the Family Division,
and Dyson and Maurice Kay LJJ

Headnote

The Court of Appeal has reversed the decision of Mackay J reported at [2008] 6 Costs LR 948, deciding that, on the facts, the solicitors were entitled to determine the "entire contract" retainer.

Judgment

1. DYSON LJ: The principal issues that arise on this appeal are whether (i) the appellant solicitors were entitled to terminate their retainer and (ii) whether they were entitled to their profit costs and disbursements up to the date of termination.

2. The appellants were retained by Mr Mills-Owens to advise upon and prosecute a statutory appeal under s 288 of the Town and Country Planning Act 1990 ("the 1990 Act") against a decision to grant planning permission by the Planning Inspector on behalf of the First Secretary of State. They terminated the retainer because Mr Mills-Owens insisted that they and counsel who had been instructed in the

case should advance certain points which neither they nor counsel considered to be properly arguable.

3. Following the termination of the retainer, the appellants submitted their final fee account which showed a balance due of £6,605.41. Mr Mills-Owens wanted the fees to be assessed by a costs judge. The assessment came before Master O'Hare who on 31 January 2008 held that the appellants should not have terminated their retainer, but should have carried out the instructions of Mr Mills-Owens even though they were of the view that "such instructions were doomed to disaster". In the result, since "they were retained for the entire business", Master O'Hare held that they were not entitled to recover any costs other than for disbursements.

4. The appellants appealed. In a reserved judgment given on 28 July 2008, Mackay J, sitting with Master Simons and Mr Martin Cockx as assessors, dismissed the appeal. In agreement with Master O'Hare, he held that the appellants were not entitled to terminate their retainer. This was an entire contract which could only be terminated for "just cause". Importantly, he said that, if a client wants a claim to be advanced on a particular basis which does not involve impropriety on the part of the solicitor or counsel, it is no answer for the solicitor to say that he believes that the claim, if so advanced, is bound to fail. He cannot refuse to advance the claim for that reason. He cannot terminate the retainer unless to continue would involve impropriety or misleading the court. On the facts of this case, the appellants were not entitled to any profit costs, although, with minor exceptions, they were entitled to their disbursements. Mr Mills-Owens had already made substantial payments on account of profit costs and disbursements. The appellants appeal with the permission of Waller LJ. The Law Society were given permission to intervene in the appeal because in their view the case raises an issue of considerable importance to the solicitors' profession: in what circumstances can a solicitor instructed in litigation lawfully terminate his retainer prior to the conclusion of the case whilst maintaining his right to be paid for the work that he has done? Mr Richard Drabble QC submits on behalf of The Law Society that the statement by Mackay J that, absent any impropriety or misleading of the court, the solicitor is not entitled to terminate his retainer is incorrect. We have been assisted by the submissions of Mr Drabble, assistance which was not available to Mackay J.

The Retainer

5. The appellants were instructed in June 2005 to advise on and prosecute an appeal against a Planning Inspector's decision confirming the grant of planning permission in respect of Hangersley House, a property close to the Mr Mills-Owens' property at Westwood, St Aubyns Lane, Hangersley, Ringwood, Hampshire.

6. Section 288(1) of the 1990 Act provides:

"(1) If any person ...

    (b) is aggrieved by any action on the part of the Secretary of State to which this section applies and wishes to question the validity of that action on the grounds –

        (i) that the action is not within the powers of this Act, or

        (ii) that any of the relevant requirements have not been complied with in relation to that action,

he may make an application to the High Court under this section."

7. Mr Mills-Owen agreed the appellants' terms of business which included:

"2. Charges and expenses

Basis for charging.

Our charges are based on the time we spend dealing with a case. Time spent will include meetings with you and perhaps others (for example, counsel and experts); attending court; any time spent travelling; considering, preparing and working on papers; correspondence; writing and receiving letters; and making and receiving telephone calls. Charges are assessed in units of 6 minutes (1/10th of an hour). ...

Payments on account

It is normal practice to ask clients to pay sums of money from time to time on account of the charges and expenses that are expected in the following weeks or months. Such monies will be placed on client account, and will not be withdrawn from there other than to meet disbursements without our invoicing you. Prompt payment on account helps to avoid delay in the progress of their case. We particularly like to have cover for fees of people we instruct on your behalf, such as counsel and experts. We will offset any such payments against your final bill, but it is important that you understand that your total charges and expenses may be greater than any advance payments. ...

3. Billing arrangements

In longer running matters, we may send you interim bills for our charges and expenses while the work is in progress. These may be sent at agreed intervals, for example quarterly, or (it often happens) as 'milestones' in a case are passed (sic). We will send you a final bill after completion of the work ...

Termination

You may terminate your instructions to us in writing at any time. However we may keep all your papers and documents while there is money owing to us for our charges and expenses. You are still liable for those until we stop acting. In practice, appropriate arrangements will be made with your new advisers, in continuing litigation matters, particularly where these are legally aided.

In some circumstances, you may consider we ought to stop acting for you, for example, if you cannot give clear or proper instructions on how we are to proceed, or if it is clear that you have lost confidence in how we are carrying out your work.

We may decide to stop acting for you only with good reason, for example, if you do not pay an interim bill or comply with our request for a payment on account. We must give you reasonable notice that we will stop acting for you."

The Facts

8. Pursuant to their instructions, the appellants obtained the advice of specialist counsel, Mr James Findlay. In an opinion dated 1 July 2005, Mr Findlay explained that challenges to an Inspector's decision can only be made on points of law and that a difference of view as to the merits, particularly if those merits concern matters of planning judgment, does not give rise to an error of law. At para 6, he said: "The hurdles that face somebody wishing to challenge a decision are thus high. In this case, I consider there is no reasonable prospect of success for any challenge." Having considered a number of points of detail to which it is not necessary to refer, he concluded at para 15:

"Whilst I can fully appreciate Mr Mills-Owens' frustrations, which in part at least appear to be shared by the local planning authority, the

Inspector reached a decision that he was entitled to come to and there is no reasonable prospect of challenging it."

9. Despite this advice, the appellants were instructed to issue proceedings. This they did on July 5. Because of the time limits for lodging grounds of appeal, these were drafted at short notice. Four grounds were included in the claim form:

a) The Inspector failed properly to deal with the issue of exceptional circumstances in his consideration of the applicability of the policy NF-H3 and the cumulative effect and consequences of the two interdependent applications.
b) The permission granted when read together with the application gives no explanation of precisely what the permission is for.
c) The appeal process has left the claimant without the ability to make proper representations on appeal and not allowed the appeal to be considered in a proper manner.
d) There was no proper consideration or screening of the necessity for an environmental impact assessment. This was important given that the area is a National Park."

10. On September 16, the appellants instructed new counsel, Mr Peter Harrison. On September 25, he emailed the appellants and said that he considered that there was a "proper argument that the Inspector has misapplied policy NF-H3 and hence made an error of law which would justify quashing the decision". He said that there were arguments the other way and the prospects of success were "still perhaps 50/50 but I do think that the point is worth taking and should be argued".

11. Mr Harrison drafted a skeleton argument which was shown to Mr Mills-Owens on December 19. It dealt only with ground (a) of the four grounds identified in the claim form. On December 20, Mr Mills-Owens wrote a long letter to the appellants commenting in detail on the skeleton argument. He said that the skeleton argument made no mention of the development being in the New Forest National Park Area, of the importance of the environmental law in respect of it, or that the planning process had given no consideration to the effects on the environment of the development. He also said that the skeleton argument should include grounds (b), (c) and (d).

12. On December 28, he wrote again repeating that the matters

referred to in his earlier letter must be included in the skeleton argument. His concern was that the skeleton argument did not address his serious concerns about the environmental effects of the development and that the planning authorities had not given due consideration to them. He said that putting the whole emphasis on seeking to prevent an increase in the size of the development to the exclusion of environmental consequences might appear to the court to be petty. The inclusion of the devastation already caused and that would be caused might give the court a true picture of his real concern which he wished the court to address.

13. During the following weeks, correspondence continued between Mr Mills-Owens and the appellants. The appellants stated and maintained their position that grounds (b), (c) and (d) were not arguable errors of law, whereas ground (a) was. Mr Mills-Owens was adamant that all four grounds should be included in the skeleton argument and advanced at the hearing. Mr Harrison was asked to reconsider the matter. He prepared a Note dated 3 January 2006. He stated that he could only operate "within the very tight parameters set by the law". He dealt with grounds (b) to (d) in the following terms:

> "8. In ground b) Mr Mills Owens suggests that he had difficulty in determining the precise scope and detail of the planning application and what would actually be allowed by the grant of permission. It is clear that the latest application is one in series and that it is designed to be the last stage in a staged expansion of the buildings on the plot. This point was considered by the Inspector who makes clear in paras 6, 7 and 12 of the Decision Letter that he has judged that he had sufficient material before him to be clear what he was being asked to grant planning permission for and the effects of it. Unfortunately this is precisely the type of judgment that the court will say was for the decision maker and will not itself made a second decision on. This is the case even if the court itself considers that it may have come to a different view.
>
> 9. In ground c) it is suggested that the inquiry procedure did not permit Mr Mills Owens to make the most effective representations opposing the appeal. However, in this case the relevant rules and regulations were followed. Mr Mills Owens did put written representations before the Inspector and the High Court will not, in my view, be prepared to rule that the current regulations which govern all written representation appeals are unfair or that decisions taken under them should be quashed.

10. Ground d) raises the issue of whether or not an EIA [Environmental Impact Assessment] should have been required. However, despite the fact the proposals are in a National Park I do not consider that the regulations or the relevant case law would require an EIA in relation to the development for which planning permission was granted in this case."

14. He then considered whether there was any harm in raising these points anyway. He said that his experience was that it was counter-productive to raise points "which are not going to succeed". He gave a number of reasons for this, including that such points distract from the strength of clear points on which there is a strong argument. Judges look less favourably on a case "where they feel that points which are clearly outside the scope which the law allows are being set up alongside points supported by arguments which the law supports." He added that ground (a) was the only argument which "has any proper chance of succeeding and that to put forward the other points would be wrong in law and not helpful to the case overall." He concluded by saying that his skeleton argument should be amended to give some more context for ground (a) by making clear that it was Mr Mills-Owens' concern to protect the environment which was the motivation behind the challenge.

15. The skeleton argument was amended to reflect this advice and Mr Mills-Owens' concern to protect the environment was amplified, but in its amended form the skeleton argument was still unacceptable to Mr Mills-Owens. On January 6, he insisted that it should not be lodged with the court since it was "fundamentally flawed". He instructed the appellants to seek an adjournment of the hearing to enable him to consider the matter fully.

16. In his reply of January 7, Mr Buxton said that an impasse had been reached. The skeleton argument had to be lodged by January 16. A request for an adjournment was "unrealistic". He then said this:

"Perhaps I have not made it clear that counsel is constrained in what can be said in the skeleton argument. Quite apart from the likely effect on costs, he will personally be criticised by the court if he makes points that he considers unarguable.

I enclose a transcript of a decision by Sullivan J one of the most respected planning judges, which sets out the court's approach in these types of circumstances. You will gather why we take the view we do. I refer to the sidelined sections towards the beginning of the judgment.

Your underlying concern relates as you quite understandably put it to the 'legal responsibility of the relevant authorities to conserve and enhance the natural beauty wildlife and cultural heritage' in the National Park. You must understand that such responsibilities have been dealt with already in the development plan. It is *that* which the inspector has, we say, failed to adhere to. If you get the decision quashed, then the matter goes back for reconsideration on a proper basis, taking those points properly into account – as you require. It is not the High Court's job to do that now, and it will not.

The above reflects my and counsel's opinion. We entirely respect your views and of course have to respect your instructions. In such circumstances there are three possible courses of action:

- To accept what we say and allow the skeleton to go in as amended (as sent to you with my last letter) though you are welcome to make suggestions as to *specific* amendments you consider should be made to the text e.g. to correct what you say are inaccuracies.

- To take a second opinion from another barrister experienced in this field. Time is relatively tight, but this is nevertheless easily done. You could even do this via another firm of solicitors though it would be more efficient for me to do so.

- Withdraw your instructions to us and simply go elsewhere. This would be disappointing but we cannot act for you if we are at cross purposes.

Please let me know what you want to do."

17. On January 11, Mr Mills-Owens replied that he had been to London to request the adjournment. He said: "I am sorry that you have left me at this late stage to do my Skeleton Argument myself. I will of course pay your bill where monies are owing but would like it taxed."

18. On January 14, Mr Buxton suggested that the skeleton argument as drafted should be lodged by the 16th. That would leave open the option of putting a supplementary skeleton argument in at a later stage. On January 16, Mr Mills-Owens replied that he expected Mr Buxton to follow his "abundantly clear" instructions. He said that he would prepare his own skeleton argument which he would submit to the court shortly.

19. On January 17, Mr Buxton wrote that the instructions of Mr Mills-Owens were not clear "(a) as to whether you wish us to continue acting for you and if so (b) whether to instruct counsel to appear on your behalf on February 6 and if so (c) what is to become of the skeleton argument". He asked what Mr Mills-Owens wanted him to do.

20. Mr Mills-Owens lodged his own skeleton argument with the court. The first Mr Buxton knew of this was when he received a communication from the Treasury Solicitor. Mr Buxton had drafted a letter to be sent by his firm to the court explaining why he had not submitted a skeleton argument. On January 24, he spoke to the Law Society and was advised that he could not send the letter or even disclose the existence of another skeleton argument without the authority of Mr Mills-Owens. Mr Buxton explained the facts to the Law Society representative and was told that, on those facts, the appellants' position was "untenable" and that they had "good reason" to terminate the retainer.

21. On January 25, Mr Buxton wrote to Mr Mills-Owens saying that, unless he authorised him to send the letter to the court or gave revised instructions "such that we do indeed represent you along the lines we recommend", he would have to terminate the retainer and apply to the court to come off the record. Mr Buxton said that he had read Mr Mills-Owens' skeleton argument and said that it did not "properly address the legal point in the case".

22. On January 26, Mr Mills-Owens said that Mr Buxton did not have his permission to discuss his (Mr Mills-Owens') skeleton argument or any other document with the defence. He said that the letter to the court "is not correct and therefore prejudicial to me". He had made it abundantly clear that he did not and would not approve of the skeleton argument drafted by counsel. He said: "At the risk of being blunt may I suggest you read my letters and address and follow my instructions."

23. On January 27, Mr Buxton said that he had not sent the letter to the court because he had decided to obtain Mr Mills-Owens' authority before doing so. Mr Mills-Owens' skeleton argument was unlikely to find favour with the court. "I am not saying that it will certainly fail, that would be dangerous, but from quite a lot of experience of these types of cases, which are very difficult in the first place, I believe that this is a likely outcome." Later in the letter, he said:

> "If you entirely decline to advance any legal argument along the lines of the first skeleton argument (whether the document is put in or not) it seems to me that we will simply be unable to act."

The letter concluded as follows:

> "What I need from you in the immediate future, please, are instructions as to whether you want us to continue to act for you, and if so we must discuss on what terms in relation to arguments that may be advanced.
>
> I may need firmly to clarify with the Law Society what our professional obligations and possibilities are in this very unusual situation, but I suspect that unless you are prepared to take our advice and permit counsel to argue as he sees fit – even on the basis of your skeleton argument while otherwise relying on the witness statement – it will be necessary to come off the court record so that you will have to appear on February 6 as a litigant in person (or with other representation).
>
> Please could you clarify that you understand this. I repeat, please also confirm whether or not you do wish to continue to instruct us (and counsel): if so, we believe it will be vital during the course of next week to have a conference in London with counsel firmly to agree what can and cannot be said. We will also need further putting in funds as previously advised. I should also advise that this recent work has taken us over the monies paid on account to some degree. I will advise in more detail next week following your response."

24. On January 30, Mr Buxton wrote again to Mr Mills-Owens enclosing a copy of the skeleton argument submitted by the Treasury Solicitor. He said:

> "the slow speed of communication by post combined with your recent approach to the case has put us in an impossible position in terms of representing you ... We have however now given you notice at many points that we will have to terminate the retainer if you do not take our advice and we do not received adequate instructions ... So there is just one last chance to try to get matters on to a proper footing and to argue the case as the court would expect at the hearing next week."

25. On January 31, Mr Mills-Owens repeated many of the points he had already made. He was "appalled and dismayed" to see from the letter of January 27 that Mr Buxton had been discussing his witness statement and skeleton argument with one of the defendants and

requested "a typescript of all such conversations and/or copy of the letter(s) with time(s) and date(s) by return and ensure that any statements made which are contrary to my instruction are withdrawn". He went on: "I should make it clear that while you do not follow my instructions you are clearly not acting for me. My instructions are clear and concise and straightforward." He insisted that the skeleton argument drafted by Mr Harrison which he had not accepted was "flawed, factually incorrect and prejudicial to my case". However, he failed to identify any such flaw, error or prejudice. He instructed Mr Buxton to apply to the court for an adjournment so that he had time either to prepare all four grounds of appeal and not just ground (a) or to have time to instruct someone who was prepared to address the true environmental case that he wished to place before the court.

26. In his first letter of February 1, Mr Buxton wrote that, since he had not heard from Mr Mills-Owens, he was making an application to take his firm off the record. In a second letter of the same date, he wrote:

> "I do not like to do it, but professionally have no alternative (unless you are prepared to sit down with me and counsel and discuss the ground rules within which we have to work) to do other than stand down and suggest you seek alternative advice."

27. On February 3, the appellants wrote to Mr Mills-Owens saying that the appeal was fixed to be heard by Ouseley J on February 6. They intended to attend in order to assist the judge in case he had questions about the procedural position. Counsel was not instructed to attend, but would be available at short notice should Mr Mills-Owens or the judge so require. Mr Mills-Owens replied on the following day saying: "You are not my solicitor. You do not have my permission to act for me or represent me ... I do not want to be approached by you or counsel or indeed anyone representing your firm in court. I would consider that a gross interference in my case."

28. On February 6, Ouseley J refused Mr Mills-Owens' request for an adjournment. Mr Mills-Owens represented himself. His appeal was dismissed as was his subsequent application for permission to appeal. Ouseley J dealt with ground (b) at paras 8 to 19 of his judgment. At para 19, he said that the understanding of the extent of the demolition could be gleaned from the plans which were incorporated as part of

the application. The contention that there was a permission for an unknown or unspecified number of dwelling units was "a simple misreading of the documents". The concerns which Mr Mills-Owens had raised "over the, to him, alarming extent of the permission, are all misconceived".

29. Ouseley J rejected ground (a) at paras 28 to 32. As the appellants were willing to advance this ground of challenge, there is no need to consider what the judge said about it. Ouseley J dealt with ground (d) in the following way:

> "36. Mr Mills-Owens next argued that a screening opinion was necessary because this development was development in a National Park which is a sensitive area for the purposes of the Town and Country Planning (Environmental Impact Assessment)(England and Wales) Regulations 1999 SI No 293. However, a screening opinion is necessary to see whether development is EIA development. EIA development has to be schedule 2 development, likely to have a significant effect on the environment. Schedule 2 development means development 'of a description mentioned in Column 2 of the table in Schedule 2 where – (a) any part of that development is to be carried out in a sensitive area or (b) any applicable threshold or criterion in the corresponding part of Column 2 of that table is respectively exceeded or met in relation to that development'. Therefore, if the development does not appear in column 1 of schedule 2, no screening opinion is required even though the development is in a sensitive area.
>
> 37. The raising of the roof, or even the raising of the roof and the infill link extension, does not come within any of the heads of development set out in column 1 to schedule 2. This could not remotely be described as an urban development project. Nor could it be described as a change or extension to an urban development project. That point is misconceived."

30. It seems that Ouseley J did not deal separately with ground (c).

The Relevant Professional Codes of Conduct

31. The Solicitors' Practice Rules 1990 (as amended to 1 October 1999) provided at para 12.12 that "a solicitor must not terminate his or her retainer with the client except for good reason and upon reasonable notice". The notes to rule 12.12 in the Guide to the Professional Conduct of Solicitors 1999 include:

"1. It is open to a client to terminate a solicitor's retainer for whatever reason. A solicitor must complete the retainer unless he or she has a good reason for terminating it.

2. Examples of good reasons include where a solicitor cannot continue to act without being in breach of the rules or principles of conduct, or where a solicitor is unable to obtain clear instructions from a client or where there is a serious breakdown in confidence between them."

32. With effect from 1 July 2007, the Solicitors' Code of Conduct 2007 came into force. This is not directly applicable in the present case, because it post-dates the appellants' retainer. Nevertheless, it is worth noting that rule 2.01(2) provides that a solicitor "must not cease acting for a client except for good reason and on reasonable notice". The Guidance to rule 2 provides at para 8 that examples of good reasons for ending a retainer include "where there is a breakdown in confidence" and where the solicitor is "unable to obtain proper instructions". Rule 11(3) provides: "you must not construct facts supporting your client's case or draft any documents relating to any proceedings containing: (a) any contention which you do not consider to be properly arguable".

33. The Bar Code of Conduct provides so far as material:

"603. A barrister must not accept any instructions if to do so would cause him to be professionally embarrassed and for this purpose a barrister will be professionally embarrassed: ...

(c) if the instructions seek to limit the ordinary authority or discretion of barrister in the conduct of proceedings in court or to require a barrister to act otherwise than in conformity with law or with the provisions of this Code; ...

Drafting documents

704. A barrister must not devise facts which will assist in advancing the lay client's case and must not draft any statement of case, witness statement, affidavit, notice of appeal or other document containing: ...

(b) any contention which he does not consider to be properly arguable;
...

provided that nothing in this paragraph shall prevent a barrister drafting a document containing specific factual statements or contentions included by the barrister subject to confirmation or their accuracy by the lay client or witness. ...

Conduct in Court

708. A barrister when conducting proceedings in court: ...

(f) must not make a submission which he does not consider to be properly arguable."

34. Although the Civil Procedure Rules ("CPR") are not formally part of the Solicitors' Rules or Code of Conduct, in discharging their professional obligations in the conduct of litigation, solicitors must also have regard to the CPR. In particular, CPR 1.3 requires the parties to "help the court to further the overriding objective". That duty extends to the legal advisers of the parties, including advocates: see *Geberan Trading Co Ltd v Skjevesland* [2002] EWCA Civ 1567, [2003] 1 WLR 912 at para 37. The overriding objective is defined in CPR 1.1 as enabling the court to deal with cases justly. In my judgment, it is clear that the overriding objective is not furthered by the parties advancing hopeless arguments.

The Judgment of Master O'Hare

35. At para 10 of his judgment, Master O'Hare said:

"Nevertheless, I think the solicitors (although undoubtedly in difficult circumstances) ultimately adopted a course which, I think, was the wrong course. I think they should not have terminated the instructions as they did. I do not think they had just cause, regardless of what notice they gave. I think what they should have done was carry out the client's instructions, even though they had given (and would no doubt repeat) that such instructions were doomed to disaster. Because they have failed to carry out the client's instructions, I do not think they are entitled to charge him fees in this matter. They were retained for the entire business; that is conducting a statutory appeal. That has to be a statutory appeal on the basis of the instructions made by the client, so long as they are legal, honest and decent. Clients cannot instruct solicitors to do anything improper but (however unwise I might think they were) I do not think this client's instructions were, in any way, improper."

36. At para 11, he said:

"There is no reason for cross purposes. So long as the solicitors advise the client that his course of instruction is doomed to failure, I think they ought to follow his instructions. Also, I think it is wrong when [the appellants' letter of 7 January] says, at the start, 'We entirely respect your views and, of course, have to respect your instructions'. Well, it is more than respect for instructions which is needed; so long as they are proper instructions (however misguided solicitors think them) they should not just respect them, they ought to follow them."

The Judgment of Mackay J

37. Having summarised the correspondence to which I have referred above, Mackay J recorded the submission of Mr Buxton that Mr Mills-Owens was instructing him to advance an improper case and that, for that reason, he was not only entitled to cease acting, but had a professional obligation to do so by reason of rule 12.12 of the Solicitors' Practice Rules (as amended). At para 21 of his judgment, the judge said that there are occasions where the line is difficult to draw between an argument which is "improper" and one which, though bound to fail, can nevertheless be properly advanced. He then said: "but in my judgment at the end of the day if a client who is prepared to pay for a case to be advanced, wants the claim advanced on a particular basis, which does not involve impropriety on the part of the solicitor or counsel, then it is no answer for the solicitor to say that he believes it is bound to fail and therefore he will not do it". At para 22, the judge expressly endorsed the observations of Master O'Hare quoted above.

38. At para 23, he concluded this part of the judgment as follows:

"I have very considerable sympathy for the solicitors here who had a very difficult problem and a difficult client. But the litigator's back must be broad, and provided that he has given clear advice to that client, if that client wishes to pursue a case which the solicitor honestly believes is going to lose, the client is entitled to instruct him to do so, absent any impropriety or misleading of the court. It is my judgment, assisted by but not dependent on the solicitor assessor sitting with me that the position here fell short of the line where the solicitor would have been entitled to terminate the retainer and that the costs judge here was right to assess the matter in the way he did."

Were the Appellants Entitled to Terminate the Retainer?

39. I am in no doubt that the retainer was an "entire contract". In

Underwood, Son, & Piper v *Lewis* [1894] 2 QB 306, Lord Esher MR explained:

> "when a man goes to a solicitor and instructs him for the purpose of bringing or defending such an action, he does not mean to employ the solicitor to take one step, and then give him fresh instructions to take another step, and so on; he instructs the solicitor as a skilled person to act for him in the action, to take all necessary steps in it, and to carry it on to the end."

40. The appellants were retained to institute and take the statutory appeal to the end. But that did not mean that the retainer could not be terminated before the end. The position at common law is that a solicitor may terminate his retainer before the end on reasonable notice and if he has a "reasonable ground for refusing to act further for the client": per Lord Esher in *Underwood* at p. 313. Where the parties have agreed in what circumstances the solicitor may terminate the retainer, then the matter is governed by their contract. In this case, the parties agreed that the appellants could terminate "only with good reason". That reflects the common law position. Unsurprisingly, it also reflects rule 12.12 of the Solicitors' Practice Rules (as amended) and rule 2.01(2) of the 2007 Code of Conduct.

41. Did the appellants have a good reason to terminate the retainer? There is no comprehensive definition of what amounts to a good reason to terminate in the Solicitors' Practice Rules or the Code of Conduct (although examples are given in both documents), or in any of the authorities that have been cited to us. That is not surprising, since whether there is a good reason to terminate is a fact-sensitive question. I accept the submission of Mr Drabble that it is wrong to restrict the circumstances in which a solicitor can lawfully terminate his retainer to those in which he is instructed to do something improper. I accept that solicitors should not lightly be able lawfully to terminate their retainers, leaving their clients with the task of finding fresh solicitors to complete the job. But the desirability of protecting a client from an arbitrary and unreasonable termination is not a sufficient justification for giving such a narrow interpretation of the phrase "good reason" as the judge has given in this case. Indeed, the 1999 Guide to rule 12.12 of the 1990 Rules (as amended) and the Guidance to the 2007 Code of Conduct give the examples of a solicitor being unable to obtain clear instructions from the client or where there

is a serious breakdown in confidence between solicitor and client. Further, s 65(2) of the Solicitors Act 1974 deems a failure by a client within a reasonable time to pay a reasonable sum on account of the costs of contentious business to be "good cause whereby the solicitor may, upon giving reasonable notice to the client, withdraw from the retainer".

42. In *Underwood*, AL Smith LJ said at p. 314:

> "On the other hand, it is clear that the solicitor may be placed in such a position by the client as to absolve him from the further performance of that contract. It appears to me from the case of *Vansandau v Browne* and the subsequent cases which have been cited, that the client may put the solicitor in such a position as to entitle him to decline to proceed; for instance, if the solicitor asks for necessary funds for disbursements, and such funds are refused by the client, the solicitor is not bound to go on; and, speaking for myself, I should say that the solicitor is not bound to go on acting for the client if the client insists on some step being taken which the solicitor knows to be dishonourable; and many other cases may be supposed in which the solicitor may be entitled to refuse to act for the client any further. I should say that, when a solicitor is in a position to show that the client has hindered and prevented him from continuing to act as a solicitor should act, then upon notice he may decline to act further, and in such case the solicitor would be entitled to sue for the costs already incurred. But we have not now to deal with such a case. The sole question here is, whether the solicitor is entitled without rhyme or reason to throw up his retainer, having given due notice of his intention to do so. I do not think that he is so entitled."

43. The particular question that arises on this appeal is whether a solicitor has good reason for terminating a retainer if a client insists on his putting forward a case and instructing counsel to argue a case which is "doomed to disaster" (Master O'Hare) or which the solicitor believes "is bound to fail" (Mackay J). I agree with Mackay J that it may be difficult to draw the line between an argument which can properly be articulated and put forward (but which has little, if any, prospect of success) and an argument which cannot properly be articulated and which is believed to be bound to fail. The Bar Code of Conduct puts the matter very clearly. Counsel may not draft any document (which must include a skeleton argument) containing a contention which he does not consider to be properly arguable; and he

may not make any submission in court which he does not consider to be properly arguable. A corresponding provision appears at rule 11.01(3) of the 2007 Code of Conduct for Solicitors. It must be acknowledged that there is no express provision in those terms in the 1990 Rules (as amended). Nevertheless, I am in no doubt that even before the point was spelt out in the 2007 Code, it would have been understood by all solicitors that, as officers of the court, they were under a professional duty (i) not to include in the court documents that they drafted any contention which they did not consider to be properly arguable and (ii) not to instruct counsel to advance contentions which they did not consider to be properly arguable. That duty was reinforced by CPR 1.3.

44. Our attention was drawn to page 6 of *Cook on Costs* (2010) where there is a reference to the decision of Mackay J in the present case. The author says:

> "If a client is prepared for a case to be advanced and wants the claim advanced on a particular basis which did not involve impropriety on the part of the solicitor or counsel, then it is no answer for the solicitor to say that he believes it is bound to fail and therefore he will not do it. Whatever one thought about the client's stance, his instructions were firm and unequivocal as to how the case was to be presented and the solicitor ought to have followed them. The situation fell short of the line where the solicitor would have been entitled to terminate the retainer and the solicitors were not entitled for any fees for the work they had done. I suggest the solicitor should have continued to act and adopted the traditional coded message to the court used in these circumstances: 'I am instructed to say'."

45. For reasons that I am about to give, I consider that the appellants were entitled to terminate the retainer in this case. But I refer to this passage in *Cook* because I do not agree with the last sentence. In my judgment, if an advocate considers that a point is properly arguable, he should argue it without reservation. If he does not consider it to be properly arguable, he should refuse to argue it. He should not advance a submission but signal to the judge that he thinks that it is weak or hopeless by using the coded language "I am instructed that". Such coded language is well understood as conveying that the advocate expects it to be rejected. In my judgment, such language should be avoided.

46. I now turn to the facts of this case. The contentions which the appellants and both counsel were unwilling to advance were ones which they all considered not to be properly arguable. They were ones which they believed they could not properly articulate as legal arguments and which were hopeless. Mackay J was right to say at para 10 of his judgment that:

> "The application was from the start bedevilled by what the costs judge found was a fundamental problem. The client did not understand and still does not understand the limited basis upon which such a planning appeal is possible. He wanted the appeal to be presented on a much wider basis by reference to the merits of the case and the need for the safeguarding of an environment of which he is understandably protective. He found it difficult, indeed impossible, as the costs judge below found, and as I find, to accept that for such an appeal to succeed it is necessary to point to a procedural error or some other legal flaw in the approach of the planning inspector. This was the thrust of an initial advice from counsel received within a week of two of the first instruction of the solicitors, to the effect that there was no reasonable prospect of challenging the decision."

47. To the extent that Mr Mills-Owens insisted (as he did) that a challenge should be made to the Planning Inspector's decision on the planning merits of the case, such a challenge could not, as a matter of law, be made under s 288 of the 1990 Act. Mackay J seems to have recognised this at para 10 of his judgment. Mr Mills-Owens would not accept that a challenge could only be made for legal error. It would be improper in a s 288 appeal to advance an argument based on the merits of the decision of the Planning Inspector; and if Mr Mills-Owens insisted that such an argument be advanced, the appellants had good reason for terminating the retainer. Mackay J did not explain why it would not be improper to advance an argument which sought to challenge a decision on the facts when such a challenge is not permitted by s 288.

48. In fact, although the main concern of Mr Mills-Owens was to challenge the Planning Inspector's decision on the facts and although at para 11 of his judgment Mackay J described grounds (b), (c) and (d) in the claim form "as going more to the general merits of the planning decision", in fact those grounds as pleaded were not expressed as going to the merits of the planning decision.

49. The reason why neither Mr Harrison nor the appellants were willing to include grounds (b) to (d) in the skeleton argument was that they considered that they were hopeless and were not properly arguable. In my judgment, they were right to do so. I have already set out at para 14 above what Mr Harrison said about these grounds in his Note dated 3 January 2006. Mr Harrison rightly said in relation to ground (b) that it was a matter of planning judgment for the Inspector whether there was sufficient material for him to be clear as to the subject matter of the application for planning permission. In any event, this ground was dismissed by Ouseley J because the extent of the proposed development was obvious from the plans which were incorporated as part of planning application. Ground (c) was hopeless for the reasons given by Mr Harrison and was not, it seems, pursued before Ouseley J in any event. Ground (d) was hopeless for the reasons given by Ouseley J: see para 30 above.

50. Thus the appellants and Mr Harrison were of the opinion that grounds (b) to (d) could not properly be put forward because they were hopeless arguments. They shared the view expressed by Mr Findlay who (unlike the appellants and Mr Harrison) had not been able to find a single argument which had any prospect of success. Mr Findlay had said that the case had "no reasonable prospect of success" and that it was "doomed to fail". Mr Harrison (who considered that there was a 50:50 chance of success on ground (a)) had similarly said in his Note dated January 3 that grounds (b) to (d) were "outside the scope which the law allows" and were "wrong in law". It is true that in his letter dated January 27, Mr Buxton said that he was not saying that the skeleton argument drafted by Mr Mills-Owens would certainly fail, but he believed this to be the "likely outcome". That sentence, if taken in isolation, would suggest that Mr Buxton did not consider that grounds (b) to (d) were unarguable and bound to fail. But if the correspondence is viewed as a whole, it is clear that Mr Buxton did not consider that he could properly submit a skeleton argument which included grounds (b) to (d) or instruct counsel to argue those grounds and Mr Harrison agreed with him.

51. I conclude, therefore, that the appellants had good reason to terminate the retainer.

Are the Appellants Entitled to Be Paid for Work Done and Disbursements Incurred Up to the Date of Termination?

52. The appellants had received payments on account which, in accordance with their terms of business, had been placed in their client account and had not been withdrawn except to meet disbursements. No invoices had been submitted to Mr Mills-Owens before the termination. The appellants' terms of business are silent as to the payment of fees in the event of termination by the appellants for good reason.

53. It is, therefore, necessary to look to the general law to see whether the appellants were entitled to be paid for the work they had done even though they had not completed the "entire contract". It has long been established that, where a solicitor terminates an "entire contract" before completion and does so for good cause or on reasonable grounds, he is entitled to be paid for the work that he has done. In *Vansandau and Tindale v Browne* (1832) 9 Bing 402, it was held that an attorney is not compelled to proceed to the end of a suit in order to be entitled to his costs, but may for reasonable cause and on reasonable notice abandon the conduct of the suit and recover his costs for the period during which he was employed.

54. In *Underwood,* solicitors had declined to continue to act for their client before the litigation in which they were acting had been completed. They brought an action for the amount of their bill of costs for work done to date. The trial judge held that a solicitor may terminate his retainer without cause and judgment was entered in favour of the solicitors. As we have seen, the Court of Appeal said that the retainer could only be lawfully terminated on reasonable grounds. They ordered a retrial. It was implicit in the decision to order a retrial that, if the solicitors were able to show that they had a reasonable ground for terminating the retainer, their claim for costs would in principle succeed. In his judgment, Lord Esher said:

> "it seems to me that from [the time of *Cresswell v Byron* (1807) 33 ER 525] downwards it has been held that a solicitor cannot sue for his costs until his contract has been entirely fulfilled, unless the case is brought within some recognised exception to the general rule."

An exception to this general rule is where the solicitor terminates the retainer on reasonable grounds.

55. None of the cases cited to us contains a statement of the legal

basis for the principle that, where a solicitor terminates his retainer for good reason, subject to any relevant provision contained in the agreement between the parties, he is entitled to be paid his profit costs and disbursements for work done prior to the termination. One possible analysis is that, at any rate in a case such as the present, where the client insists on the solicitor putting forward contentions which the solicitor does not consider to be properly arguable, the client repudiates the retainer and the solicitor accepts the repudiation by terminating. The solicitor may then elect to claim the fees due (if any) under the agreement or on a *quantum meruit*. It is, however, unnecessary to consider this further, since the common law rule that a solicitor is entitled to be paid for all the work he has done prior to termination if he terminates for good reason has been part of our law for almost 200 years. It follows that the appellants are entitled to be paid their profit costs and disbursements for the work done prior to the termination. There should in principle be no difficulty in calculating these, since the basis for charging was clearly defined in the appellants' terms of business: see para 8 above.

Overall Conclusion

56. For the reasons I have given, the appellants were entitled to terminate their retainer and entitled to their proper costs and disbursements for work done prior to the termination. I should add that Mr Mills-Owens has permission to cross appeal in relation to the issue of disbursements, but that issue does not now arise. Finally, I should record my view that, throughout his dealings with Mr Mills-Owens, Mr Buxton has acted in a thoroughly professional manner and has shown conspicuous patience.

57. MAURICE KAY LJ: I agree.

58. THE PRESIDENT OF THE FAMILY DIVISION: I also agree.

Richard Buxton appeared for the appellant.

Mr Mills-Owens appeared in person.

Richard Drabble QC and *David Holland* (instructed by Mills & Reeve) appeared for the Intervener.

Case 33
HR Trustees Ltd
v
German and Another
(In the Matter of the IMG Pension Plan)

[2010] 3 Costs LR 443

Neutral Citation Number: [2010] EWHC 321 (Ch)
High Court of Justice, Chancery Division
26 February 2010

Before:
Arnold J

Headnote

An important decision on when it is appropriate to make a prospective costs order for an appeal in "friendly" pension fund litigation.

Judgment

Introduction

1. ARNOLD J: On 10 November 2009 I gave judgment ("the first judgment", [2009] EWHC 2785 (Ch)) on an application by the claimant ("the Present Trustee") for the determination of seven questions arising out of the purported conversion of the IMG Pension Plan ("the Plan") from a "final salary" scheme to a "money purchase" scheme by a deed dated 3 March 1992 ("the 1992 Deed").

2. As I recorded in the first judgment at para 2, the Present Trustee was neutral in these proceedings. The first defendant ("Mr German") is a deferred member of the Plan. During the trial I appointed Mr

German to act as a representative beneficiary under an "issues-based" representation order pursuant to CPR rule 19.7(2)(d)(ii) i.e. to represent those beneficiaries in whose interests it would be to argue for particular answers to the questions raised. The second defendant ("IMG") is the Plan's Principal Employer. Although the point was not mentioned in the first judgment, because it was not necessary to do so, for present purposes it is important to note that the effect of the representation order so far as question 5 was concerned was that Mr German represented two classes of beneficiary. The first class was the class of existing active members as at the date of the 1992 Deed. The second class was the class of members who joined the Plan after the 1992 Deed, but before the coming into effect of a new Definitive Deed and Rules dated 30 December 2004 on 1 January 2005 ("the 2004 Deed"). The reason for this is that the effect of complete success by Mr German on question 5 would be that the Plan continued to be a final salary scheme until the 2004 Deed came into effect.

3. Broadly speaking, the effect of the first judgment was that I ruled in favour of Mr German on questions 1, 2, 4 and 6 and I ruled in favour of IMG on questions 5 and 7. (There turned out to be no real dispute on question 3.) Thus the first class of members represented by Mr German on question 5 benefit under my judgment, but the second class do not.

4. On 2 December 2009 I gave a supplemental judgment ([2009] EWHC 3410 (Ch)) in which I determined an additional issue that had arisen and ruled upon applications for permission to appeal. I granted IMG permission to appeal on questions 1, 2, 4 and 6. I granted Mr German permission to appeal on question 5 limited to arguing the legal consequences of the facts that I had found. I gave that permission because I considered it arguable that there was either no effective exercise by IMG of its power to appoint four new trustees who were appointed by a deed of appointment dated 2 March 1992 ("the New Trustees") or a failure on the part of the New Trustees to exercise their discretion to amend the Plan when executing the 1992 Deed in the manner that they should have done.

5. Counsel for Mr German made it clear when applying for permission to appeal that Mr German would only wish to appeal if IMG appealed. I was assured by counsel for Mr German during the hearing of the present application that in reaching that decision those advising Mr German gave careful consideration to the position of the

second class of members represented by him with respect to question 5. Accordingly, para 8(b) of my order dated 2 December 2009 provided that Mr German's permission to appeal was conditional upon IMG filing an appellant's notice and extended his time for filing his respondent's notice until 21 days after service of IMG's Appellant's Notice on him.

6. In the event, IMG did file an appellant's notice on 6 January 2010. Accordingly, Mr German wishes to file a cross-appeal. By consent, his time for doing so has been extended until 14 days after judgment on the present application.

7. Mr German's representation at first instance was funded by IMG under the terms of a costs agreement dated 10 September 2008. That agreement has now expired. IMG has agreed to fund Mr German's representation for the purposes of resisting IMG's appeal under a new costs agreement. IMG has not agreed to fund Mr German to pursue his proposed cross-appeal. Accordingly, Mr German has applied for a prospective costs order in the form of the model costs agreement set out in PD64 para 11. In short, Mr German seeks an order that IMG pay his costs of the cross-appeal to be assessed on the indemnity basis, and that he should not pay IMG's costs of the cross-appeal, regardless of the outcome of the cross-appeal. IMG opposes such an order being made.

8. It is common ground that I have jurisdiction to make a prospective costs order in respect of the costs of an appeal from this court to the Court of Appeal, as held by Laddie J in *Laws v National Grid plc* [1998] 20 PBLR (1). It is also common ground that the jurisdiction extends to making an order that the costs be paid by IMG as the Principal Employer rather than out of the assets of the Plan, the Plan being a balance of cost scheme and moreover one that is now a money purchase scheme. There is a dispute between the parties, however, as to the principles to be applied in exercising my discretion as well as to how to exercise that discretion.

Previous Case Law

9. The leading authority on the principles to be applied to applications for prospective costs orders in pension fund cases is the decision of the Court of Appeal in *McDonald v Horn* [1995] 1 All ER 961. In that case the plaintiffs were members of an occupational pension scheme which provided final salary benefits. The plaintiffs commenced

proceedings against their employers, the pension fund trustees and others alleging improper use of powers in the trust deeds and breaches of trust in the investment of trust funds. Initially the plaintiffs' action was financed by their trade union, but in due course that support was withdrawn. The plaintiffs then applied for a pre-emptive costs order requiring that their costs, and any costs which they might be ordered to pay to the defendants, should be paid on an indemnity basis out of the pension fund whether they won or lost. The judge granted the order down to the end of discovery and inspection. The defendants appealed, contending that the court had no jurisdiction to make the order, alternatively that the judge's exercise of his discretion was flawed. The Court of Appeal dismissed the appeal.

10. The principal judgment was given by Hoffmann LJ (as he then was). After setting out the background in sections (1)–(4) of his judgment, in section (5) he considered the statutory basis for the court's jurisdiction to deal with litigation costs in s 51 of what is now the Senior Courts Act 1981. He said that the decision of the House of Lords in *Aiden Shipping Co Ltd* v *Interbulk Ltd* [1986] AC 969 showed that the discretion conferred by s 51 was broad, but not untrammelled. As he said at 969d, "It must be exercised in accordance with the rules of court and established principles". In section (6) he dealt with the general principle which is applicable, namely that costs follow the event. Although the advent of the Civil Procedure Rules has modified the principles applicable to costs in various respects, this remains the general rule: see CPR 44.3(2)(a).

11. In section (7) of his judgment, Hoffmann LJ considered the special principle concerning payment of costs out of a fund under four sub-headings: (i) "Costs of trustees and other fiduciaries"; (ii) "Extension of special principle to beneficiaries"; (iii) "Extension of special principle to derivative action"; and (iv) "Extension of *Wallersteiner* to pension funds".

12. Under the first sub-heading, he noted that in the case of proceedings concerning a fund held on trust, the trustee is entitled to his costs out of the fund on an indemnity basis, provided that he has not acted unreasonably or in substance for his own benefit rather than that of the fund.

13. Under the second sub-heading, he noted that the courts had been willing in certain circumstances to extend to other parties to trust

litigation an entitlement to costs in any event by analogy with that accorded to trustees. As he said at 970j–971b:

> "The classic statement of the principles upon which the court acts is by Kekewich J, who was acknowledged in his time as a master of Chancery procedure, in *Re Buckton* [1907] 2 Ch 406 at 413–415. While warning that it was 'well nigh impossible to lay down any general rules which can be depended on to meet the ever varying circumstances of particular cases', he said that trust litigation could be divided into three categories. First, proceedings brought by trustees to have the guidance of the court as to the construction of the trust instrument or some question arising in the course of administration. In such cases, the costs of all parties are usually treated as necessarily incurred for the benefit of the estate and ordered to be paid out of the fund. Secondly, there are cases in which the application is made by someone other than the trustees, but raises the same kind of point as in the first class and would have justified an application by the trustees. This second class is treated in the same way as the first. Thirdly, there are cases in which a beneficiary is making a hostile claim against the trustees or another beneficiary. This is treated in the same way as ordinary common law litigation and costs usually follow the event."

14. Hoffmann LJ went on to say at 971e–972a (emphasis added):

> "The court may sometimes feel sufficiently confident that the case is clearly within the first or second category to be able to make a prospective order that parties other than the trustees are to have their costs in any event. ... This is not an interference with discretion because it is clear that the discretion can only be exercised in one way. ...
>
> I think that before granting a pre-emptive application *in ordinary trust litigation or proceedings concerning the ownership of a fund held by a trustee or other fiduciary*, the judge must be satisfied that the judge at the trial could properly exercise his discretion only by ordering the applicant's costs to be paid out of the fund."

15. He then held at 972b–e (emphasis added):

> "If one applies these principles to the instant case, they do not in my judgment assist the plaintiffs. ... This is hostile litigation if ever there was. ... I do not think it likely that *if this were ordinary trust litigation* and the plaintiffs are unsuccessful, the judge would order their costs to

come out of the fund. They therefore cannot rely upon Ord. 62 r. 6(2) as extended to beneficiaries by the principles in *Re Buckton*."

16. Under the third sub-heading, Hoffmann LJ said at 972f–g that in *Wallersteiner* v *Moir (No. 2)* [1975] QB 373 the Court of Appeal had held that:

> "a minority shareholder bringing a derivative action on behalf of a company could obtain the authority of the court to sue as if he were a trustee suing on behalf of a fund, with the same entitlement to be indemnified out of the assets against his costs and any costs he may be ordered to pay to the other party. The court said that the minority shareholder could make a *Beddoe* application in the same way as a trustee and so secure an assurance that he would not be personally liable for any costs."

17. Under the fourth sub-heading, he held that the principle established in *Wallersteiner* should be extended to cover a beneficiary suing on behalf of a fund in which he and many others have interests. His reasoning at 972j–973e was as follows (emphasis added):

> "... if one looks at the economic relationships involved, there does seem to me a compelling analogy between a minority shareholder's action for damages on behalf of the company and an action by a member of a pension fund to compel trustees or others to account to the fund. In both cases a person with a limited interest in a fund, whether the company's assets or pension fund, is alleging injury to the fund as a whole and seeking restitution on behalf of the fund. And what distinguishes the shareholder and pension fund member, on the one hand, from the ordinary trust beneficiary, on the other, is that the former have both given consideration for their interests. They are not just recipients of the settlor's bounty which he, for better or worse, has entrusted to the control of trustees of his choice. The relationship between the parties is a commercial one and the pension fund members are entitled to be satisfied that the fund is being properly administered. Even in a non-contributory scheme, the employer's payments are not bounty. They are part of the consideration for the services of the employee.
>
> *Pension funds are such a special form of trust, and the analogy between them and companies with shareholders is so much stronger than in the case of ordinary trusts*, that, in my judgment, it would do no violence to established authority if we were to apply to them the *Wallersteiner* v

Moir (No. 2) procedure. Mr Sher QC, who appeared for the defendants, said that this court had no jurisdiction to do this. He referred us to the statement of the limits of the court's inherent jurisdiction over trusts in the decision of the House of Lords in *Chapman* v *Chapman* [1954] AC 429. But I say that the jurisdiction is to be found in s 51 of the Supreme Court Act 1981, which is subject only to rules of court and established principles. For the reasons I have given, I think that no such rule or principle would be violated."

18. In section (8) of his judgment, Hoffmann LJ rejected the defendants' attack on the judge's exercise of his discretion. In this connection he said at 973e–g:

> "The judge identified various factors which he regarded as material to the exercise of the discretion. He said that in the case of a pension fund the trust beneficiaries were not mere volunteers. They had contributed to the fund and had a moral right to be satisfied that it was being properly administered. The plaintiffs were bringing an action on behalf of the trust estate and should therefore enjoy the same right to an indemnity out of the fund as if they were trustees. As appears from what I have already said, I think that these are the features which, in combination, enable the case to be brought within the *Wallersteiner* principle. They are pre-conditions of the existence of the discretion rather than factors to be taken into account in its exercise."

19. In section (9) he made observations on the practice to be followed in pension fund cases, saying that the power to make a *Wallersteiner* order should be exercised with caution due to "the dangers of too easily making orders which allow minority shareholders to litigate at the cost of the company", but this did not mean undertaking a close examination of the merits of the dispute.

20. My attention was drawn to three first instance decisions since *McDonald*. The first is that of Rimer J (as he then was) in *Laws* v *National Grid*. That case concerned a surplus in the Electricity Supply Pension Scheme for National Grid. The trustees allocated 70% of the surplus to National Grid and 30% to fund benefit improvements. A Mr Laws and a Mr Mayes challenged this by complaints to the Pensions Ombudsman. The Ombudsman upheld the complaints, and the trustees and National Grid appealed to the High Court. Mr Laws

and Mr Mayes applied for pre-emptive costs orders to enable them to resist the appeals.

21. Rimer J held that, if the case fell within the third class identified in *Buckton*, the applicants faced considerable difficulties. In that event, he could only make the order sought if he were satisfied that the judge hearing the appeals would order the applicants' costs to be paid out of the scheme assets; but he could not be so satisfied. He went on to hold, however, that that was not the end of the matter because the Court of Appeal in *McDonald* had held that a pre-emptive costs order could be justified in contributory pension scheme cases by analogy with derivative actions. He then noted that the analogy was not an exact one in the instant case because the applicants had not commenced actions in the High Court, but had instead complained to the Pensions Ombudsman and were now seeking to resist appeals. He continued:

> "But I do not regard that difference as ruling the applicants out of court on their present application. The complaints to the Pensions Ombudsman can, in a sense, be regarded as the equivalent of a successful claim by the applicants in proceedings in the Chancery Division, and the present appeals can be regarded as the equivalent of appeals to the Court of Appeal by the trustees and NGC against the orders made in such proceedings. If the applicants could have obtained pre-emptive costs order to pursue an action for the benefit of the pension fund, I cannot see why in principle they could not equally apply for a like order so as to enable them to resist an appeal against the judgment they had obtained in such action. I understood both counsel to accept that they could."

22. Rimer J then considered whether to make the order sought and concluded that it was appropriate to do so. In reaching this conclusion, he addressed the four considerations set out in the following passage from the judgment of Lightman J in *Alsop Wilkinson v Neary* [1995] 1 All ER 431 at 437:

> "The court has an exceptional jurisdiction in hostile litigation to make an order at an early stage in the proceedings regarding the ultimate incidence of costs. For the purpose of this application, all parties are agreed that the relevant principles are sufficiently set out in the judgment of Mary Arden QC (sitting as a deputy High Court judge in the Chancery Division) in *Re Biddencare Ltd* [1994] 2 BCLC 160 and that

the four relevant considerations for this purpose are (1) the strength of the party's case; (2) the likely order as to costs at the trial; (3) the justice of the application; and (4) any special circumstances. I would only add that since the decision of the Court of Appeal in *McDonald* v *Horn*, the second requirement has been tightened up and (save the presently recognised exceptions namely derivative actions and actions relating to pension funds), it must appear that the judge at the trial could properly exercise his discretion only by ordering that the applicants' costs be paid out of the trust estate."

23. The second decision is that of Carnwath J (as he then was) in *Laws* v *National Grid*. This was another decision in the *National Grid* proceedings and in related proceedings concerning the Electricity Supply Pension Scheme for National Power. In those proceedings a Mr Machin had been made a representative defendant to a claim by the trustees for a determination that they had correctly treated the surplus in that scheme. Both sets of proceedings had come before Robert Walker J (as he then was), who had reversed the Pensions Ombudsman's determinations in favour of Mr Laws and Mr Mayes in the National Grid proceedings and ruled in favour of the trustees in the National Power proceedings. Each of Mr Laws, Mr Mayes and Mr Machin appealed, and applied for pre-emptive costs orders in respect of the appeals.

24. In his judgment Carnwath J considered the judgment of Hoffmann LJ in *McDonald* in some detail. Having referred to the discussion of *Buckton*, he noted that the first and second classes in that case were concerned with non-hostile proceedings, seeking the guidance of the court on issues of difficulty in relation to the construction or management of the trust. Even in such cases preemptive orders were only made where it was clear that the trial judge would order costs out of the fund. He then said that the *National Power* proceedings at first instance could be categorised as non-hostile. He went on:

"However, as Mr Warren says, in the *Buckton* type of case the same considerations do not normally apply to an appeal. He referred me to what was said in *Re Earl of Radnor's Will Trusts* (1890) 45 ChD 423. The Master of the Rolls at 423 referred to the right of the trustees in that case to seek the opinion of the judge as to what was right to be done, but he continued:

'... but when they appeal to this court from him, being absolutely protected as trustees by his decision – I do not say they are wrong in appealing, but they appeal to this court under the ordinary conditions of Appellants, and they fail in the appeal; therefore this appeal must be dismissed with costs.'

So one sees that where there is a genuine difficulty, trustees, and by analogy beneficiaries, may be able to seek authoritative guidance of the High Court at the expense of the fund, but once such guidance has been obtained from the High Court's decision, then in the absence of some special circumstances, such for example as difficulties arising from that decision itself, the parties have the authoritative guidance they need. The fact that they do not like it is not a reason for litigating further at the expense of the fund. That principle would apply equally in this case. The judgment provides the sort of clear guidance which is required under the *Buckton* approach, and the fact that some of the parties do not like it would not justify the cost of the appeal."

25. Carnwath J then turned to consider the *Wallersteiner* extension. After citing from the judgments of Buckley LJ and Lord Denning in that case, he quoted a number of passages from sections (7), (8) and (9) of Hoffmann LJ's judgment in *McDonald*.

26. Carnwath J next recorded a submission by Mr Warren, counsel for the employers, that *Wallersteiner* and *McDonald* were cases of alleged wrongdoing by those in control of the company or trust and had no relevance to an ordinary administration or construction case, but said that he did not think that Hoffmann LJ had in mind any such clear-cut criterion. He went to refer to the earlier decision of Rimer J and cited a section from his judgment, including the passage I have quoted in para 21 above. He continued:

"Although that was based partly on a concession, no-one before me has argued that Rimer J's approach was wrong. Having reached that point, at least in the *National Grid* case, it seems to me impossible to argue that the *McDonald* principle is as narrowly confined as Mr Warren submits. Furthermore, once it has been decided that the case is of the kind which justifies a *McDonald* order at the first stage, it cannot be right, in my view, for the jurisdiction of the court (as opposed to the exercise of its discretion) to continue that order at a later stage depends on who won or lost. That, it seems to me, must depend on the nature of the case, and the circumstances will differ widely."

27. Carnwath J then turned to consider the cases before him, and concluded that it was appropriate to make the order sought by the applicants subject to a costs cap.

28. The third decision is that of Laddie J in *Chessels v British Telecommunications plc* [2002] PLR 141. In that case the trustees of the BT Pension Scheme had applied to the court for guidance. There were about 320,000 employees or former employees who were entitled to pensions under the scheme. The issues raised arose out of the fact that some members were formerly employed by the Post Office, which had been a government department, and thus they had civil service pension rights. In 1987 the civil service arrangements were revised, but the benefit of the former rules (referred to as "reserved rights") was preserved for those in what was called a "mobile grade". From 1990 to 1995 BT had reduced its workforce by means of an early release scheme which did not offer relevant members reserved rights. Four questions were raised for determination by the court, the second of which was what, if anything, was the BT equivalent of the civil service mobile grades. Two members were joined as representative defendants. One had left under an early release scheme and one was a current member. Both had the benefit of a pre-emptive costs order made by consent.

29. On the second question, BT argued that none of the relevant BT employees qualified as being of mobile grade while the representative members argued that all or most did. Both advanced the same fallback position, namely that the mobile grade was a reflection of a particular grade of seniority within the civil service and that BT employees of equivalent seniority were to be treated as being of the mobile grade for the purpose of the reserved rights. Jonathan Parker J (as he then was) ruled in favour of the mutual fallback position, and held that anyone at a BT grade equivalent to the EO grade in the civil service or above was entitled to reserved rights. This decision had an effect which had not been anticipated. Both the representative members had been employed in grades equivalent to EO or above. They were thus content with the judge's demarcation and had no interest in arguing for the interests of those in lower grades, referred to as "the excluded members". Thus the excluded members, estimated to number around

12,000, were left unrepresented. As a stop-gap measure, a Mr Cooper, who was a partner in the firm of solicitors who represented the two representative members, was joined as an additional defendant to represent the excluded members until a suitable representative excluded member could be found and joined.

30. Mr Cooper then applied to Laddie J (Jonathan Parker LJ having been elevated to the Court of Appeal) on behalf of the excluded members for permission to appeal and, if that was granted, for a pre-emptive costs order in respect of the appeal. It is important to note that the application for a pre-emptive costs order was made on the footing that, if no such order was made, Mr Cooper would not pursue the proposed appeal. It is also important to note that BT's response was that, if but only if permission to appeal was granted to Mr Cooper and pursued, it wanted permission to cross-appeal on the first and third questions which Jonathan Parker J had decided adversely to it. It was estimated that the effect of BT succeeding on the proposed cross-appeal would be to deprive about 5,000 members of increased benefits secured for them by Jonathan Parker J's judgment. Laddie J granted both Mr Cooper and BT permission to appeal, saying that he was prepared to assume in Mr Cooper's favour that he had substantial grounds.

31. Counsel for Mr Cooper submitted to Laddie J that he had a broad discretion under s 51 of the 1981 Act, while counsel for the trustees and BT submitted that the discretion could only be exercised in one way, namely to refuse the order sought. In the alternative they submitted that the court's discretion should be exercised against Mr Cooper. Laddie J appears to have accepted the primary submission of counsel for the trustees and BT. It is therefore important to try to understand the reasoning which led him to that conclusion.

32. Laddie J began at paras 35–37, by setting out s 51 of the 1981 Act, referring to *Aiden* v *Interbulk* and quoting the statement of Hoffmann LJ in *McDonald* that I have quoted in para 10 above. At paras 38–42 he made some observations about the general principles relating to costs. At paras 43–44 he set out the order sought by Mr Cooper and considered its effect. At para 45 he said that Hoffmann LJ's judgment in *McDonald* indicated that the relationship between the trust and the trustees was the proper starting point for an analysis of when and why pre-emptive costs orders can be made against the trust estate.

33. At paras 46–47 Laddie J considered applications by trustees under *Re Beddoe* [1893] 1 Ch 547 for pre-emptive indemnity out of the estate in respect of claims brought by the estate against third parties or claims by third parties against the estate. At para 48 he referred to cases in which trustees sought guidance from the court as to their powers or duties. At para 49 he observed:

> "Mr Nugee helpfully referred to the first class of cases as 'external' and the second as 'internal'. In each the same principle applies namely that the trustees are indemnified out of the estate because they will be acting properly for and on behalf of and for the benefit of the estate as a whole."

34. At para 50 Laddie J noted that Hoffmann LJ had pointed out in *McDonald* that the principles underlying the payment of the trustees' costs out of the estate had been extended to beneficiaries, and quoted his summary of *Buckton*. At para 51 he commented:

> "The guiding principle is that the special entitlement of the trustee to be indemnified out of the estate is extended to third parties where, in substance, they are performing the same function as the trustees or are assisting them to do so. Where that is the case, the third parties' costs are treated as necessarily incurred for the benefit of the estate."

35. At para 52 he noted that Hoffmann LJ had explained in *McDonald* that the favourable costs treatment of trustees had been extended by analogy to other types of cases. In minority shareholders' actions, the minority were treated as if they were bringing proceedings on behalf of and for the benefit of the company. He continued:

> "Similarly in *McDonald* v *Horn* itself, the principle was extended to actions for breach of trust brought by members of a pension scheme against the trustees. In such cases it is clear that if the members' allegations are true, the trustees themselves will not bring the proceedings on behalf of the estate. The members are therefore taking action for and on behalf of the estate and may be viewed as standing in the shoes of the trustees."

It may be noted that Laddie J did not quote, or refer to, Hoffmann LJ's reasoning which I have quoted in para 17 above.

36. At para 53, Laddie J said that two other points came out of *McDonald*, the second of which concerned whether such orders for

indemnification should be made pre-emptively. He continued at para 54:

> "As I have pointed out above in relation to litigation commenced by trustees on behalf of the trust against third parties, it is prudent, but not essential, for the trustees to seek a pre-emptive indemnification. That is part of the *Beddoe* application. Similarly, the fact that a third party may be entitled to indemnification does not, of itself, determine whether he should be entitled to it pre-emptively. This subject was addressed by Hoffmann LJ in *McDonald v Horn* [1995] 1 All ER 971d–972a: ..."

He then set out the passage from which I have quoted in para 14 above. It may be noted that Laddie J did not quote, or refer, the passage of Hoffmann LJ's judgment which I have quoted in para 15 above.

37. Laddie J concluded as follows (emphasis added):

> "55. It follows that a pre-emptive order indemnifying a third party should only be made where the court hearing the costs application is satisfied that no other order could properly be made by the court which is to hear the proceedings in respect of which the costs order is sought.
>
> 56. The question I have to decide is how the above principles apply to a case where what is sought by a group of beneficiaries is a pre-emptive costs order in respect of an appeal. Taking the last point first, for me to make such an order now it must be clear that an order for indemnification of the beneficiaries out of the fund, even if they lose the appeal, is the only order the Court of Appeal could make. I cannot be so satisfied. Although it is possible that the Court of Appeal may exercise its discretion to make such an order, I do not consider it to be inevitable or even particularly likely for the reasons set out below.
>
> 57. This case started life as an application by the trustees of BTPS for guidance as to how to interpret some of the rules of the scheme. All the parties agree that it was, as such, a classic *Buckton 1* application in which it was appropriate to indemnify not only the trustees but also the representative defendants out of the fund. But the trustees have now received guidance from Jonathan Parker LJ. They have no desire nor need to take the matter further. They happen to believe that the judge was correct in his analysis. So the position now is that there is no requirement that further guidance be given by the court. It might be that such guidance would be necessary if the judgment was clearly and

indubitably wrong, but Mr Topham goes nowhere near making any such suggestion. If that is right then even the trustees cannot assume that any appeal brought *by them* would be on the basis of an indemnity out of the fund (see *In re Earl of Radnor's Will Trusts* (1890) 45 Ch D 402, 423). If they were to appeal it would be at the risk of being ordered to pay the costs personally. The fourth defendant cannot be in a better position. On the contrary, the fourth defendant's position is worse. He cannot argue that the appeal has been rendered necessary by clear error of the judge, nor does he or can he say that he should be funded for any such appeal because the trustees' refusal to appeal is unreasonable or contrary to the interests of the beneficiaries of the scheme as a whole. These factors illuminate why the fourth defendant wants to appeal. *It is to secure an interpretation of the rules of the scheme which would be more advantageous to a group of members, which happens to be small in number compared to the total number of members of the scheme. It is not to clarify the meaning of the rules for the benefit of the scheme as a whole.* Any such appeal is most like hostile litigation of the *Buckton 3* type.

58. It seems to me, with respect, that the approach adopted by Carnwath J in *Laws v National Grid plc* [1998] PLR 295 is correct and applies here as well: ..."

Laddie J proceeded to quote the last paragraph of the passage which I have quoted in para 24 above. It may be noted that he did not quote, or refer to, the remainder of Carnwath J's judgment. Nor did he refer to Rimer J's earlier judgment.

38. Before proceeding, it is perhaps worth pointing out, for the avoidance of confusion, that the terminology employed in these earlier cases is that of "pre-emptive" costs orders. That terminology has subsequently been replaced by that of "prospective" costs orders: see PD64 para. 6.3. This makes no difference to the principles to be applied.

What Is the Correct Approach?

39. Before turning to the dispute as to the principles to be applied, it is convenient to begin with two points which are common ground. The first is that, even disregarding the fact that this is a pension fund case, the first instance proceedings fell within the first class of case identified in *Buckton*: it was a claim by a neutral trustee seeking the court's

guidance. Mr German was joined as a representative beneficiary so that the court could be assisted by adversarial argument. Accordingly, if there had not been a costs agreement, the court would inevitably have exercised its discretion to order that Mr German be indemnified in respect of his costs. The order would most likely have been for IMG to pay the costs, rather than for the costs to be paid out of the Plan assets for the reasons identified in para 8 above. An order for payment out of the Plan assets would have the result of requiring IMG to make extra contributions to the scheme *pro tanto*. The only difference would be to IMG's cash flow.

40. The second point is that, even where first instance proceedings fall within the first or second class identified in *Buckton*, the special principle which protects trustees and beneficiaries at first instance does not apply to appeals for the reasons articulated by Carnwath J in the passage I have quoted in para 24 above.

41. Counsel for Mr German submitted, in summary, that the principles I should apply were those applied by Rimer and Carnwath JJ in the *National Grid* case. Accordingly, I should consider the four factors which Rimer J derived, via Lightman J's judgment in *Alsop Wilkinson*, from the judgment of Mary Arden QC (as she then was) in *Biddencare*. He submitted that it was not correct to apply the test applied by Laddie J in *Chessels* at para 56, namely to ask whether the court is satisfied that the only order the Court of Appeal could make even if the appellant loses the appeal was for the appellant to be indemnified. He sought to distinguish the present case from *Chessels* on a number of grounds. He conceded that, if the correct test was that applied by Laddie J in *Chessels* at para 56, Mr German could not satisfy it.

42. Counsel for IMG submitted, in summary, that the correct test was that applied by Laddie J in *Chessels* at para 56. In support of that submission he contended that there were two distinct lines of authority, (i) the *Buckton* line and (ii) the *Wallersteiner* and *McDonald* line. He argued that *National Grid* and *Chessels* showed that: (i) where there was hostile litigation or a hostile appeal and the *Buckton* line applied, a prospective costs order would only be made if the trial judge or the Court of Appeal could only properly exercise his or its discretion by ordering that costs be paid out of the trust fund; and (ii) the *Wallersteiner* and *McDonald* line only applied to pension fund cases in which the trustees were not neutral, but actively opposed the

members who sought the prospective costs order. He submitted that the present case was on all fours with *Chessels*.

43. In my judgment counsel for Mr German is correct. I consider that Laddie J's reasoning in *Chessels* is difficult to reconcile with that of Rimer and Carnwath JJ in *National Grid*. I prefer the latter, since I consider it more accurately reflects the judgment of Hoffmann LJ in *McDonald*. My reasons are as follows.

44. The starting point is the passage in Hoffmann LJ's judgment which I have quoted in para 15 above. This makes it clear that, if that case had been ordinary trust litigation, the principles stated in *Buckton* would not have justified a prospective costs order: it was hostile litigation and it was not possible to say that the trial judge could only properly exercise his discretion to order the plaintiffs to be indemnified.

45. It is clear from the passages in Hoffmann LJ's judgment which I have quoted in paras 17 and 18 above that he was saying that a claim by a member of a pension fund to compel trustees or others to account to the fund was different to ordinary trust litigation for the reasons he gave. Accordingly, in such a case the court had a discretion to make a prospective costs order even though such an order could not be justified on *Buckton* principles for the reasons previously given.

46. It is also clear that Rimer and Carnwath JJ both understood *McDonald* in this way. As noted in para 21 above, Rimer J held that the applicants could not justify a prospective costs order on *Buckton* principles, because he could not be satisfied that the judge would order their costs to be paid out of the scheme assets, but that that was not the end of the matter because of the Court of Appeal's decision in *McDonald*. It can be seen from para 22 above that, in deciding whether to make an order on the basis of *McDonald*, he did not proceed on the basis that the applicants had to show that the judge would order their costs to be paid out of the scheme assets, but on the basis that he had a broader discretion to exercise. Moreover, he considered the position to be analogous to an appeal to the Court of Appeal (although he was considering the position of parties resisting the appeal and not pursuing it).

47. As can be seen from para 24 above, Carnwath J again held that the applicants before him could not justify a prospective costs order on *Buckton* principles, because they were appealing from the High Court's determination and therefore he could not be satisfied that the

Court of Appeal would order their costs to be paid out of the scheme assets. Again, however, that was not the end of the matter because of the Court of Appeal's decision in *McDonald*. As can be seen from para 26 above, he went on to follow Rimer J's approach, no one having argued that it was wrong, and to reject the submission that *McDonald* was limited to cases of trustee wrongdoing. He then decided that it was appropriate to make the order sought.

48. If one considers Laddie J's reasoning in *Chessels* at paras 55–57, it can be seen that he treated the principles which apply to cases of ordinary trustee litigation, and in particular the principle that a prospective order will only be granted where the court is satisfied that the ultimate tribunal can only properly exercise its discretion to order an indemnity, as equally applicable to a claim or an appeal by a member in a pension fund case. For the reasons given above, I do not think that that is correct.

49. That is not say to that Laddie J reached the wrong conclusion. As he noted in the passage towards the end of para 57 that I have italicised in para 37 above, the proposed appeal was an appeal purely for the benefit of a small group of members. It can be seen from my summary of the facts that the group in question numbered about 12,000 out of a total of around 320,000. Moreover, if the appeal proceeded, it would expose around 5,000 other members to losing benefits gained under Jonathan Parker J's judgment as a result of a cross-appeal by BT that would otherwise not be brought. It follows that Laddie J was right to say that the proposed appeal was not for the benefit of the fund as a whole. In those circumstances he would have been justified in concluding that the threshold conditions for bringing the case within the *McDonald* principle were not satisfied. Alternatively, he would have been justified in exercising his discretion to refuse to make a prospective cost order.

50. In the present case, the situation is quite different. As noted above, so far as question 5 is concerned, Mr German represents not only the existing members as at the date of the 1992 Deed, but also those who joined after the purported conversion but before 1 January 2005. Thus Mr German represents the interests of the majority of the membership. Indeed, as counsel for Mr German submitted, one can regard the Plan as being divided into two sections, the first section comprising those who joined down to 31 December 2004 and the second section comprising those who joined after 1 January 2005. Mr

German represents the vast majority of the members in the first section. He does not represent a small handful of existing deferred members as at 3 March 1992, but their interests are not affected by these proceedings anyway. If Mr German is successful on the proposed cross-appeal, then (subject to the further issues discussed below) the consequence will be that IMG will have to make increased contributions to the Plan for the benefit of all those represented by Mr German. In these circumstances Mr German can fairly be considered to be, as Hoffmann LJ put it, "a person with a limited interest in a ... pension fund [who] is alleging injury to the fund as a whole and seeking restitution on behalf of the fund" .

51. Finally, I do not accept that the *McDonald* jurisdiction is limited to cases where the trustee is actively opposing the members as opposed to maintaining a neutral stance. In my judgment such a limitation is inconsistent with Hoffmann LJ's reasoning in *McDonald* and with Carnwath J's reasoning in *Laws* v *National Grid*. In any event, in relation to question 5, Mr German is attacking the actions of the Present Trustee's predecessors.

52. For these reasons, I consider that Mr German satisfies the threshold conditions for the exercise of the *McDonald* jurisdiction. I shall therefore apply the principles applied by Rimer and Carnwath JJ in *National Grid*. That said, I do not myself consider it particularly helpful to try separate out the four factors identified in the *Alsop Wilkinson* case. The key factor is the third one, and it seems to me that the other three factors are really aspects of it. I remind myself that, as Laddie J put it in *Chessels* at para 59, "the court should be careful not to be generous with someone else's money".

How Should the Discretion Be Exercised?

53. Counsel for Mr German relied upon the following factors as supporting the making of the order sought:

i) The merits of the proposed cross-appeal.
ii) The fact that there will be an appeal to the Court of Appeal anyway, in respect of which IMG had agreed to pay Mr German's costs. Thus this application only relates to the increased costs of the parties having to argue the cross-appeal as well.
iii) The fact that Mr German is only cross-appealing because IMG

appealed. If IMG had accepted this court's judgment, so would have Mr German.

iv) The issues on the cross-appeal are closely related to, although distinct from, those on the appeal. In particular, the factual background is the same.

v) Success on the cross-appeal could result in a substantial financial benefit for a substantial number of members.

vi) If the order was not granted, Mr German would not be in a position to pursue the cross-appeal.

54. Although counsel addressed me at some length on (i), I do not think it is either possible or desirable for me to say any more than that I consider that the cross-appeal has a real prospect of success.

55. So far as (ii), (iii) and (iv) are concerned, I agree that these are factors which support the making of the order. It may be noted that, in this respect, the present case is the precise converse of *Chessels*.

56. I also agree that (v) favours the making of the order, but I shall return to this below. I shall consider (vi) below.

57. Counsel for IMG relied upon the following factors as supporting the refusal of the order sought:

i) Success on question 5 would not necessarily result in increased benefits for the members. Two points were left undecided in the first judgment (see paras 208 and 209). Moreover, by agreement a further issue as to whether the members were barred by contract or estoppel had been carved out of the trial and would then require to be decided.

ii) The extra costs of the cross-appeal were likely to be substantial.

iii) IMG is a company of relatively modest resources. It would be unfair that IMG should have to pay for the risk of being saddled with a substantial liability, whereas the members could gamble on obtaining a substantial benefit at no cost to themselves.

iv) The order sought exposed IMG to immediate liability, whereas an eventual order for the costs of the cross-appeal to be paid out of the Plan assets would have a reduced impact on IMG's cash flow.

v) It had not been shown that the members could not find an alternative means of funding the cross-appeal.

58. I agree that (i) is a relevant consideration, and goes some way to neutralising Mr German's factor (v), but in my view it does not go all

the way. None of those three issues have been decided. I have to approach the matter on the basis that they could be decided either way.

59. So far as (ii) is concerned, I am not persuaded that the extra costs of the cross-appeal are particularly substantial in context. IMG's evidence on this application reveals that it has already spent £1,882,263 (including VAT) on its own, the Present Trustee's and Mr German's representation in these proceedings. To that must in event be added the costs of IMG and Mr German, and perhaps the Present Trustee, on the appeal. The appeal is estimated at 2½ days. Adding the cross-appeal should only add half a day, or at most one day, to the estimate. As a result of the limitation on the scope of Mr German's permission, the cross-appeal is confined to issues of law based on the facts found in the first judgment. In my view, the extra costs of the cross-appeal should be relatively small in the context of the total costs incurred and to be incurred by IMG.

60. As to (iii), I accept that IMG has relatively modest resources, but it is able to afford this litigation and there is no evidence that success by Mr German on question 5 will expose IMG to such a large liability that it will inevitably have to be placed in administration or liquidation. As for the one-sided nature of the risk, that is the inevitable effect of any prospective costs order.

61. I do not regard (iv) as a significant factor for the reasons discussed above.

62. IMG's factor (v) is the flip side of Mr German's factor (vi). There was some debate between counsel as to who bore the burden of proof on this question. I do not think it is satisfactory to resolve this aspect of the matter on the burden of proof. Taking a realistic view, I think it would be difficult for Mr German and those he represents to put in place an alternative funding mechanism, particularly in the time available. Accordingly, I consider that this factor favours Mr German and not IMG.

63. Looking at the matter in the round, I consider that it is likely, although not inevitable, that the Court of Appeal would order IMG to pay the costs of the cross-appeal in any event. Furthermore, I am satisfied that the justice of the case means that it is appropriate to exercise my discretion to make a prospective order now.

Conclusion

64. I shall make the order sought by Mr German.

Richard Hitchcock and *Farhaz Khan* (instructed by Baker & McKenzie LLP) appeared for the first defendant.

Keith Rowley QC and *Elizabeth Ovey* (instructed by Macfarlanes LLP) appeared for the second defendant.

Case 34
R
v
Splain

[2010] 3 Costs LR 465

Neutral Citation Number: [2010] EWCA Crim 49
Court of Appeal (Criminal Division)
12 January 2010

Before:
Maurice Kay LJ, David Clark J and Sharp J DBE

Headnote

The Criminal Division of the Court of Appeal stated that a full order for prosecution costs following conviction should not have been made against a defendant who had not been convicted on most of the counts charged.

Judgment

1. MAURICE KAY LJ: David Clarke J will give our judgment.

2. DAVID CLARKE J: On 24 July 2009, the appellant was convicted on three counts of what had become a 17-count indictment for offences contrary to the Trade Marks Act 1994. On July 27, he was fined £2,000 on each of those three counts, together with the statutory victim surcharge, and was ordered to pay the prosecution costs amounting to £22,045. That was the full amount of the costs sought by the prosecuting authority, which was Swansea City Council. This appeal, brought with leave of the single judge, is against the order for costs only.

3. The prosecution arose from the seizure of items from a street seller in Swansea who was selling counterfeit Swansea City Football Club merchandise on 20 March 2006. The seller refused to name his supplier, but on further enquiries it was established that the merchandise had originated from this appellant, who was the proprietor of a business called Eclipse Flags carrying on business in Essex.

4. On 28 April 2006, a search warrant was executed at those business premises. A large quantity of goods was found ready for dispatch at the factory door. Items were seized, including computer and printing equipment, and various goods were identified which officers believed bore false marks, that is to say marks identical to, or likely to be mistaken for, registered trademarks. The appellant was not present at the time of the search, but was arrested on his return to the premises.

5. The three counts on which the jury convicted him were counts 1 and 2, which relate to a T shirt and flag seized from the street vendor in Swansea, and count 7, which concerned a Chelsea football T shirt, which was one of the numerous items seized at his premises.

6. All the remaining counts, on which he was acquitted, concerned items similarly seized, all which were alleged to be counterfeit goods in the sense that they bore marks which the Crown alleged to be identical to, or likely to be mistaken for, registered trade marks. They were not all football related items. They included items bearing the logos of various pop groups, and the like. The jury acquitted the appellant on eight of those counts. The remainder were withdrawn by the judge, apparently because of absence of proof of the registration of the trade marks.

7. No complaint is made about the level of fines, which was carefully considered by the judge. The complaint is made that although counsel had submitted that he should reflect in his costs order the fact that the appellant had only been convicted on three of the counts, he was nevertheless ordered to pay the full amount of the costs.

8. The court's power to award costs arises from s 17(1) of the Prosecution of Offences Act 1985, and it is to make such order as the court considers just and reasonable. The submission here is that to impose this very large order for costs, which so far exceeded the amount of the fines imposed, was to impose a substantial additional penalty on the appellant, which was wrong in principle.

9. It has been argued in writing that a more detailed breakdown of the costs should have been provided by the Crown, but, in the absence of any point taken in the court below to that effect, we do not consider that any proper criticism can be made. The information provided was not detailed, but it was quite sufficient for the court to proceed in the absence of any complaint on this score.

10. It is further submitted with more force that the Crown's case had shifted as the proceedings unfolded. The indictment underwent a number of changes. There was the addition and deletion of various counts until the indictment reached its final form with 17 counts, of which the appellant was convicted of only three.

11. Reliance is placed on the decision of this court in *R v B&Q plc* [2005] EWCA Crim 2297, a Health and Safety Act prosecution arising from a fatal accident to a customer at retail premises. There was a substantial contested trial in that case. The appellants were convicted of some of the counts on the indictment, but not all. Those on which they were convicted included the important one arising from the death of the customer. The company were fined a total of £550,000 and ordered to pay the costs of £250,000. This court in a lengthy judgment dismissed the appeals against conviction and fines, but did reduce the order for costs.

12. There was a significant issue there which did not arise here, which was the defendants had sought, but had been refused, a defendant's cost order in respect of those counts on which they were acquitted. No appeal against that could be pursued.

13. It was an unusual case in the sense that the trial had twice been aborted for reasons that were in no way the defendant's fault, but in which they had incurred substantial costs in respect of which they were also seeking relief. This court did make a deduction for the fact that the appellants were acquitted on some of the counts.

14. In our judgment it was wrong in principle for the judge to make an order for the totality of the costs against the defendant when he was only convicted on three of the counts. The fact that the amount of the costs was disproportionate to the amount of the fines is not, in our judgment, the crucial factor. There may well be cases in which in the totality of the sentencing process the court is justified in weighting the penalty on to the costs more than on to the fine.

15. The point here which carries weight with us is the appellant's acquittal on so many of the counts on the indictment. It does not

follow that a mathematical approach should be taken. Mr Roughton does not pursue his submission, based on pure mathematics, that the order for costs should have been three seventeenths of the total costs claimed. This was a man who was conducting a substantial commercial enterprise, which, on the finding of the court, involved the commission of criminal offences. The judge remarked in his sentencing observations that what the defendant was really doing for commercial purposes was to test the regulations, as found by the jury, to beyond the limits of the criminal law. The prosecution and the trial were clearly in the public interest. This was not a case of a sledgehammer being used to crack a nut.

16. We consider that it is right for this court to take an overall view. It accords with the general approach commonly taken in civil proceedings where issues are decided differently in respect of the opposing parties. We have concluded that fairness and proportionality here would be achieved by reducing the order for costs to £10,000 in place of that made by the learned judge. The appeal is allowed to that extent.

17. MAURICE KAY LJ: Thank you, Mr Roughton.

18. MR ROUGHTON: My Lords and My Lady, the order that the judge made was on 27 July 2009. All I simply seek is the substitution of the £10,000 with the time to pay remaining being twelve months from 27 July 2009, so that it is payable by the next 26 July 2010. I would ask for that order.

19. MAURICE KAY LJ: Yes. I am much obliged. Thank you very much, indeed. Mr Roughton, are you publicly funded?

20. MR ROUGHTON: I am publicly funded, my Lord.

Mr A Roughton appeared on behalf of the appellant.

Editorial Note: The following are decisions of costs judges on criminal cases and therefore do not have the same authority as those at higher judicial level. However, they are included because it is thought they will be of use to the profession.

Case 35
R
v
Jones

[2010] 3 Costs LR 469

Senior Courts Costs Office
2 February 2010

Before:
J Simons, Costs Judge

Headnote

The costs judge, whilst allowing a "special preparation" fee claim on its facts, refused to distinguish the very recent decision of the High Court judge in *Lord Chancellor* v *Michael J Reed Ltd* [2010] 1 Costs LR 72 on the point of principle advanced by the appellant as an alternative ground of appeal.

Reasons For Decision

1. Mr John Dodd QC and his Junior, Mr Richard Kelly, appeal in respect of the decision by the Determining Officer at the National

Taxing Team in Eastleigh to refuse their claims for fees for special preparation.

2. Counsel represented Luke Jones who, together with James Franks, was charged with the murder of Jack Large. At the time of the murder, Jones was aged 13 and Franks was aged 14. The victim was also aged 14. The parties were known to each other, and there was animosity from the victim towards Franks, which included racist elements. On the evening in question, there had been further trouble and the victim was said to be armed with a knife. Jones, who was the best friend of Franks, passed to his friend a small kitchen knife to defend himself. Franks then stabbed the victim twice, once in his back, and once in his head. The victim died from the resulting injuries. Franks was acquitted of murder, but was convicted of manslaughter, and Jones was acquitted, although he was sentenced in respect of his being in possession of the knife.

3. When counsel submitted their claims for costs, they claimed special preparation fees for consideration of the Achieving Best Evidence ("ABE") videos of the child witnesses, and consideration of the CCTV footage. Mr Dodd claimed 30.5 hours special preparation, and Mr Kelly claimed 69 hours special preparation. Mr Kelly broke down his time for the special preparation as being 48 hours, 35 minutes for consideration of the CCTV footage, and 20 hours 21 minutes for considering the ABE video interviews.

4. The Determining Officer rejected these claims. She rejected counsel's submission that the ABE and CCTV evidence was of an exceptional kind, and that the factual issues that arose as a result of it were very unusual, and required preparation of an exceptional nature. She also rejected counsel's alternative submission that as the CCTV footage was served in electronic format only, a special preparation fee was payable pursuant to para 14(1)(c) of Schedule 1 to the Criminal Defence Service (Funding) Order 2007.

5. The Determining Officer stated that she was not persuaded that the consideration of the video evidence of the juvenile witnesses or the CCTV footage, amounted to a very unusual or novel factual issue, so as to support a claim for special preparation. She further stated that an allowance had already been made in the page count for the transcripts of the ABE video interviews, and that the time taken for viewing the video interviews themselves was not something that was payable under special preparation. Whilst she acknowledged that there may have

been a large number of interviews conducted in this way due to the ages of the witnesses involved that did not make it a very unusual factual issue. Similarly with regard to the CCTV footage, although she accepted that viewing the CCTV footage was important to the case, it was not unusual for CCTV footage to be important in many other cases that come before the courts, and that did not amount to a very unusual factual issue.

6. The Determining Officer acknowledged that under the Criminal Defence Service (Funding) Order 2001, a separate fee could be claimed in respect of the viewing of disk, tape or video evidence, but that was not the case under the 2007 Order, and the Determining Officer speculated as to whether or not graduated fees payable under the 2007 Funding Order incorporated such fees.

7. The Determining Officer also rejected counsel's alternative claim that as the CCTV footage was served in electronic form, a special preparation fee was payable pursuant to reg 14(1)(c). She stated that the intention behind that particular paragraph was to recompense counsel for the consideration of documentation that had been served by the prosecution solely on CD-ROMs or in other electronic format, which would otherwise have been served in paper format. This was because without the actual physical documents being served, they could not form part of the allowance for the page count, so a method was devised to allow payment for their consideration in electronic format only. It was not however introduced to cover claims for viewing CCTV footage.

8. Mr Kelly had annexed detailed Grounds of Objection to his Notice of Appeal, and these grounds have been adopted by Mr Dodd.

9. Counsel submit that it is not for the Determining Officer to compare the differences between the 2001 and 2007 Orders, as each claim for special preparation must be considered on its individual merits as to whether or not it fulfils the criteria laid down in para 14(1)(a) of the Order. In this particular case the claim was made as the ABE interviews of the young witnesses and the CCTV footage was exceptionally voluminous, and was of crucial importance to the case. The only direct evidence of the actions of either defendant on the night in question came from those two sources. The CCTV footage both supported and contradicted crucial parts of the young witnesses' evidence, and that the task of examining the minutiae of the CCTV footage and cross-referencing all the strands of evidence was of an

exceptional nature, even in a case of murder, where one expects there to be complexities and a large volume of material. Accordingly, counsel submit that the factual issues which arose, were very unusual and required preparation, substantially in excess of the normal amount done for cases of this type. Accordingly, the full amount of the claims for special preparation for both counsel should be allowed.

10. In the alternative, counsel submits that as the CCTV footage was served on CD-ROMs, a claim for special preparation can be made under para 14(1)(c) of the Order. Counsel acknowledge that some parts of the CCTV footage were printed up, but those frames that were not printed, were served on CD-ROMs. Under the Regulation, the Determining Officer can make a payment for special preparation if she considers it reasonable to do so. Counsel submit that the test of reasonableness cannot be determined by reference to the Determining Officer's perceptions as to the reasons behind the changes between the 2001 and 2007 Orders. The test of reasonableness should focus on whether it was reasonable for the advocate to undertake this special preparation and in this respect, counsel refer to the acknowledgement by the Determining Officer that she accepted that the CCTV footage was important to the case.

11. Consequently, counsel submit that if a special preparation fee is not to be payable under para 14(1)(a) of the Order, it should be payable in respect of the CCTV footage only, pursuant to para 14(1)(c) of the Order, which in the case of Mr Kelly, amounted to 48 hours and 35 minutes.

12. Mr Kelly attended before me at the hearing of this appeal, and made representations on behalf of himself and Mr Dodd. He explained to me that the prosecution case was that his client had encouraged Franks to commit the murder. Jones' case was that, although he admitted that he had passed the knife to Franks, this had been some time before the offence was committed. Certain witnesses gave evidence about the time when they had seen Jones hand the knife to Franks. The CCTV footage that was available, whilst not showing the killing itself, identified the victims, the defendants, and many of the witnesses in a 2½ hour period prior to the actual killing. Mr Kelly explained that although he had claimed 48 hours 35 minutes for his initial perusal of the CCTV footage, his actual time that he spent looking at the footage was very much longer. Furthermore, the CCTV footage was not clear and had to be looked at many times. As a result

of his detailed consideration of the footage, he was able to persuade one of the main prosecution witnesses to acknowledge that his evidence at a crucial point was disproved by the CCTV evidence, and consequently that witness lost his creditability.

13. Mr Kelly submitted that the ABE evidence and the CCTV footage were inextricably linked as the ABE evidence showed the demeanour of the young witnesses, and also showed how they gave demonstrations as to what happened.

14. Mr Kelly's submission was that the factual issue was very unusual as, whilst the facts might not have been unusual, the issue with regard to the extent of the CCTV footage linked with the ABE evidence, was something that was completely unusual, even for a murder case, let alone a murder case where the victim, the defendants, and the witnesses were all juveniles.

15. With regard to his alternative claim for special preparation under 14(1)(c) of the Order, Mr Kelly submitted that this case was distinguishable from the *Lord Chancellor* v *Michael J Reed Ltd,* [2009] EWHC 2981 (QB) in that some of the CCTV footage was actually served as pictorial exhibits. That issue was not addressed by Penry-Davey J in *Reed.*

Criminal Defence Service (Funding) Order 2007 Schedule 1, para 1(2):

> "For the purposes of this schedule, the number of pages of prosecution evidence served on the court shall include:
>
> (a) witness statements;
>
> (b) documentary and pictorial exhibits;
>
> (c) records of interviews with the assisted person; and
>
> (d) records of interviews with other defendants,
>
> which form part of the committal or served prosecution documents or which are included in any Notice of Additional Evidence, but does not include any document provided on CD-ROM or by other means of electronic communication."

Paragraph 14 – Fees for Special Preparation:

> "(1) This paragraph applies where, in any case on indictment in the

Crown Court, in respect of which a graduated fee is payable under Part 2 or Part 3

(a) it has been necessary for an advocate to do work by way of preparation, substantially in excess of the amount normally done for cases of the same type, because the case involves a very unusual or novel point of law or factual issue;

(b) ...

(c) Any or all of the prosecution evidence, as defined in para 1(2) is served in electronic form only, and the appropriate officer considers it reasonable to make a payment in excess of the guarantee fee payable under this schedule."

16. The Determining Officer is correct when she states that CCTV footage is important in many cases, and that does not usually amount to a very unusual factual issue, regardless of how fundamental it may have been to the preparation. However, each case must be judged on its own merits. I am satisfied that in this particular case, the novelty, that is essential for work to come within the Regulation, was the combination of the sheer extent, complexity and importance of the CCTV footage, combined with its linkage with the ABE evidence, and the fact that the defendants, the victims and the witnesses were all juveniles. Whilst individually, none of these matters would normally indicate a novel factual issue, in this particular case, the combination of all these factors which clearly contributed to the acquittal of Jones on the murder charge, leads me to my conclusion that both counsel carried out work by way of preparation, substantially in excess of the amount normally done for cases of the same type, because the case involved very unusual factual issues. Accordingly, both appeals succeed and I direct the Determining Officer to pay counsel their fees for special preparation as claimed.

17. Although I have allowed these appeals, I must still deal with Mr Kelly's alternative argument that a special preparation fee is payable pursuant to reg 14(1)(c). I do not accept Mr Kelly's submission that this particular case is distinguishable from *Lord Chancellor* v *Michael J Reed Ltd*. In that case Penry-Davey J decided that as the prosecution evidence, as defined in para 1(2) of the Regulation, does not and cannot include DVD footage, a special preparation fee cannot be claimed. Whilst I accept that 78 pages were converted into a printed

document, and served as part of the prosecution evidence (which has been included in the page count for which counsel have been paid), for the reasons given by Penry-Davey J, the CCTV footage not reduced to printed form, cannot be regarded as a document, and consequently is not eligible for a special preparation fee under reg 14(1)(c).

18. Accordingly, this alternate appeal for a special preparation fee pursuant to para 14(1)(c) of the 2007 Order does not succeed and must be dismissed.

Case 36

R

v

O'Cuneff

[2010] 3 Costs LR 476

Senior Courts Costs Office
17 February 2010

Before:
C. Campbell, Costs Judge

Headnote

The costs judge re-affirmed the principle that the LSC in calculating the PPE count in a litigator fee claim had to follow the provisions of para 1(2) of Part 1 of Schedule 2 of the Criminal Defence Service (Funding) Order 2007, and not simply to accept as conclusive the paginated list of pages of PPE provided by the CPS.

Reasons For Decision

1. This is an appeal against of the decision of the Legal Services Commission to recoup £2,525.04 in accordance with paras 26(1) and 26(2)(a) of the Criminal Defence Service (Funding) Order 2007, from the account of the appellant firm, Leslie Franks, solicitors. The appellant had acted for the defendant, Russ O'Cuneff in the Southwark Crown Court in respect of a Class B offence and been paid on the basis of a cracked trial with Pages of Prosecution Evidence ("PPE") at 1938. However, according to the LSC, the correct PPE was 1322 and for that reason the overpayment was recouped under the Funding Order.

2. The amount originally paid was £12,019.18 but on 12 November 2009, the LSE gave its reasons for recouping the overpayment as follows:

"During a recent review of Crown Court cases, a number of matters have been identified where the ... PPE recorded on the court's records and/or PPE form, do not correspond with the details held by the prosecuting authorities.

We have recently contacted the Revenue and Customs Prosecutions Office regarding this case and they have confirmed that the number of pages of this case that fall within the definition of PPE was 1322 pages. This page count comprises of 186 statements, 740 exhibits, 232 interview transcripts, and 164 photographs. We have been unable to verify that the additional pages meet the PPE criteria and therefore should be excluded from payment."

3. In this appeal the appellant contests the LSC's calculation. In written submissions, the appellant has stated that the 1938 pages was based upon the number of pages paid to counsel, and following confirmation from Southwark Crown Court, on 22 and 27 October 2009, that that figure was the correct page count. In addition, the appellant relies on a note from Mr Graham Blower of counsel, in which he confirmed that the total figures for PPE were agreed between the court and counsel involved. That calculation had been accepted by the LSC as Mr Blower had been paid £1,270 based upon 1938 pages of PPE.

4. I have received written submissions in response from the LSC dated 27 November 2009. The letter says this:

"The solicitors claim 1938 PPE. The PPE claimed was based on the figure held by Southwark Crown Court. The firm submitted a fax from Southwark Crown Court stating 1938 PPE. Upon receipt of this document, Leslie Franks were informed that we no longer rely solely on court records to verify the PPE in a case, and as from 1 October 2009 it is a requirement that all litigator fee claims are submitted with documentation served by the prosecuting authority, such as paginated statements and exhibit lists, committal bundle, front sheets and/or Notices of Additional Evidence. Leslie Franks subsequently supplied paginated statement and exhibit lists to account for 1080 PPE. It was agreed with Leslie Franks that the LSC caseworker would contact the prosecuting authority to confirm the remaining number of pages before authorising payment. Unfortunately the claim was processed incorrectly, and the claim was paid in accordance with the PPE figure recorded by the court.

When authorising payment for a co-defendant in this matter, it was highlighted that the case had been paid incorrectly as when paying the co-defendant, the Revenue and Customs Prosecution Office were contacted and the PPE for the case was confirmed to be 1322 pages. This figure comprises 186 statements, 740 exhibits, 232 interview transcripts, and 164 photographs. As a result of this information, Leslie Franks were contacted and were informed that part of their payment would be recouped (£2,520.04) in the light of the PPE confirmed by RCPO, unless they could provide any further documentation to support the page count of 1938 from the prosecuting authority.

Leslie Franks could not provide any further information to support their claim of 1938 PPE, and therefore the recoupment of £2,520.04 was carried out."

5. The appellant made further written submissions in reply to the LSC's letter of 27 November 2009, as follows:

"It is worthy of note that the Crown Court used two systems to record PPE figures. The first is CREST which the LSC used to determine the PPE figure for solicitors, the second system is EXHIBIT which court use to update the PPE figures for the payment of counsel, and which records the agreed PPE figure at the end of the case with the court and counsel. It is the EXHIBIT system which is used to pay counsel, not the CREST system, which is often not updated at the end of the proceedings with the correct PPE figure. The EXHIBIT system, once updated, takes into account un-paginated pages used in evidence, and any evidence which was previously unused but becomes used material during the course of the case. This is why, when we ask the court to confirm the PPE count in the matter of O'Cuneff, we have asked for the agreed figure as recorded on the EXHIBIT system, and not the CREST system, in order to obtain an accurate PPE figure."

6. At the hearing of the appeal, I heard from Mr Nicholas Rosenfeld, the solicitor of the appellant with overall responsibility for the case, and from Mr Graham Blower, counsel briefed on behalf of the defendant. Mr Blower has explained to me that under the EXHIBIT system, at the conclusion of the case, the page count is agreed between

prosecution and defence advocates, and a "PPE form" is then submitted to the Clerk of the court for his approval. In the present case, this arrangement had led to the court approving 1938 PPE in respect of which Mr Blower received payment from the Southwark Crown Court under the EXHIBIT system.

7. Mr Rosenfeld explained to me that litigator fee claims are paid differently. The court also runs the CREST system. Into this system are inputted the number of pages, but whereas EXHIBIT updates the page count as and when new documents are served, CREST does not, indeed it was Mr Rosenfeld's submission that the system was never designed to be updated on a regular basis. It follows that problems have occurred where counsel is paid for a particular number of pages which have been logged on the EXHIBIT system and approved by the Clerk of the court, but where CREST has not been updated, and his firm has received lower fees.

8. In the present case, form LF1 was lodged on 14 October 2009 on the basis of 1938 pages of PPE. Payment was made based upon this figure, but was subsequently recouped in the manner I have set out above. Accordingly, it was not appropriate in this case for the firm to lodge a form LF2 because the shortfall (if it be that) occurred by way of recoupment rather than disallowance.

9. The problem, as submitted to me, has been that the LSC will only accept a paginated list of pages of PPE. However, there is no requirement on the Crown Prosecution Service when serving evidence to do so by way of paginated list, still less does the Crown deliver its evidence all at once. On the contrary, where, as here, evidence is served right up to the commencement of the trial, there cannot be a paginated list. In the present case, telephone records and additional statements were served at the last minute and material that had previously been unused became used when it was relied on and served upon the court. However, notwithstanding that form LF1 now has a tick box as to whether the PPE form agreed by the Court Clerk has been submitted, it was Mr Rosenfeld's submission that in the LSC's latest Guidance, such a form is not accepted as proof of the page count. The LSC will only accept a paginated list, which, for the reasons set out above, it is not possible to provide in every case.

10. Having made these factors, I am satisfied that the appeal must be allowed. To qualify as PPE, para 1(2) of Part 1 of Schedule 2 of the Criminal Defence Service (Funding) Order 2007, provides:

"For the purposes of this schedule, the number of pages of prosecution evidence served on the court includes all –

(a) witness statements;

(b) documentary and pictorial exhibits;

(c) records of interviews with the assisted person; and,

(d) records of interviews with other defendants, which form part of the committal or serve prosecution documents for which are included in any notice of additional evidence, but does not include any document provided on CD-ROM or by other means of electronic communication."

11. Prior to the appeal, Mr Rosenfeld had lodged copies of the telephone records, etc, which had been served other than with a paginated list. He submitted that these documents accounted for the difference between the 1938 pages agreed by the Crown Court and the 1322 pages which the LSC had remunerated. I accept his submission on this point, and accordingly the appeal must be allowed. I am satisfied that the correct page count, as agreed between prosecuting and defence counsel, and approved by the court was 1938 pages and the LSC must accordingly repay the amount of £2,525.04 previously recouped to the appellant. In reaching this decision, it is appropriate that I should express concern that this is yet another appeal in which counsel have been paid by the Crown Court on the basis of the PPE form approved by the Clerk, but the solicitors have had to make do with a significantly lesser sum because the LSC has either not been willing to accept the PPE form, or has declined to pay out in the absence of a paginated list. In my view, very considerable weight should be given to the figure agreed in the Crown Court at the end of a case, when the papers served under para 1.2 of Part 1, will be in court, as will be the advocates with their own papers, who can then agree the correct PPE figure with the Clerk of the court. So far as the Guidance is concerned, it is appropriate to re-state what Sir Christopher Holland said in *Lord Chancellor* v *Purnell* [2009] EWHC 3158 (QB) that the GFS Guidance published on behalf of the Lord Chancellor is not a source of law, but is "no more and no less than 'Guidance'".

Index of Reported Cases
(1910–2010)

1-800 Flowers Inc v
Phonenames Ltd
[2001] 2 Costs LR 286

A B and Others v Leeds Teaching
Hospitals NHS Trust
(In the Matter of the
Nationwide Organ Group
Litigation)
[2003] 3 Costs LR 405

A Local Authority v
A Mother and Child
[2001] 1 Costs LR 136

A v The Chief Constable
of South Yorkshire Police
[2008] 6 Costs LR 935

Aaron v Okoye
[1998] 2 Costs LR 6

Aaron v Shelton
[2004] 3 Costs LR 488

Abedi v Penningtons
[2000] 2 Costs LR 205

Admiral Management Services Ltd
v Para-Protect Europe Ltd and
Others
[2003] 1 Costs LR 1

Adrian Alan Ltd v Fuglers (a Firm)
[2003] 4 Costs LR 518

Aehmed and Others v The Legal
Services Commission
[2009] 3 Costs LR 425

Aerospace Publishing Ltd and
Another v Thames Water
Utilities Ltd
[2007] 3 Costs LR 389

AF v BG
[2010] 2 Costs LR 164

Agassi v Robinson (HM Inspector
of Taxes) (Bar Council and Law
Society Intervening)
[2006] 2 Costs LR 283

Al Fayed v Hamilton and Others
[2002] 3 Costs LR 389

Ali and Others v Lord Chancellor's
Department
[2002] 2 Costs LR 258

Ali Reza-Delta Transport Co Ltd v
United Arab Shipping Co Sag
[2004] 1 Costs LR 18

Al-Koronky and Another v
Time-Life Entertainment Group
Ltd and Another
[2007] 1 Costs LR 57

Amber Construction Services Ltd v
London Interspace HG Ltd
[2008] 5 Costs LR 715

Amber v Stacey
[2001] 2 Costs LR 325

Andrews and In the Matter of the Criminal Justice Act 1988
[1999] 2 Costs LR 133

Angel Airlines SA v Dean & Dean (CA)
[2009] 2 Costs LR 182

Angel Airlines SA v Dean & Dean (QBD)
[2009] 2 Costs LR 159

Angel Airlines SA v Dean & Dean Solicitors
[2007] 3 Costs LR 355

Anthony v Ellis & Fairbairn (a Firm)
[2000] 2 Costs LR 277

Apex Frozen Foods Ltd v Ali and Others
[2007] 6 Costs LR 818

Arkin v Borchard Lines Ltd and Others (No. 2)
[2004] 2 Costs LR 231

Arkin v Borchard Lines Ltd and Others (No. 3)
[2004] 2 Costs LR 267

Arkin v Borchard Lines Ltd and Others
[2005] 4 Costs LR 643

Armitage v Nurse
[2000] 2 Costs LR 231

Arrowfield Services Ltd v BP Collins (a Firm)
[2005] 2 Costs LR 171

Aspen Property Investment plc v Leslie Ratcliffe and Others
[1997] 2 Costs LR 1

Aspin v Metric Group Ltd
[2008] 2 Costs LR 259

Atack v Lee and Grechan; Ellerton v Harris
[2005] 2 Costs LR 308

B (Children)
[2005] 4 Costs LR 675

Bailey v IBC Vehicles Ltd
[1998] 2 Costs LR 46

Baker v Rowe
[2010] 2 Costs LR 175

Barndeal Ltd and Another v London Borough of Richmond-Upon-Thames
[2006] 1 Costs LR 47

Barr and Others v Biffa Waste Services Ltd and Another (Westmill Landfill Group Litigation)
[2010] 3 Costs LR 291

Barr and Others v Biffa Waste Services Ltd (No. 2) (Westmill Landfill Group Litigation)
[2010] 3 Costs LR 317

Baxendale-Walker v The Law Society
[2006] 5 Costs LR 696

Index of Reported Cases 1910–2010 (including this issue)

Baxendale-Walker v The Law Society
[2007] 3 Costs LR 475

Baylis v Kelly and Others
[1997] 2 Costs LR 54

BCCI v Ali and Others
[2000] 2 Costs LR 243

Begum v Klarit
[2005] 3 Costs LR 452

Bevan Ashford (a Firm) v Geoff Yeandle (Contractors) Ltd (in Liquidation)
[1998] 2 Costs LR 15

Biguzzi v Rank Leisure plc
[2000] 1 Costs LR 67

Bilkus v Stockler Brunton (a Firm)
[2010] 2 Costs LR 237

Bilkus v Stockler Brunton (a Firm)
[2009] 4 Costs LR 652

Bim Kemi AB v Blackburn Chemicals Ltd
[2004] 2 Costs LR 201

Birmingham City Council v Crook and Others
[2007] 5 Costs LR 732

Birmingham City Council v Forde
[2009] 2 Costs LR 206

Birmingham City Council v Lee
[2009] 2 Costs LR 191

Blackham v Entrepose UK
[2005] 1 Costs LR 68

Boodhoo (Harry), Solicitor (Re)
[2007] 3 Costs LR 433

Booth v Britannia Hotels Ltd
[2003] 1 Costs LR 43

Botham v Niazi (sued as Imran Khan); Lamb v Niazi (sued as Imran Khan)
[2005] 2 Costs LR 259

Bourns Inc v Raychem Corporation & Latham & Watkins
[1999] 2 Costs LR 72

Bourns Inc v Raychem Corporation
[1999] 1 Costs LR 27

Bovis Homes Ltd v Kendrick Construction Ltd
[2009] 5 Costs LR 778

Boyd & Hutchinson v Joseph
[2003] 3 Costs LR 358

Brawley v Marczynski and Another
[2003] 3 Costs LR 325

Brawley v Marczynski and Business Lines Ltd
[2003] 1 Costs LR 53

Brewer v Secretary of State for Justice
[2009] 3 Costs LR 440

Brewer v The Supreme Court Costs Office
[2009] 3 Costs LR 462

Bridgewater v Griffiths
[1999] 2 Costs LR 52

Brisset v Brisset
[2009] 4 Costs LR 641

Bromsgrove Medical Products Ltd
v Edgar Vaughan & Co Ltd
[1998] 1 Costs LR 75

Brown v MCASSO Music
Productions
[2006] 3 Costs LR 404

Brush and Another v Bower Cotton
& Bower (a Firm)
(1992) Costs LR (Core) 223

Budgens Stores Ltd v Hastings
Magistrates' Court and Rother
District Council
[2010] 2 Costs LR 153

Bufton v Hill
[2002] 3 Costs LR 381

Burchell v Bullard and Others
[2005] 3 Costs LR 507

Burkett (R) v London Borough of
Hammersmith and Fulham
[2005] 1 Costs LR 104

Burridge and Another v Stafford
and Another; Khan v Ali
[2001] 1 Costs LR 77

Burstein v Times Newspapers Ltd
[2003] 1 Costs LR 111

Burton Marsden Douglas (a Firm),
In the Matter of; Marsden and
Douglas v Guide Dogs for the
Blind Association and Others
[2004] 3 Costs LR 378

Business Environment Bow Lane
Ltd v Deanwater Estates Ltd
[2009] 4 Costs LR 672

Butt v Nizami and Kamuluden
[2006] 3 Costs LR 483

C v Merseyside Regional
Ambulance Service NHS Trust
[2004] 3 Costs LR 363

C v W
[2009] 1 Costs LR 123

Callery v Gray (HL)
[2002] 2 Costs LR 205

Callery v Gray (No. 1)
[2001] 2 Costs LR 163

Callery v Gray (No. 2)
[2001] 2 Costs LR 205

Campbell v MGN Ltd
[2006] 1 Costs LR 120

Cantor Fitzgerald International and
Another v Tradition (UK) Ltd
and Others
[2003] 4 Costs LR 614

Capewell v Her Majesty's Revenue
and Customs and Another
[2007] 2 Costs LR 287

Carver v BAA plc
[2008] 5 Costs LR 779

Cavaliere v Legal Services
Commission
[2003] 3 Costs LR 350

Index of Reported Cases 1910–2010 (including this issue)

Child Abduction and Custody Act 1985, In the Matter of the, and in the Matter of R (Minors) Taxation of Costs – Solicitors' Hourly Rate and Care and Conduct Mark Up
[1997] 1 Costs LR 1

Chohan v Times Newspaper Ltd
[2001] 1 Costs LR 127

Chohan v Times Newspapers Ltd
[2002] 1 Costs LR 1

Chrulew and Others v Borm-Reid & Co (a Firm)
(1991) Costs LR (Core) 150

CIBC Mellon Trust Company and Another v Stolzenberg and Others
[2005] 4 Costs LR 617

CIBC Mellon Trust Company Ltd and Another v Mora Hotel Corporation NY and Others
[2003] 3 Costs LR 334

Claims Direct Test Cases, In the Matter of
[2003] 2 Costs LR 254

Clifford Harris & Co v Solland International Ltd and Others
[2005] 3 Costs LR 414

Codent Ltd v Lyson Ltd
[2007] 2 Costs LR 185

Cole v British Telecommunications plc
[2000] 2 Costs LR 310

Colley v Council for Licensed Conveyancers
[2002] 1 Costs LR 147

Colour Quest Ltd and Others v Total Downstream UK plc and Others
[2010] 2 Costs LR 140

Commissioners for Her Majesty's Revenue and Customs v Xicom Systems Ltd
[2009] 1 Costs LR 45

Compton (R) v Wiltshire Primary Care Trust
[2008] 6 Costs LR 898

Cope v United Dairies (London) Ltd
(1963) Costs LR (Core) 23

Cox and Carter v MGN Ltd and Others
[2006] 5 Costs LR 764

Crane v Canons Leisure Centre
[2008] 1 Costs LR 132

Crosbie v Munroe and Motor Insurers' Bureau
[2003] 3 Costs LR 377

Crouch v King's Healthcare NHS Trust; Murry v Blackburn Hyndburn & Ribble Valley Health Care NHS Trust
[2005] 2 Costs LR 200

Currey v Currey
[2007] 2 Costs LR 227

D Pride & Partners v Institute for Animal Health and Others
[2009] 5 Costs LR 803

Dadourian Group International Inc and Others v Simms and Others
[2010] 1 Costs LR 89

Daniels v London Borough of Lambeth
[1997] 1 Costs LR 64

Dart v Dart
[2002] 2 Costs LR 312

Davey v Aylesbury Vale District Council
[2007] 3 Costs LR 452

Davey v Aylesbury Vale District Council
[2008] 1 Costs LR 60

David Truex, Solicitor (a Firm) v Kitchin
[2007] 4 Costs LR 587

Davidsons (a Firm) v Jones-Fenleigh
(1980) Costs LR (Core) 70

Days Healthcare UK Ltd v Pihsiang Machinery Manufacturing Co Ltd and Others
[2006] 5 Costs LR 788

Dean & Dean Solicitors v Angel Airlines SA
[2007] 6 Costs LR 795

Dean & Dean v Angel Airlines SA
[2008] 6 Costs LR 866

Dempsey v Johnstone
[2004] 1 Costs LR 41

Designers Guild Ltd v Russell Williams (Textiles) Ltd (t/a Washington DC)
[2003] 1 Costs LR 128

Designers Guild Ltd v Russell Williams (Textiles) Ltd
[2003] 2 Costs LR 204

Dickinson (t/a John Dickinson Equipment Finance) v Rushmer (t/a F J Associates)
[2002] 1 Costs LR 128

Dolphin Quays Developments Ltd (in Administrative and Fixed Charge Receivership) v Mills and Others
[2008] 2 Costs LR 220

Douglas and Others v Hello! Ltd and Others
[2004] 2 Costs LR 304

Drew v Whitbread
[2010] 2 Costs LR 213

Dymocks Franchise Systems (NSW) Pty Ltd v Todd and Others (No. 2)
[2005] 1 Costs LR 52

Dyson Technology Ltd v Strutt
[2007] 4 Costs LR 597

E C-L v DM
[2005] 4 Costs LR 576

Earles v Barclays Bank plc
[2009] 6 Costs LR 906

Index of Reported Cases 1910–2010 (including this issue)

East Coast Aggregates Ltd and
Para-Pagan and Others; Ross
and
(1) The Owners of the Ship
"Bowbelle" (2) The Owners of
the Ship "Marchioness"
[1997] 1 Costs LR 90

Eastwood (Deceased), Re, Lloyds
Bank Ltd v Eastwood and
Others
(1974) Costs LR (Core) 50

Easyair Ltd (t/a Openair) v Opal
Telecom Ltd
[2009] 6 Costs LR 882

Electricity Supply Nominees Ltd v
Farrell and Others
[1998] 1 Costs LR 49

Eversheds v Osman
[2000] 1 Costs LR 54

Eweida v British Airways plc
[2010] 1 Costs LR 43

Fattal and Fattal v Walbrook
Trustees (Jersey) Ltd and
Another
[2009] 4 Costs LR 591

Federal Bank of the Middle East v
Hadkinson and Hadkinson and
Others v Saab and Others
[2000] 1 Costs LR 94

Federation Against Copyright Theft
(FACT) v Broomhall and Others
[2007] 4 Costs LR 640

Federation Against Copyright Theft
(FACT) v North West Aerials
and Others
[2006] 2 Costs LR 361

Fenton v Holmes
[2008] 2 Costs LR 238

Finley v Glaxo Laboratories Ltd
(1989) Costs LR (Core) 106

Fitzpatrick Contractors Ltd v Tyco
Fire and Integrated Solutions
(UK) Ltd (No. 3)
[2010] 2 Costs LR 115

Fleming v Chief Constable of the
Sussex Police Force
[2005] 1 Costs LR 1

Flynn v Scougall
[2005] 1 Costs LR 38

Forcelux Ltd v Binnie
[2009] 5 Costs LR 825

Fosberry v Her Majesty's Revenue
& Customs
[2008] 3 Costs LR 380

Fosse Motor Engineers Ltd and
Others v Conde Nast and
National Magazine Distributors
Ltd and Others
[2009] 3 Costs LR 377

Galandauer v Snaresbrook
Crown Court
[2007] 2 Costs LR 205

Garbutt and Another v Edwards
and Another
[2006] 1 Costs LR 143

Garrett v Halton Borough Council;
  Myatt and Others v National
  Coal Board
  [2006] 5 Costs LR 798
Gaynor v Central West London
  Buses Ltd
  [2007] 1 Costs LR 33
Gazley v Wade and News Group
  Newspapers Ltd
  [2005] 1 Costs LR 129
General Mediterranean Holdings
  SA v Patel
  [1999] 2 Costs LR 10
General of Berne Insurance Co
  (The) v Jardine Reinsurance
  Management Ltd and Others
  [1997] 2 Costs LR 66
General of Berne Insurance Co v
  Jardine Reinsurance
  Management Ltd
  [1998] 1 Costs LR 1
Geraghty & Co v Awwad and
  Another
  [2000] 1 Costs LR 105
Giambrone and Others v JMC
  Holidays Ltd
  [2003] 2 Costs LR 189
Giambrone and Others v JMC
  Holidays
  [2002] 2 Costs LR 294
Gil v Baygreen Properties Ltd
  (in Liquidation) and Others
  [2005] 1 Costs LR 75

Glossop v The Lord High
  Chancellor
  [2005] 3 Costs LR 359
Gloucestershire County Council v
  Evans and Others
  [2008] 2 Costs LR 308
Gold v Mincoff Science & Gold (a
  Firm)
  [2005] 1 Costs LR 30
Goldman v Hesper
  (1988) Costs LR (Core) 99
Goodman and Farr v The Secretary
  of State for Constitutional
  Affairs
  [2007] 3 Costs LR 366
Goodwood Recoveries Ltd v Breen;
  Breen v Slater
  [2007] 2 Costs LR 147
Governing Body of St Albans Girls'
  School and Hertfordshire
  County Council v Neary
  [2010] 2 Costs LR 191
Gower Chemicals Group Litigation
  (Various Claimants in the) v
  Gower Chemicals Ltd and
  Another
  [2008] 4 Costs LR 582
Gray v Going Places Leisure
  Travel Ltd
  [2005] 3 Costs LR 405
Griffiths and Others v Solutia (UK)
  Ltd
  [2001] 1 Costs LR 99

Index of Reported Cases 1910–2010 (including this issue)

Grupo Torras SA v Al-Sabah
 [2003] 2 Costs LR 294
Gundry v Sainsbury
 (1910) Costs LR (Core) 1
Haji-Ioannou and Others v Frangos
 and Others
 [2006] 2 Costs LR 315
Haji-Ioannou v Frangos and Others
 [2007] 2 Costs LR 253
Hall and Others v Stone
 [2008] 3 Costs LR 450
Hall v Rover Financial Services Ltd
 (GB) t/a Land Rover Financial
 Services
 [2003] 1 Costs LR 70
Hallam-Peel & Co v The Mayor
 and Burgesses of the London
 Borough of Southwark
 [2009] 2 Costs LR 269
Halloran v Delaney
 [2002] 3 Costs LR 503
Halsey v Milton Keynes General
 NHS Trust; Steel v Joy
 and Halliday
 [2004] 3 Costs LR 393
Harold v The Lord Chancellor
 [1999] 1 Costs LR 14
Harris and Hartless v Moat
 Housing Group-South Ltd
 [2008] 2 Costs LR 294
Harrison and Others v Tew
 (1990) Costs LR (Core) 124

Hart v Aga Khan Foundation (UK)
 (1984) Costs LR (Core) 87
Hatton v Hopkins and Another
 [2007] 2 Costs LR 172
Hawley v Luminar Leisure plc; ASE
 Security Services Ltd v Mann
 [2006] 5 Costs LR 687
Hazlett v Sefton Metropolitan
 Borough Council
 [2001] 1 Costs LR 89
Hedrich and Another v Standard
 Bank London Ltd
 [2008] 5 Costs LR 679
Henry v British Broadcasting
 Corporation
 [2006] 3 Costs LR 412
Hickman v Blake Lapthorn
 and Fisher
 [2006] 3 Costs LR 452
Higgs v Camden & Islington
 Health Authority
 [2003] 2 Costs LR 211
Hill v Bailey
 [2004] 1 Costs LR 135
Hinde v Harbourne and Others
 [2004] 2 Costs LR 289
HLB Kidsons (a Firm) v Lloyds
 Underwriters
 [2008] 3 Costs LR 427
HM Revenue & Customs v
 Viewtopia Ltd
 [2006] 2 Costs LR 344

Hodgson and Others v Imperial
 Tobacco Ltd & Gallaher
 [1998] 1 Costs LR 14
Hodgson and Others v Imperial
 Tobacco Ltd and Others (No. 2)
 [1998] 2 Costs LR 27
Hollins v Russell and Related
 Appeals
 [2003] 3 Costs LR 423
Holmes v Alfred McAlpine Homes
 (Yorkshire) Ltd
 [2006] 3 Costs LR 466
Home Office v Lownds
 [2002] 2 Costs LR 279
Homes Assured Corporation plc, In
 the Matter of: The Official
 Receiver v Dobson and Others
 and Sampson and Kohlbacher v
 Wilson and Others
 [2002] 1 Costs LR 71
Hornsby and Others v Clark
 Kenneth Leventhal (a Firm) and
 Others
 [2000] 2 Costs LR 295
Horsford v Bird and Others
 [2007] 2 Costs LR 245
Howarth v Green
 [2003] 2 Costs LR 160
HR Trustees Ltd v German and
 Another (In the Matter of the
 IMG Pension Plan)
 [2010] 3 Costs LR 443

HSS Hire Services Group plc v
 BMB Builders Merchants Ltd
 and Grafton Group (UK) plc
 [2006] 2 Costs LR 213
Huck v Robson
 [2003] 1 Costs LR 19
Hunt v East Dorset Health
 Authority
 (1992) Costs LR (Core) 174
Hunt v R M Douglas (Roofing) Ltd
 (1988) Costs LR (Core) 136
Hurst v Leeming
 [2003] 2 Costs LR 153
Ikarian Reefer, The
 [2000] 1 Costs LR 37
Ilangaratne v British Medical
 Association
 [2006] 1 Costs LR 101
Ilangaratne v British Medical
 Association
 [2008] 3 Costs LR 367
Inline Logistics Ltd v UCI
 Logistics Ltd
 [2002] 2 Costs LR 304
Investment Invoice Financing Ltd v
 Limehouse Board Mills Ltd
 [2006] 4 Costs LR 632
Irvine v Commissioner of Police for
 the Metropolis and Others
 [2005] 3 Costs LR 380

Index of Reported Cases 1910–2010 (including this issue)

Irwin Mitchell v The Revenue and
 Customs Prosecutions Office
 and Allad
 [2009] 1 Costs LR 34

J Murphy & Sons Ltd v Johnston
 Precast Ltd (formerly Johnston
 Pipes Ltd) (No. 2 – Costs)
 [2009] 5 Costs LR 745

Jackson v The Lord Chancellor
 [2003] 3 Costs LR 395

Jefferson v National Freight
 Carriers plc
 [2001] 2 Costs LR 313

Jemma Trust Company Ltd v
 Liptrott and Others (No. 2)
 [2004] 4 Costs LR 610

Jemma Trust Company Ltd v
 Liptrott and Others
 [2004] 1 Costs LR 66

Jenkins v Young Brothers
 Transport Ltd
 [2006] 3 Costs LR 495

Johnson and Others v Reed
 Corrugated Cases Ltd
 (1990) Costs LR (Core) 180

Jonathan Alexander Ltd v Proctor
 (1995) Costs LR (Core) 399

Jones and Jones and Secretary of
 State for Wales and The Vale of
 Glamorgan Borough Council
 [1997] 1 Costs LR 34

Jones v Caradon Catnic Ltd
 [2006] 3 Costs LR 427

Jones v Wrexham Borough Council
 [2008] 1 Costs LR 147

Joseph v Boyd & Hutchinson
 [1999] 1 Costs LR 74

Kamenou & Another (t/a Regency
 Developments) v Pariser
 and Others
 [1999] 2 Costs LR 117

Kasir v Darlington & Simpson
 Rolling Mills Ltd
 [2001] 2 Costs LR 228

Kastor Navigation Co Ltd and
 Another v Axa Global Risks
 (UK) Ltd and Others;
 The "Kastor Too"
 [2004] 4 Costs LR 569

Kellar and Carib West Ltd
 v Williams
 [2005] 4 Costs LR 559

Kew v Bettamix Ltd and Others
 [2007] 4 Costs LR 527

Khan v Lord Chancellor
 [2003] 2 Costs LR 228

Kier Tankard v John Fredricks
 Plastics Ltd and Others
 [2009] 1 Costs LR 101

Kilby v Gawith
 [2008] 6 Costs LR 959

King v Telegraph Group Ltd
 [2004] 3 Costs LR 449

Kitchen v Burwell Reed
 & Kinghorn Ltd
 [2006] 1 Costs LR 82

Knight v Beyond Properties Pty Ltd
and Others
[2007] 1 Costs LR 5

Kostic v Chaplin and Others
[2008] 2 Costs LR 271

Kris Motor Spares Ltd v Fox
Williams LLP
[2009] 6 Costs LR 931

KU (a Child, By Her Mother and
Litigation Friend PU) v
Liverpool City Council
[2005] 4 Costs LR 600

Kundrath v Harry Kwatia &
Gooding
[2005] 2 Costs LR 279

Kuwait Airways Corporation v
Iraqi Airways Company (Body
Corporate) and Others
[2003] 1 Costs LR 130

L v L
[1997] 1 Costs LR 9

Lahey v Pirelli Tyres Ltd
[2007] 3 Costs LR 462

Lamont v Burton
[2007] 4 Costs LR 574

Landau and Cohen v The Lord
Chancellor's Department (R v
Abraham)
[1999] 2 Costs LR 5

Latimer Management Consultants
v Ellingham Investments Ltd
(Mr Peires)
[2008] 1 Costs LR 1

Laurence and Laurence v Singh (t/a
K & T Investments)
[1997] 1 Costs LR 58

Law Society v Persaud
(1990) Costs LR (Core) 114

Lay and Others v Drexler and
Others
[2007] 5 Costs LR 695

Ledward Claimants v Kent &
Medway Health Authority and
East Kent Hospitals NHS Trust;
Cost Capping Application
[2004] 1 Costs LR 101

Leeds City Council v Carr and
Coles & Wells v Barnsley
Metropolitan Borough Council
[2000] 1 Costs LR 144

Legal Services Commission v
Rasool
[2008] 4 Costs LR 529

Leigh v Michelin Tyre plc
[2004] 1 Costs LR 148

Leopold Lazarus Ltd v Secretary of
State for Trade and Industry
(1976) Costs LR (Core) 62

Less and Others v Benedict
[2005] 4 Costs LR 688

Lifeline Gloves Ltd v Richardson
and Richardson
[2006] 1 Costs LR 58

Index of Reported Cases 1910–2010 (including this issue)

Liverpool Freeport Electronics Ltd and Others v Habib Bank Ltd and The Legal Services Commission
[2009] 3 Costs LR 434

Lloyds TSB Bank plc v Lampert
[2003] 2 Costs LR 286

Lobster Group Ltd v Heidelberg Graphic Equipment Ltd and Another
[2008] 5 Costs LR 724

Locabail (UK) Ltd v Bayfield Properties and Others and Emmanuel v Locabail (UK) Ltd and Another
[2000] 2 Costs LR 169

London Borough of "A" v M and SF
(1994) Costs LR (Core) 374

London Borough of Enfield v P
[1997] 1 Costs LR 73

London Borough of Southwark v Nejad and Others
[1999] 1 Costs LR 62

Lord Chancellor (The) v John Charles Rees QC and Others
[2009] 2 Costs LR 334

Lord Chancellor v Frieze
[2007] 5 Costs LR 684

Lord Chancellor v Haggan and Others
[2007] 5 Costs LR 722

Lord Chancellor v Michael J Reed Ltd
[2010] 1 Costs LR 72

Lord Chancellor v Purnell and McCarthy [2010] 1 Costs LR 81

Lord Chancellor v Singh
[2003] 1 Costs LR 62

Lord Chancellor v Taylor
[2000] 1 Costs LR 1

Loveday v Renton and Another (No. 2)
(1991) Costs LR (Core) 204

Lownds v Home Office
[2002] 2 Costs LR 279

Lynch v Paul Davidson Taylor (a Firm)
[2004] 2 Costs LR 321

Macdonald v Taree Holdings
[2001] 1 Costs LR 147

Macdougall v Boote Edgar Esterkin (a Firm)
[2001] 1 Costs LR 118

MacPherson v Bevan Ashford
[2003] 3 Costs LR 389

Macro (Ipswich) Ltd, In re
[1997] 1 Costs LR 128

Maes Finance Ltd v WG Edwards & Partners
[2000] 2 Costs LR 198

Mainwaring and Lisle and
  Goldtech Investments Ltd;
  Goldtech Investments Ltd and
  Mainwaring and Lisle
  [1997] 1 Costs LR 143
Mainwaring and Lisle v Goldtech
  Investments Ltd
  [1999] 1 Costs LR 96
Malkinson v Trim
  [2002] 3 Costs LR 515
Malmesbury (James Carleton,
  Seventh Earl of Malmesbury)
  and Others v Strutt & Parker
  (a Partnership)
  [2008] 5 Costs LR 736
Maltby and Another v D J Freeman
  & Co (a Firm)
  (1977) Costs LR (Core) 64
Mamidoil – Jetoil Greek Petroleum
  Company SA and Moil – Coal
  Trading Company Ltd v Okta
  Crude Oil Refinery AD
  [2003] 2 Costs LR 175
Manches LLP v Green; Green v
  Manches LLP and the Former
  Partners in Marshall Ross &
  Prevezer (a Firm)
  [2008] 6 Costs LR 881
Mars UK Ltd v
  Teknowledge Ltd
  [1999] 2 Costs LR 44
Martin v Holland and Barrett
  [2002] 3 Costs LR 530

Mastercigars Direct Ltd v
  Withers LLP
  [2008] 1 Costs LR 72
MasterCigars Direct Ltd v
  Withers LLP
  [2009] 3 Costs LR 393
MasterCigars Direct Ltd v
  Withers LLP
  [2010] 3 Costs LR 374
McCarthy v Essex Rivers
  Healthcare NHS Trust [2010] 1
  Costs LR 59
McGlinn v Waltham Contractors
  Ltd and Others
  [2006] 1 Costs LR 27
McIlwraith v McIlwraith
  [2004] 4 Costs LR 533
McLinden v Redbond
  [2006] 4 Costs LR 651
McPherson v BNP Paribas (London
  Branch)
  [2004] 4 Costs LR 596
McPhilemy v Times Newspapers
  Ltd and Others (No. 4)
  [2001] 2 Costs LR 295
Mealing-McLeod v The Common
  Professional Examination Board
  [2000] 2 Costs LR 223
Medcalf v Mardell
  [2002] 3 Costs LR 428

Index of Reported Cases 1910–2010 (including this issue)

Medway Oil and Storage Co Ltd v Continental Contractors Ltd and Others
(1928) Costs LR (Core) 5

Meeke and Taylor v Secretary of State for Constitutional Affairs
[2006] 1 Costs LR 1

Meretz Investments NV and Britel Corporation NV v ACP Ltd and Others
[2008] 1 Costs LR 42

Metalloy Supplies Ltd v MA (UK) Ltd
[1998] 1 Costs LR 85

Michaelides, Re
[2005] 2 Costs LR 191

Miller Gardner v The Lord Chancellor
[1997] 2 Costs LR 29

Miller v Hales and Others
[2007] 4 Costs LR 521

Mills v Birchall and Gilbertson
[2008] 4 Costs LR 599

MMR/MR Vaccine Litigation; Afrika and Others v Cape plc; X, Y, Z and Others v Schering Health Care Ltd; Sayers and Others v Merck and Smithkline Beecham plc
[2003] 4 Costs LR 503

Mohammadi v Shellpoint Trustees Ltd and Anston Investments Ltd
[2009] 3 Costs LR 486

Mohammed v Alaga & Co
[1999] 2 Costs LR 169

Montlake and Others (as Trustees of Wasps Football Club) v Lambert Smith Hampton Group Ltd
[2004] 4 Costs LR 650

Moon v Garrett and Others
[2007] 1 Costs LR 41

Morgan and Baker v Hinton Organics (Wessex) Ltd and CAJE [2010] 1 Costs LR 1

Morgan and Others v Legal Aid Board
[2001] 1 Costs LR 57

Morgan v UPS
[2009] 3 Costs LR 384

Morris v Lord Chancellor
[2000] 1 Costs LR 88

Morris v Wiltshire and Woodspring District Council and the Supreme Court Costs Office
[2002] 1 Costs LR 167

Mount Cook Land Ltd and Another (R) v Westminster City Council
[2004] 2 Costs LR 211

Mullings v (1) Boahemaah (2) Kudum-Bradley (3) Toppin
[1998] 1 Costs LR 57

Multiplex Constructions (UK) Ltd
v Cleveland Bridge UK Ltd and
Another (No. 7)
[2009] 1 Costs LR 55

Murphy and Another v Young &
Co's Brewery and Another
[1998] 1 Costs LR 94

Murria v Lord Chancellor
[2000] 1 Costs LR 81

Myatt and Others v National Coal
Board
[2007] 4 Costs LR 564

Myler and Mirror Group
Newspapers v Williams
[2003] 4 Costs LR 566

National Westminster Bank plc v
Rabobank Nederland
[2008] 3 Costs LR 396

National Westminster Bank plc v
Rabobank Nederland (No. 3)
[2008] 6 Costs LR 839

National Westminster Bank
v Kotonou
[2010] 2 Costs LR 193

Nederlandse Reassurantie Groep
Holding NV v (1) Bacon and
Woodrow (a Firm) (2) Ernst
and Young (a Firm) (3) Swiss
Bank Corp (4–47,45–59)
Anderton and Others
[1998] 2 Costs LR 32

Nedlloyd Lines UK Ltd and
Another v CEL Group Ltd
[2004] 2 Costs LR 286

Newall v Lewis and Others
[2008] 4 Costs LR 626

Nicholas Drukker & Co v Pridie
Brewster & Co
[2006] 3 Costs LR 439

Norris v Norris; Haskins v Haskins
[2003] 4 Costs LR 591

Northstar Systems Ltd and Others
v Fielding and Others
[2007] 2 Costs LR 264

Nossen's Patent, Re
(1968) Costs LR (Core) 36

Nugent and Killick v Michael Goss
Aviation and Others
[2002] 3 Costs LR 359

Nykredit Mortgage Bank plc v
Edward Erdman Group Ltd
(formerly Edward Erdman (an
Unlimited Company)) (No. 2)
[1998] 1 Costs LR 108

O'Beirne v Hudson
[2010] 2 Costs LR 204

Official Receiver (The)
v Brunt and Others
[1998] 2 Costs LR 38

Official Receiver (The) v Brunt and
Others
[1999] 2 Costs LR 97

Index of Reported Cases 1910–2010 (including this issue)

Oliver v Whipps Cross University Hospital NHS Trust and Waltham Forest Primary Care Trust
[2009] 3 Costs LR 474

Onay v Brown
[2010] 1 Costs LR 29

Ortwein v Rugby Mansions Ltd
[2004] 1 Costs LR 26

Painting v University of Oxford
[2005] 3 Costs LR 394

Palmer v The Estate of Kevin Palmer (Deceased) and Others
[2008] 4 Costs LR 513

Pankhurst v White and Another
[2010] 3 Costs LR 402

Paragon Finance plc v Noueiri
[2002] 1 Costs LR 12

Patten (t/a Anthony Patten & Co) v Lord Chancellor
[2001] 2 Costs LR 233

Paturel v Marble Arch Services Ltd
[2006] 4 Costs LR 556

Pauls Agriculture Ltd v Smith and Others
(1992) Costs LR (Core) 218

Peacock v MGN Ltd
[2009] 4 Costs LR 584

Pearce v Ove Arup Partnership Ltd and Others
[2004] 4 Costs LR 631

Persaud v Persaud and Others
[2004] 1 Costs LR 1

Petromec Inc v Petroleo Brasileiro SA Petrobras
[2007] 2 Costs LR 212

Petrotrade Inc v Texaco Ltd
[2002] 1 Costs LR 60

Phillips and Others v Symes (a Bankrupt) and Others; in the matter of an issue ordered to be tried between: Symes (a Bankrupt) v Phillips and Others
[2005] 2 Costs LR 224

Pilbrow v Pearless de Rougemont & Co
[1999] 2 Costs LR 109

Pine v The Law Society
[2002] 3 Costs LR 347

Piper Double Glazing Ltd v DC Contracts
(1992) Costs LR (Core) 256

Platt v GKN Kwikform Ltd
(1992) Costs LR (Core) 250

Plender v Hyams
[2001] 1 Costs LR 109

Powell v Herefordshire Health Authority
[2003] 2 Costs LR 185

PR Records Ltd v Vinyl 2000 Ltd and Owlett (Susan) and Owlett (Adrian)
[2008] 1 Costs LR 19

Pritchard v Ford Motor Co Ltd; Riccio v Ford Motor Co Ltd
[1997] 1 Costs LR 39

Available online at www.CostsLawReports.co.uk

Property and Reversionary Investment Corporation Ltd v Secretary of State for the Environment
(1975) Costs LR (Core) 54

R (Brewer) v Supreme Court Costs Office
[2007] 1 Costs LR 20

R (Buglife – The Invertebrate Conservation Trust) v Thurrock Thames Gateway Development Corp and Another
[2009] 1 Costs LR 80

R (Bullmore) v West Hertfordshire Hospitals NHS Trust
[2007] 6 Costs LR 844

R (Corner House Research) v The Secretary of State for Trade and Industry
[2005] 3 Costs LR 455

R (Davies) (No. 2) v HM Deputy Coroner for Birmingham
[2004] 4 Costs LR 545

R (E) v Governing Body of JFS and Others
[2009] 4 Costs LR 695

R (Factortame and Others) v Secretary of State for Transport
[2002] 3 Costs LR 467

R (Roudham and Larling Parish Council) v Breckland Council and Paul Rackham Ltd (Interested Party)
[2009] 2 Costs LR 282

R (Spiteri) v Basildon Crown Court
[2009] 5 Costs LR 772

R (Wulfsohn) v Legal Services Commission
[2002] 3 Costs LR 341

R v Agbobu
[2009] 2 Costs LR 374

R v Ainsworth
[2007] 6 Costs LR 865

R v Alays and Others
[2007] 2 Costs LR 321

R v Al-Goni and Ataya
[2009] 2 Costs LR 356

R v Ali and Others
(1984) Costs LR (Core) 434

R v Alwan
[2000] 2 Costs LR 326

R v Amin
[2009] 1 Costs LR 149

R v Armstrong
[2008] 5 Costs LR 794

R v Austin
[2006] 5 Costs LR 857

R v Ayres
[2002] 2 Costs LR 330

R v Backhouse
(1986) Costs LR (Core) 445

Index of Reported Cases 1910–2010 (including this issue)

R v Baker and Fowler
  [2004] 4 Costs LR 693
R v Balme
  [2008] 6 Costs LR 988
R v Bell
  [2003] 1 Costs LR 144
R v Bellas and five other appeals
  (1986) Costs LR (Core) 479
R v Bhatti
  [2006] 2 Costs LR 356
R v Bishop and Others
  [2007] 3 Costs LR 506
R v Bishop
  [2008] 5 Costs LR 808
R v Bolton (Stephen George)
  [2005] 2 Costs LR 334
R v Bolton
  [2006] 4 Costs LR 659
R v Bond (Michael)
  [2005] 3 Costs LR 532
R v Boswell; R v Halliwell
  (1987) Costs LR (Core) 507
R v Bowles
  [2007] 3 Costs LR 514
R v Bowman
  [2007] 1 Costs LR 1
R v Brewer
  [2007] 4 Costs LR 662
R v Briers (Michael)
  [2005] 1 Costs LR 146
R v Brinkworth
  [2006] 3 Costs LR 512

R v Brook
  [2004] 1 Costs LR 178
R v Brown
  [2002] 3 Costs LR 539
R v Cadogan
  [2009] 5 Costs LR 853
R v Carlyle
  [2002] 1 Costs LR 192
R v Carty
  [2009] 3 Costs LR 500
R v Cevik
  [1998] 2 Costs LR 1
R v Chapple
  [2007] 2 Costs LR 310
R v Cheng and Chen
  [2007] 4 Costs LR 626
R v Cheng
  [2008] 1 Costs LR 180
R v Cheng, Chen and Miah
  [2007] 4 Costs LR 634
R v Chowdhury
  [2009] 3 Costs LR 514
R v Chubb
  [2002] 2 Costs LR 333
R v Clarke
  (1991) Costs LR (Core) 496
R v Comer
  [2009] 6 Costs LR 972
R v Conboy
  (1990) Costs LR (Core) 493
R v Conroy
  [2004] 1 Costs LR 182

Available online at www.CostsLawReports.co.uk

R v Coutts (Graham)
   [2007] 6 Costs LR 878
R v Cowie
   [2006] 2 Costs LR 375
R v Crocker
   [2001] 1 Costs LR 25
R v Crucefix
   [2007] 5 Costs LR 770
R v Dalziell
   [2003] 4 Costs LR 651
R v Davies (Benjamin)
   [2007] 1 Costs LR 116
R v Davies
   (1985) Costs LR (Core) 472
R v Davies
   [2008] 5 Costs LR 813
R v Davis
   [2010] 1 Costs LR 108
R v Dawson
   [1999] 1 Costs LR 4
R v Despres
   [2005] 4 Costs LR 750
R v Dhaliwal
   [2004] 4 Costs LR 689
R v Dhesi
   [2003] 4 Costs LR 645
R v Dodd and Ward
   [2009] 2 Costs LR 368
R v Dunlop
   [2008] 5 Costs LR 803
R v Duxbury
   (1983) Costs LR (Core) 423

R v Duzgun and Another
   [2000] 2 Costs LR 316
R v Edwards
   [2004] 4 Costs LR 679
R v Evans-Southall and Others
   [1998] 1 Costs LR 68
R v Fairhurst
   [2000] 1 Costs LR 34
R v Farrell and Selby
   [2007] 3 Costs LR 495
R v Faulkner and Others
   [1998] 1 Costs LR 66
R v Faulkner
   [2003] 1 Costs LR 148
R v Findlay and McGregor
   [2002] 2 Costs LR 322
R v Finn
   [2006] 3 Costs LR 525
R v Foot
   [2004] 3 Costs LR 525
R v Ford-Lloyd
   (1984) Costs LR (Core) 424
R v Frampton
   [2005] 3 Costs LR 527
R v Franks
   [2008] 5 Costs LR 819
R v Ghadhim Gerhards
   (1984) Costs LR (Core) 463
R v Ghaffar
   [2009] 6 Costs LR 980
R v Gill (Steven)
   [2006] 5 Costs LR 837

Index of Reported Cases 1910–2010 (including this issue)

R v Gittins and Khan
 [2007] 4 Costs LR 549
R v Goodwin
 (1984) Costs LR (Core) 425
R v Goodwin
 [2008] 3 Costs LR 497
R v Grant
 [2006] 1 Costs LR 173
R v Gray (Richard)
 [2009] 6 Costs LR 967
R v Great Western Trains
 Company Ltd
 [2004] 2 Costs LR 331
R v Greenwood
 [2010] 2 Costs LR 268
R v Griffin
 [2008] 3 Costs LR 483
R v Hadley
 [2005] 3 Costs LR 548
R v Halcrow
 (1984) Costs LR (Core) 436
R v Hameed
 [2001] 2 Costs LR 343
R v Hann
 [2009] 5 Costs LR 833
R v Hardev Singh
 [2002] 1 Costs LR 196
R v Harper
 [2007] 6 Costs LR 862
R v Harris
 [2009] 3 Costs LR 507
R v Hashash
 [2008] 4 Costs LR 646

R v Hayes
 [2008] 1 Costs LR 186
R v Hendy-Freegard
 [2007] 5 Costs LR 776
R v Henshaw
 [2006] 1 Costs LR 191
R v Hill and Dalton
 [2007] 5 Costs LR 788
R v Hindle
 (1987) Costs LR (Core) 486
R v Hudson
 (1985) Costs LR (Core) 456
R v Huggett
 (1988) Costs LR (Core) 488
R v Hussain and Others
 (1984) Costs LR (Core) 426
R v Islami
 [2009] 6 Costs LR 988
R v Ismail
 [2006] 3 Costs LR 530
R v Jacobs
 [2010] 1 Costs LR 99
R v Johnson (Craig)
 [2007] 2 Costs LR 316
R v Johnson (L)
 [2005] 1 Costs LR 153
R v Johnson and 13 Others
 [2008] 2 Costs LR 337
R v Johnson and 13 Others
 [2009] 4 Costs LR 710
R v Johnson
 [2006] 5 Costs LR 852

R v Johnson
    [2008] 6 Costs LR 983
R v Jones
    [2010] 3 Costs LR 469
R v Jones (John Ivor)
    [2007] 6 Costs LR 873
R v Judd
    [2006] 2 Costs LR 340
R v K, G and M
    [2005] 4 Costs LR 571
R v Kayani
    [2007] 3 Costs LR 490
R v Kelly and Others
    [2004] 2 Costs LR 344
R v Kennedy (Francis)
    [2006] 4 Costs LR 662
R v Khair (Lee)
    [2005] 3 Costs LR 542
R v Khan (Zulfi Al)
    [2005] 1 Costs LR 157
R v Knight
    [2003] 3 Costs LR 496
R v Larsh
    [2007] 5 Costs LR 783
R v Lawrence
    [2000] 2 Costs LR 334
R v Lawrence
    [2007] 1 Costs LR 138
R v Leigh (John)
    [2008] 1 Costs LR 191
R v Long
    [2009] 1 Costs LR 151

R v Macatonia
    [2010] 2 Costs LR 262
R v Maguire
    [2006] 4 Costs LR 678
R v Mahmood
    [2008] 2 Costs LR 326
R v Mahon
    [1999] 2 Costs LR 151
R v Marandola
    [2006] 1 Costs LR 184
R v Martin and Others
    [2007] 1 Costs LR 128
R v Martin
    [2004] 1 Costs LR 167
R v Mashhour
    [2003] 2 Costs LR 318
R v Matthews (Rosalind) and Others
    [2007] 2 Costs LR 328
R v McClean
    [2005] 4 Costs LR 740
R v McGunigle (Thomas)
    [2005] 3 Costs LR 537
R v Miller
    (1984) Costs LR (Core) 431
R v Mills and Morris
    (1993) Costs LR (Core) 498
R v Mold Crown Court ex parte Khan
    [2001] 2 Costs LR 336
R v Moss
    (1984) Costs LR (Core) 437

Index of Reported Cases 1910–2010 (including this issue)

R v Neil
 [2010] 2 Costs LR 283
R v Neil and five other appeals
 (1986) Costs LR (Core) 475
R v Newport
 [2009] 6 Costs LR 983
R v O'Brien and Ollife
 (1984) Costs LR (Core) 505
R v O'Brien
 (1985) Costs LR (Core) 440
R v O'Brien
 [2003] 4 Costs LR 625
R v O'Cuneff
 [2010] 3 Costs LR 476
R v Oates
 [2002] 3 Costs LR 375
R v Oldcorn
 [2003] 2 Costs LR 310
R v Ortiz-Ortega
 [2008] 6 Costs LR 976
R v Osagie
 (1984) Costs LR (Core) 433
R v Ozen
 [2006] 5 Costs LR 847
R v Panice
 (1984) Costs LR (Core) 462
R v Phillips
 [2007] 1 Costs LR 121
R v Phillips
 [2009] 6 Costs LR 993
R v Pickett
 [2004] 3 Costs LR 529

R v Pitchforth and Brighouse (CPS Appeal)
 [2005] 4 Costs LR 721
R v Plews
 (1984) Costs LR (Core) 466
R v Prenga
 [2004] 4 Costs LR 699
R v Preston Crown Court ex parte Lancashire County Council
 [1999] 1 Costs LR 58
R v Pullum
 (1983) Costs LR (Core) 413
R v Raji
 [2003] 4 Costs LR 636
R v Ranjit
 [2006] 3 Costs LR 541
R v Richardson
 [2008] 2 Costs LR 320
R v Rigelsford
 [2006] 3 Costs LR 518
R v Roberts
 [2008] 2 Costs LR 323
R v Rose
 [2008] 1 Costs LR 198
R v Russell (Sebastian Lee)
 [2006] 5 Costs LR 841
R v Russell
 [2008] 3 Costs LR 501
R v Rycott
 (1992) Costs LR (Core) 449
R v Sandhu
 (1984) Costs LR (Core) 451

R v Sanghera and Others
[2008] 5 Costs LR 823

R v Secretary of State for the Home Department ex parte Gunn
[2001] 2 Costs LR 263

R v Shacklady (Andrew)
[2005] 4 Costs LR 716

R v Shaw (Mark Anthony)
[2005] 2 Costs LR 326

R v Slessor
(1984) Costs LR (Core) 438

R v Smith (Philip)
[2008] 4 Costs LR 656

R v Smith (Thomas)
[2006] 1 Costs LR 167

R v Smith
[2004] 2 Costs LR 348

R v Solomka
[2007] 6 Costs LR 868

R v Sood
[2004] 3 Costs LR 520

R v Splain
[2010] 3 Costs LR 465

R v Staniland (Craig)
[2005] 2 Costs LR 337

R v Starr
[2009] 5 Costs LR 841

R v Stewart
[2004] 3 Costs LR 501

R v Sturdy
[1999] 1 Costs LR 1

R v Sturmer and Lewis
[2009] 2 Costs LR 364

R v Sullivan
(1989) Costs LR (Core) 490

R v Supreme Court Taxing Office ex parte John Singh and Co
[1997] 1 Costs LR 49

R v Syed
[2004] 4 Costs LR 686

R v Tanimowo
[2008] 2 Costs LR 331

R v Taylor
[2000] 1 Costs LR 32

R v Taylor
[2005] 4 Costs LR 712

R v Theobald
[2008] 4 Costs LR 662

R v Thomas; R v Davidson; R v Hutton
(1985) Costs LR (Core) 469

R v Thompson
[2006] 4 Costs LR 668

R v Tooth (David Christopher) (CPS Appeal)
[2007] 2 Costs LR 302

R v Tucker
[2009] 5 Costs LR 850

R v Uddin
[2010] 2 Costs LR 274

R v Umezie
[2010] 1 Costs LR 93

R v Villiers
[2005] 4 Costs LR 732

R v Wallace
[2008] 3 Costs LR 494

Index of Reported Cases 1910–2010 (including this issue)

R v Walpole
  [2002] 1 Costs LR 199
R v Wanklyn
  (1985) Costs LR (Core) 443
R v Ward-Allen
  [2005] 4 Costs LR 745
R v Warren
  [2006] 2 Costs LR 336
R v Wellman and Others
  [2009] 1 Costs LR 137
R v White
  [2008] 3 Costs LR 479
R v Winskill
  [2008] 4 Costs LR 651
R v Zemb
  (1985) Costs LR (Core) 442
Rackham v Sandy and Others
  [2006] 1 Costs LR 34
Radu v Houston and Another
  [2007] 5 Costs LR 671
Ralph Hume Garry (a Firm) v
  Gwillim
  [2003] 1 Costs LR 77
Read v Edmed
  [2006] 2 Costs LR 201
Reed Executive plc and Reed
  Solutions plc v Reed Business
  Information Ltd, Reed Elsevier
  (UK) Ltd and Totaljobs.com Ltd
  [2004] 4 Costs LR 662
Reeves v Sprecher and Others
  [2009] 1 Costs LR 1

Reid Minty (a Firm) v Taylor
  [2002] 1 Costs LR 180
Reid v The Capita Group plc
  [2006] 4 Costs LR 564
Report from the Appeal Committee
  of the House of Lords
  [2000] 1 Costs LR 7
Reynolds v Stone Rowe Brewer (a
  Firm)
  [2008] 4 Costs LR 545
Rezvi and Rezvi v Brown Cooper
  (a Firm)
  [1997] 1 Costs LR 109
Richard Buxton (Solicitors)
  v Mills-Owens
  [2008] 6 Costs LR 948
Richard Buxton (Solicitors) v Mills-
  Owens and The Law Society
  [2010] 3 Costs LR 421
Richards & Wallington (Plant Hire)
  Ltd v Monk & Co Ltd
  (1984) Costs LR (Core) 79
Richardson Roofing Company Ltd
  v Ballast plc (Dissolved) and
  Others
  [2009] 1 Costs LR 14
Richardson Roofing Company Ltd
  v The Colman Partnership Ltd
  [2009] 4 Costs LR 521
Ridehalgh v Horsefield and
  Another
  (1994) Costs LR (Core) 268

Available online at www.CostsLawReports.co.uk

Riniker v University College London
[2001] 1 Costs LR 20

RM Broudie & Co v The Lord Chancellor
[2000] 2 Costs LR 285

Roach and Roach v The Home Office; Matthews v The Home Office
[2009] 2 Costs LR 287

Rogers v Merthyr Tydfil County Borough Council
[2007] 1 Costs LR 77

Rosling King v Rothschild Trust
[2005] 2 Costs LR 165

Ross v Bowbelle (Owners) and Another
[1998] 1 Costs LR 32

Ross v Stonewood Securities Ltd
[2005] 1 Costs LR 89

Roundstone Nurseries Ltd v Stephenson Holdings Ltd
[2009] 5 Costs LR 787

Royal Bank of Scotland v Allianz International Insurance Co and Others
(1994) Costs LR (Core) 344

Russell Young & Co v Brown and Others
[2007] 4 Costs LR 552

Ruttle Plant Hire Ltd v Department For Environment, Food & Rural Affairs
[2007] 5 Costs LR 750

Sarwar v Alam
[2002] 1 Costs LR 37

Scribes West Ltd v Relsa Anstalt and Another (No. 1)
[2005] 1 Costs LR 18

Seaga v Harper
[2009] 4 Costs LR 607

Secretary of State for Constitutional Affairs v Stork
[2006] 1 Costs LR 69

Serious Organised Crime Agency v Szepietowski and Others
[2009] 4 Costs LR 532

Serious Organised Crime Agency v Szepietowski and Others
[2009] 4 Costs LR 615

SES Contracting Ltd and Others v UK Coal plc
[2007] 5 Costs LR 758

Shah v Ul-Haq and Others
[2010] 3 Costs LR 336

Sharratt and Others and Rowe Cohen (a Firm) v London Central Bus Company Ltd and Others
[2006] 4 Costs LR 584

Shepherds Investments Ltd v Walters and Others
[2007] 6 Costs LR 837

Index of Reported Cases 1910–2010 (including this issue)

Sheppard v Essex Strategic Health Authority
[2006] 1 Costs LR 8

Shirley v Caswell
[2001] 1 Costs LR 1

Sibley & Co v Reachbyte Ltd and Kris Motor Spares Ltd
[2009] 2 Costs LR 311

Simms and Others v The Law Society
[2006] 2 Costs LR 245

Simpson v Bowker
[2007] 6 Costs LR 850

Simpsons Motor Sales (London) Ltd v Hendon Corporation (No. 2)
(1964) Costs LR (Core) 29

Sims v Hawkins
[2008] 5 Costs LR 691

Sinclair (in His Capacity as the Former Receiver) v Glatt and Others
[2009] 4 Costs LR 568

Sinclair v British Telecommunications plc
[2001] 1 Costs LR 40

Sisu Capital Fund Ltd and Others v Tucker and Others
[2006] 2 Costs LR 262

Skuse v Granada Television Ltd
(1993) Costs LR (Core) 333

Slatter v Ronaldsons
[2002] 2 Costs LR 267

Smart v East Cheshire NHS Trust
[2004] 1 Costs LR 124

Smith Graham v The Lord Chancellor's Department (R v Carr)
[1999] 2 Costs LR 1

Smithkline Beecham plc and Glaxosmithkline UK Ltd v Apotex Europe Ltd and Others; Apotex Europe Ltd and Others v Beecham Group plc and Smithkline Beecham plc
[2005] 2 Costs LR 293

Smiths Dock Ltd v Edwards and Others
[2004] 3 Costs LR 440

Snowden v Ministry of Defence
[2002] 2 Costs LR 249

Solutia UK Ltd v Griffiths and 165 Others
[2001] 2 Costs LR 247

Sony Music Entertainment Inc and Sony Music Entertainment (UK) Ltd v Prestige Records Ltd and Dancebuy Ltd (t/a Slam Music)
[2000] 2 Costs LR 186

South Coast Shipping Company Ltd v Havant Borough Council
[2002] 1 Costs LR 98

Spath Holme Ltd v Chairman of
the Greater Manchester and
Lancashire Rent Assessment
Committee and Others; Curtis v
Chairman of the London Rent
Assessment Committee
& Another
[1998] 1 Costs LR 40

Spencer v Wood and Wood t/a
Gordons Tyres (a Firm)
[2004] 3 Costs LR 372

Stacy v Player
[2004] 4 Costs LR 585

Sterling Publications v Burroughs
[2000] 2 Costs LR 155

Strachey v Ramage
[2009] 1 Costs LR 9

Straker v Tudor Rose (a Firm)
[2008] 2 Costs LR 205

Strydom v Vendside Ltd
[2009] 6 Costs LR 886

Stubblefield and Others v Kemp
and Others
[2001] 1 Costs LR 30

Stubbs v Board of Governors of
the Royal National
Orthopaedic Hospital
(1988) Costs LR (Core) 117

Suisse Security Bank and Trust Ltd
v Governor of the Central Bank
of the Bahamas (The Bahamas)
[2007] 2 Costs LR 222

Sulaman v Axa Insurance
plc and Another
[2010] 3 Costs LR 391

Sullivan v The Co-Operative
Insurance Society Ltd
[1999] 2 Costs LR 158

Supperstone v Hurst and Hurst
[2008] 4 Costs LR 572

Sutton v Horsham District Council
[2005] 2 Costs LR 344

Symes v Phillips and Others
[2006] 4 Costs LR 553

Symphony Group plc v Hodgson
(1993) Costs LR (Core) 319

Szekeres v Alan Smeath & Co
[2005] 4 Costs LR 707

Tanfern Ltd v Cameron-Macdonald
[2000] 2 Costs LR 260

Thai Trading Co (a Firm) v Taylor
[1998] 1 Costs LR 122

The Accident Group Test Cases:
Sharratt v London Central Bus
Company and Other Cases
[2004] 3 Costs LR 422

Thomas Joyce v Kammac Ltd
(1988) Costs LR (Core) 353

Thomas v Bunn, etc
(1990) Costs LR (Core) 161

Thomas Watts & Co (a Firm) v
Smith
[1998] 2 Costs LR 59

Index of Reported Cases 1910–2010 (including this issue)

Thomson v Berkhamsted Collegiate School and Others
[2009] 6 Costs LR 859

Thornley v Lang
[2004] 1 Costs LR 91

Three Rivers District Council and Others v The Governor and Company of the Bank of England
[2006] 5 Costs LR 714

Tierney v News Group Newspapers Ltd
[2006] 4 Costs LR 606

Treasury Solicitor v Regester and Another
(1977) Costs LR (Core) 42

Truex v Toll
[2009] 5 Costs LR 758

Truscott v Truscott; Wraith v Sheffield Forgemasters Ltd
[1997] 2 Costs LR 74

Trustees of Stokes Pension Fund v Western Power Distribution (South West) plc
[2006] 2 Costs LR 226

Turner & Co v O Palomo SA
[1999] 2 Costs LR 184

University of East London Higher Education Corporation v London Borough of Barking and Dagenham and Others (No. 2)
[2005] 2 Costs LR 287

Utaniko Ltd v P&O Nedlloyd BV; East West Corp v Dampskibsselskabet AF, 1912 Aktieselskab and Another
[2003] 4 Costs LR 531

Utting v McBain
[2008] 3 Costs LR 442

Various Claimants v Gower Chemicals Ltd and Others
[2007] 4 Costs LR 647

Various Ledward Claimants v Kent & Medway Health Authority and East Kent Hospitals NHS Trust; Cost Capping Application
[2004] 1 Costs LR 101

Venture Finance plc v Mead and Another
[2006] 3 Costs LR 389

W (a Child), Re; D and DW v Portsmouth Hospital NHS Trust
[2006] 5 Costs LR 742

Wagstaff v Colls
[2003] 4 Costs LR 535

Wakeling v Harrington (Liquidator of Chelmsford City Football Club (1980) Ltd)
[2007] 5 Costs LR 710

Walker v Walker
[2005] 3 Costs LR 363

Wallace and Wallace v Brian Gale & Associates (a Firm)
[1998] 2 Costs LR 53

Available online at www.CostsLawReports.co.uk

Wallace and Wallace v Brian Gale
& Associates
[1997] 2 Costs LR 15

Waterson Hicks v Eliopoulos
and Others
(1995) Costs LR (Core) 363

Weaver v London Quadrant
Housing Trust
[2009] 6 Costs LR 875

Westland Helicopters Ltd v Sheikh
Salah Al-Hejailan
[2006] 4 Costs LR 549

Westminster City Council v Porter
and Weeks; Citroen Wells (a
Firm) and Chorles
(Respondents)
[2005] 2 Costs LR 186

Widlake v BAA Ltd
[2010] 3 Costs LR 353

Wills and Others v The Crown
Estate Commissioners and
Others
[2003] 4 Costs LR 581

Wilson v The Specter Partnership
and Others
[2007] 6 Costs LR 802

Wilson v William Sturges & Co
(a Firm)
[2006] 4 Costs LR 614

Wong v Vizards
[1997] 2 Costs LR 46

Wraith and Sheffield
Forgemasters Ltd
[1997] 1 Costs LR 23

Young v JR Smart (Builders) Ltd
[2004] 2 Costs LR 298

Index

ATE insurance,
  disclosure of, 291–316, 317–335
CCTV, 469–475
CD-ROMs, 469–475
Civil Procedure Rules,
  Part 36 offers, 402–420
Conditional fee agreements,
  291–316, 317–335
Costs capping, 443–464
  group litigation orders, 317–335
Costs,
  effect of lying to the court,
  391–401
CPS,
  providing pages of prosecution
  evidence count, 476–480
Detailed assessment, 374–390
Disclosure,
  ATE insurance, 291–316,
  317–335
Dishonesty, 391–401
Entire contract rule, 421–442
Estimates, 317–335
  reliance upon,
    whether amounts payable
    should be limited, 374–390
Exaggerated claims,
  effect on costs, 353–373
Fraud,
  in related claim, 336–352

Group litigation orders, 291–316
  cost capping, 317–335
Legal Services Commission,
  476–480
Lying to the court,
  effect on costs, 391–401
Medical expert,
  misleading the, 353–373
Misconduct, 336–352, 353–373,
  391–401
Misleading the medical expert,
  353–373
Pages of prosecution evidence,
  count provided by CPS, 476–480
Part 36 offers,
  where rules changed between offer
  and trial, 402–420
Pension funds,
  prospective costs orders, 443–464
Personal injury, 353–373
Privilege, 291–316, 317–335
Prosecution costs,
  where defendant not convicted on
  most counts, 465–468
Prospective costs orders,
  pension fund litigation, 443–464
Reliance upon estimates,
  whether amounts payable should
  be limited, 374–390
Retainers,
  termination of, 421–442

Index

Road traffic accidents, 336–352

Special preparation,
and the Michael J.
Reed case, 469–475

Strike-out,
fraud,
in related claim, 336–352

Termination of retainers, 421–442